Exploration into God

The Raymond Fred West Memorial Lectures
at Stanford University
1966

In the End, God ...
The Body: A Study in Pauline Theology
Jesus and His Coming
On Being the Church in the World
Liturgy Coming to Life
Christ Comes In
Twelve New Testament Studies
Honest to God
Christian Morals Today
The New Reformation?
But That I Can't Believe!

EXPLORATION
INTO GOD

JOHN A. T. ROBINSON

Bishop of Woolwich

1967
Stanford University Press
Stanford, California

The Raymond Fred West Memorial Lectures
on Immortality, Human Conduct, and Human Destiny
were established in 1910 by
Mr. and Mrs. Fred West of Seattle
in memory of their son

Stanford University Press
Stanford, California
© 1967 by the Board of Trustees of the
Leland Stanford Junior University
Printed in the United States of America
L.C. 67-26529

Preface

This book is a considerably expanded version of material delivered as the Raymond Fred West Memorial Lectures at Stanford University, California, in May 1966. I am most grateful
for the invitation, for the stimulus the lectures provided, and
for the hospitality accorded to my wife and myself.

My original intention had been to devote the lectures to the
subject of Christology. But it became increasingly clear that
before one could develop the theme "God was in Christ"
(which I shall be presupposing in all that follows), one must
try to explore further the meaning of "God"—for, as Thomas
Altizer has said, "Christ cannot appear as God at a time in
which God is dead."[1] And to this further exploration I was
much encouraged by some disarmingly gracious words from
Father F. C. Copleston, S.J., in an article which he called
"Probe at Woolwich":

My basic idea is this. By publishing *Honest to God* the bishop won
for himself an extremely wide circle of readers. He succeeded in
shocking or startling many people into thinking and talking about
theological matters. If therefore he could write for his public, in
similarly popular style, a book exhibiting more positively and fully
the foundations of his Christian vision of reality, he might do a

[1] T. J. J. Altizer and W. Hamilton, *Radical Theology and the Death of
God* (Indianapolis, 1966), p. 135.

v

tremendous amount of good. Perhaps this is an impertinent suggestion to make. But it seems to me that the Bishop of Woolwich
is faced with an opportunity which rarely comes to anyone in his
position.[2]

I am certain that I have not in fact matched that demand.
Indeed I am not quite sure what "my public" is. For *Honest
to God* itself did not set out to be a popular book. And the lectures that occasioned this book were prepared for university
students and so to that extent were framed for an academic
audience.[3] But they were not addressed primarily to those
with a professional interest in theology. I have therefore tried
to combine a "lay" approach with the kind of scientific rigor
which an educated public now properly expects in any field
of learning.

Nevertheless I fully expect that this work may fall between
two stools. For this is not a piece of *haute vulgarisation* in the
classical sense of taking what the scholars are saying and communicating it to an intelligent lay public. That presupposes a
relatively stable situation in which there is an agreed body of
knowledge or discussion to interpret and disseminate. This I
do not believe exists at the moment in the area of the doctrine
of God. The theologizing and the popularizing have to be
done at one and the same time.

To press on from *Honest to God,* for instance, means being
both more fundamental and more radical—not that there
should be any conflict between the two, for fundamentals and
roots are after all but two metaphors for the same thing. It

[2] *The Month,* July 1965, pp. 365f.
[3] I have attempted to write at a much more popular level on this and
other themes in a collection of pieces called *But That I Can't Believe!* (London, 1967).

means digging deeper; and this necessarily involves asking many far from superficial questions, to which profound minds over the centuries have given answers which must be taken into the account. Nevertheless, I am convinced that this digging has to be carried on, if I may so put it, on an open site, with the public looking on and being welcomed to join in. This is a relatively new and exposed place for the theologian to do his creative work, though many of the greatest contributions to theology have in fact been from men who did their best thinking on the frontier—from St. Paul, through Origen, Augustine, Aquinas, and Luther, to Paul Tillich in our own day.

Perhaps the analogy with archaeology is an illuminating one. For archaeology is a field in which there is still room for collaboration between professional and amateur, and in which there is a tradition of popular yet scientific writing of a high order. There will always be the place in theology as in archaeology for the fully annotated academic monograph. And of course there will always be the place for genuine mass communication. But what I suspect we are going increasingly to see is the marketplace rather than the library, the secular city rather than the monastery, as the *normal* place where the original work of serious theology is done. And this is liable to satisfy neither the professionals nor the public. But all one can do is to refuse to burke the difficult questions because they are difficult, to supply the references, not for armor-plating (for one must be prepared to operate more like David than Goliath) but for new openings, and above all to try to be humble in a field where the great have been before and at the same time honest to the questions that are genuinely one's own.

Contents

The human heart can go to the lengths of God.
Dark and cold we may be, but this
Is no winter now. The frozen misery
Of centuries breaks, cracks, begins to move;
The thunder is the thunder of the floes,
The thaw, the flood, the upstart Spring.
Thank God our time is now when wrong
Comes up to face us everywhere,
Never to leave us till we take
The longest stride of soul men ever took.
Affairs are now soul size.
The enterprise
Is exploration into God.

Christopher Fry: *A Sleep of Prisoners*

I should like to change the name "seekers" to "explorers" ...
We do not "seek" the Atlantic, we explore it.

Christian Faith and Practice in the Experience
of the Society of Friends, Excerpt 125.

Prologue: Quest for the Personal

In the lectures which formed the basis of this book I began, as Chapter 1 indicates, with a brief review of how the current debate about God has come to occupy the place and take the shape that it has. This review was concerned with what the research scholar calls "the state of the question," its public history. But there is also for anyone who comes to an issue after a good deal of personal involvement another train of events, an inside history, which may be equally important for interpreting the direction and thrust of the argument. This is not so appropriate for the public platform but may be a necessary preface for the reader.

I have hesitated before starting this book with what amounts to a condensed spiritual and intellectual autobiography, especially as personal histories are bound to appear tedious, if not obtrusive, to many readers. On the other hand, it has become obvious to me in the course of debate that without some understanding of the motivation behind it, what one says, and even more what one writes, is subject, apparently, to constructions and interpretations which one scarcely recognizes. In personal conversation or in the face-to-face dialogue of question and answer I find that much of this misunderstanding drops away or falls into place. That is why I always prefer if I can to respond to questions rather than to lecture or to preach. But this still leaves the much larger audience that one can reach only through the written word. And I realize that one owes it to them to declare one's presuppositions.

This is particularly true of the readership of *Honest to God*. Previous to that book it had not been my experience to find that what I had written was greeted by reviewers as confused, contradictory, or merely badly written. I am only too conscious of all these defects. But I do not think that this book was very much worse in these respects than any others of mine. Nor, I fear, will the last refuge of the ecclesiastical critic—that the Bishop was a sick man when he wrote it—really explain its deficiencies: a slipped disc cannot be held responsible for that amount of lapse. To be sure, as I freely acknowledged, it was tentative, it was thinking aloud, it was trying to find words for what was felt on the pulses. Nevertheless, I believe in retrospect that the real failure of communication, where it existed, was much more at the level of presupposition than of proposition. Where there was no failure, where, to use a distinction made by a Norwegian student at a public discussion, people felt what I meant even when they did not understand what I said, it was because they stood where I stood: they shared a common presupposition and felt a common pinch.

The room for misunderstanding was the greater because in *Honest to God* I was *taking for granted* most of what I believed. I was assuming the relatively limited audience for which I had previously written and was pushing out on the circumference rather than filling in the center. There were several areas of Christian doctrine—notably the Resurrection and Eschatology—on which I had already written extensively and so omitted because I had nothing new at the time that I wanted to say. But, above all, I was presupposing a fundamental conviction and commitment to the heart of the Christian faith—summed up in "the grace of our Lord Jesus Christ and the love of God and the fellowship of the Holy Spirit"— which I scarcely thought it necessary to state. This was the thesis from which I started. And even when questioning its expression or exploring its antithesis,[1] my base was not in doubt. Naturally if that was discounted, the whole perspective would look very different. And I could begin to understand, if still not really enter into, the supposition that I was an atheist (or at any rate trying to have it both ways), or wanted to substitute an impersonal pantheism for Biblical personalism, or immanence for transcendence, or acceptability to secular man for the truth of the Gospel. The only answer to such constructions is to fill in the center—or, rather, since this would involve an entire *apologia pro vita mea,* to draw out the leading thread which, as I see it, has been running through, and giving direction to, everything that I have sought to express.

This is, inevitably, to isolate and oversimplify. But I suppose that all my deepest concerns both in thought and in action— and I cannot separate the theological, the pastoral, and the political—find their center in a single, continuing quest. This is to give expression, embodiment, to the overmastering yet elusive conviction of the *Thou* at the heart of everything. It is a quest for the form of the personal as the ultimate reality in life, as the deepest truth about all one's relationships and com-

---

[1] As for instance in the lecture, given to urge *Christians* to take the challenge of atheism seriously, "Can a Truly Contemporary Person *Not* Be an Atheist?," *The New Reformation?* (London, 1965), Appendix I.

3

mitments. How can one give shape to the conviction that the personal is the controlling category for the interpretation of everything, both conceptually and in action? That it is this is one of those basic acts of trust of which it is impossible to say whether it comes from one's Christian commitment or whether Christianity authenticates itself because it provides its definition and vindication. At any rate it is, as near as I can determine, my central concern, that which chiefly decides what rings a bell, what I respond to as meaningful, significant, stimulating.

And I think the phrase "respond to" is the key. What I have in mind is that which makes one say, "Yes, that's true, that's real—for me." There are so many things one could not have thought up or expressed, but when one hears them or sees them one says "Yes." There is the sense that what is most deeply real is there before one: one is simply catching up on it, entering into it. Pascal's remark has always haunted me: "Thou wouldst not be seeking me if thou hadst not found me." Just *why* does this, on the face of it paradoxical, statement strike one as true—as true as, indeed much more profoundly true than, the more obvious fact that "thou wouldst not be seeking me if thou *hadst* found me"? It is one of those things of which one can simply say that it is so, reality is like that: it is prevenient, life is response—and hence responsibility—to something that encounters one, as it seems, with the claim of a *Thou*. This is the mystery that lies at its heart.

The clue to one's life can therefore be traced to those things to which one has responded, which have taken a hold on one or set up reverberations. In the realm of ideas—which, needless to say, is only a small, though decisive, part of life—I find that what has proved formative has been certain books backed

4

by the influence of persons to whom they meant much. I should never wish to underestimate the power of a person introducing a thought or a thinker to another. That is why I am unashamed to bring frequent quotations and references into my writings. Most readers may pass over them or wish that the man would predigest the matter for them in his own words: but for the occasional reader, at the right time, it may be a window opening on new worlds unknown. And one introduction leads to another. Or so it has often been with me.

I remember clearly the first time this happened to me. The first work of theology of which I recall becoming aware, as opposed to books of religious instruction, was Nicolas Berdyaev's *The Destiny of Man*. The school chaplain, a man for whom I had a great regard, had it with him at a religious discussion group because he happened to be reading it at the time. For some reason it caught my attention—was it the sweep of the title, the exotic sound of the author's name, the challenge of its obvious difficulty? At any rate its memory simmered, and some two or three years later I chose it for a College prize. The attempt to read it defeated me, and I put it aside. It had come before its time. But later I found it of consuming interest. I got other Berdyaevs. There were many ideas and allusions to further ideas which I did not understand. But I responded. For he was grappling with great issues, from a breadth of background and with a profundity of mind which fascinated me. It was to him that I owe my introduction to such deep, and near-heretical, thinkers as Origen, Meister Eckhart, and Jacob Boehme. I was fortunate to have discovered philosophy in a form that I now realize corresponded closely to my personalist and existentialist concern, even though I was not to read Berdyaev again for many years.

For though he fired me to read the philosophy of religion after I had finished classics, the reading list that then still dominated the Cambridge syllabus had not caught up on anything so recent as Berdyaev, let alone on the then new Oxford school of linguistic analysis (for which I was at the time not sorry). I was set to read John Caird's *Introduction to the Philosophy of Religion* and other products of English Hegelianism, together with a number of pre-1914 Gifford Lectures. The dominant books on the Cambridge scene were F. R. Tennant's two-volume *Philosophical Theology* and John Oman's *The Natural and the Supernatural*. The former had indeed a special lecture course entirely devoted to it by H. C. L. Heywood, subsequently Provost of Southwell; and to it I went in the autumn of 1940 with one other, a friend who was soon to leave for the R.A.F. and tragically to meet his death in the first mass raid over Cologne. This meant that I found myself in a one-to-one relationship with my lecturer; and to it I owe much. But the moment to which I owe most he has probably quite forgotten. It was one in which in passing he showed me Martin Buber's dull-brown paperback *I and Thou*. And again my curiosity was whetted by his remark that I should find it very difficult, that it would be useless for the Tripos, but that it might transform me.

It did. And, no sooner was the examination syllabus behind me and I had the never to be repeated opportunity of research on any subject that I chose, than I opted for this tiny book— and its relation to the vastness of the Christian doctrine of God —for the subject of my Ph.D. thesis. But already there had been two other influences that affected the direction in which I would go. The first was the theme for a University prize—

6

"Kant's Ethics and the Christian Moral Ideal"—which was closely related to the special subject for my Tripos examination. This made me steep myself in Kant, who remains surely one of the profoundist thinkers ever to have written on what he called "the kingdom of ends"—that whole realm that deals with the freedom, the autonomy, the unconditional integrity of the personal. The other influence was also the set subject of a prize essay, specifically entitled "The Personality of God."

Accompanying this was the discovery of Kierkegaard, who was at that time being translated into English after an interval of nearly a century. Again I remember very clearly what stimulated me to read him. It was a quotation in a sermon— was there ever so long a quotation in a sermon?—by A. D. Lindsay, the then Master of Balliol. He read the whole of the extract from the *Journals* in which Kierkegaard meditates on the infinitely delicate relationship between power and freedom which requires nothing less than omnipotence in God if man is to be free, because only omnipotence has the power so to retract itself as to leave the other completely free.[2] It was a passage that undoubtedly affected my earliest attempt at original theological writing, on the omnipotence of love to accomplish universal salvation, which later found its way into my first published book.[3] But, more importantly, it opened up Kierkegaard to me, with his vital insight into the significance of the concrete individual person and of truth as "subjectivity"

[2] S. Kierkegaard, *Selections from the Journals,* edited by A. Dru (London, 1938), No. 616.

[3] *In the End, God* .... In the newly revised edition to be published in 1968, it appears in chaps. 11 and 12.

—though one of the most formative essays I read was Buber's criticism of Kierkegaard for supposing that the *I* of "the Individual" could be understood out of relation to the *Thou*.[4]

This was a time too in which the insights of Buber's thinking were beginning to be popularized, largely through J. H. Oldham's *Christian Newsletter* and his book *Real Life Is Meeting.* Closely parallel (though, as far as I know, independent) ideas had been spread through John Macmurray's books. His *Reason and Emotion, The Structure of Religious Experience,* and *Interpreting the Universe* were to influence me most and introduced a valuable threefold distinction between "instrumental," "functional," and "personal" relationships to supplement Buber's twofold division between *I-Thou* and *I-It.* But he was never able to satisfy me, any more than John Wren-Lewis subsequently, that he really did justice to the dimension of transcendence required to make meaningful talk of divine-human encounter as distinct from purely interpersonal relationships.

The Divine-Human Encounter was in fact the translated title of a work by another author who influenced me greatly at the time, Emil Brunner. This has since been republished, with additional material, under its original title, *Truth as Encounter,* which does more justice to its thesis, namely, that the truth as the Christian knows it is always a relationship a person must be "in" if he is to understand it aright, as a subject in response to a *Thou.* It can never, without distortion, be stated objectively or propositionally. This thesis was to be reflected in the title of my Ph.D. dissertation, *Thou Who Art,* which

[4] *Die Frage an den Einzelnen,* subsequently included in *Between Man and Man* (London, 1947), pp. 40–82.

8

was chosen in conscious contrast to that of one of E. L. Mascall's books published about that time, *He Who Is*.

Brunner's name is also a reminder that the dominant influence of this period in theology was that of the Neo-orthodox school, whose whole emphasis was on the transcendent personal God of the Biblical revelation. This was the context in which my mind was shaped, and I have never had reason to doubt its basic presuppositions. My only concern has been with the way in which what Bonhoeffer called Barth's "positivism of revelation" made the presentation of this school of theology often so irrevelant to the realities of relationship from which human beings actually begin. In its more extreme form its distrust of all philosophy and its almost pathological abhorrence of natural theology seem to me to require a split, if not a sacrifice, of the intellect as intolerable as that demanded by any Biblicist fundamentalism.

I mention the influence of Continental Neo-orthodox theology mainly to make it clear that an impersonal immanentism of a pantheistic kind for which I have been thought to be arguing has never for me been a live option—though I suppose there is a part of all of us to which the philosophies of a Wordsworth or a Matthew Arnold make their appeal. For they, like the religions of the East, draw attention to an aspect of reality for which Biblical personalism must find a place if it is to satisfy the whole man.

But the main line of my thinking was firmly within the tradition represented by my supervisor for the Ph.D., H. H. Farmer. With John Baillie, who was also to be one of my examiners, he more than anyone else in Britain had assimilated the insights of the *I-Thou* philosophy to the Biblical doc-

9

trines of God and man. And it was under his guiding that I explored both the history and the implications of this tradition of thought for how one could speak of personality in God. The very phrase "personality in God," rather than talk of God as "a Person," is a reminder of another book that played a decisive part in shaping my mind, C. C. J. Webb's Gifford Lectures of 1918, *God and Personality*. These set in context how remarkably recent is the phrase "the personality of God." It only came into use as the eighteenth century passed into the nineteenth: prior to that, the category of personality was reserved for the "Persons" of the Trinity. Indeed, the clues to our modern understanding of personality all lie in the nineteenth century. The classical writers had no word for it, and Boethius' definition of *persona* which was to dominate, and indeed freeze, discussion for over a thousand years, was formulated in a *Christological* context. A person, he said, is "an individual substance of a rational nature." This definition was to have a baleful effect. Not only did it try to encompass the mystery of personality in terms of subpersonal categories like substance and nature (perhaps this was inevitable, though Augustine had opened the possibilities of much deeper psychological insight); but, above all, it attempted to define personality without any reference to relationships. An individual substance could be thought of as existing in complete isolation, and all that distinguished a person from other substances was certain qualities of rationality not possessed by things or animals.

The effect of this definition was to be seen in the discussion of the personality of God. Not only could God easily be envisaged as existing *per se* and *a se,* but all that need be predicated of him for him to be personal was certain "attributes" of goodness and knowledge, purpose and power, etc. The fact that, like a human person, such a Supreme Being could stand in quite impersonal relations with other persons did not matter. For the deism of the eighteenth and early nineteenth centuries it was sufficient that God could be shown to be the benevolent Architect and master Minder of the universe. That this watchmaker Deity, the individual Substance of a supremely rational Nature, who did nothing in particular (except for occasional acts of special providence and miracle) and did it very well, should be remote and impersonal in his relationships was in no way thought to be incompatible with his Personality. It is hardly surprising that Feuerbach (one of the earliest users, incidentally, of the *I-Thou* terminology) should have been so passionate in wanting to restore to human *relationships* the attributes which, as he saw it, had been projected onto this Being in the heavens and had there become frozen.

The ghost of deism was never finally laid by the emergence of a much warmer theism, represented at its best in the late nineteenth century by Hermann Lotze. Indeed, it haunts theology still. This was because theism, which saw that an intimate personal relationship of love and freedom between God and his creatures was essential if he was to bear any resemblance to "the God of Abraham, Isaac, and Jacob," let alone "the God and Father of our Lord Jesus Christ," nevertheless still worked with the assumption that this relationship was external rather than internal to the definition of personality. It was this assumption that the *I-Thou* philosophy challenged. The *I* of personality is possible at all only as the *I* of the *I-Thou* —or of the *I-It*—relationship.

The heart of all talk about personality is the reality of a certain quality of relatedness, of being encountered and drawn out by the grace and claim of the *Thou*. This is the center point, the existential reality, which has to be given expression. And the need to speak of "God" derives from the awareness that in and through and under every finite *Thou* comes, if we are open to it, the grace and claim of an eternal, unconditional *Thou* who cannot finally be evaded by being turned into an *It*. This was the reality which the language of "the personality of God" was trying to represent.[5] The image of a super-Person, of a celestial Being, with those rational qualities, seemed strangely peripheral and irrelevant. No doubt he had to be "there" as the invisible telephone exchange, as it were, to which all wires led. But of him in himself, apart from the wires of relationship, one could see or know nothing.

Such was the point, as I see it in retrospect, to which I had come at the stage of my doctoral thesis in 1945, which has since lain unread and unpublished. And there I left the theoretical quest for the form of the personal, to give myself first to pastoral relationships with real people and then to the teaching of New Testament theology and to liturgical and political involvement with equally real people. By the time I returned to the doctrine of God some fifteen years later and tried to gather up what in the interval had been collecting under the surface, I suppose I had come, without realizing it, to the same sort of point which Bishop Berkeley reached in his questioning of Locke's philosophy of substance. Was it really essential, in order to assert the fact of being held in this

[5] I. T. Ramsey makes the same point by insisting on the centrality of the notion of "reciprocity" in his essay "A Personal God" in F. G. Healey, ed., *Prospect for Theology: Essays in Honour of H. H. Farmer* (Welwyn, Eng., 1967), pp. 52–71.

inescapable personal relationship as the final, interpretative reality of life, to posit this concept of a divine Person behind the scenes? If his being there seemed peripheral and irrelevant, might it not be actually misleading? Might not the image of this super-Person distract from the reality-in-relationship it was seeking to express by turning people's eyes upward or outward to a Being for whose existence the evidence was to say the least doubtful, instead of focusing attention on "the beyond in the midst"?

So *Honest to God* was born. The underlying concern had not changed. It was still to give expression to the form of the personal at the level of the universe as a whole, to the overwhelming conviction of the ultimate reality of the *Thou* at the heart of all things. To say that this was atheistic because it questioned traditional theism's image of a supreme Being was surely absurd. To say that it was propounding an impersonal God because it used the phrase "the ground of being" was hardly less so. To use such language of God is no more to assert an impersonal Deity than to call him "the rock of our salvation" or, with the very ancient Christian hymn, the "strength and stay upholding all creation." Indeed, it employs the same metaphor as "substance"—that which "stands under." It is, of course, nonpersonal terminology, and as such very limited. In fact, I have since found myself using it less and less. But its point was not to say that God *is* a Substance, or a Ground, but that the utterly personal *Thou*-relationship in which God is known is (to use Buber's metaphor) the umbilical cord of man's very existence: his whole being is rooted in it. Of course, this metaphor, like any metaphor if pressed, is equally unsatisfactory. For the umbilical cord has to be cut. Or rather it has to be replaced, in the process of growth, first by a natural tie of physical response and then by a free relationship of moral and spiritual responsibility. Only so can a person become a person.

Equally beside the point was the supposition that I was trying to substitute immanence for transcendence, to replace the God "up there" or "out there" by one "in here." In fact, as I tried to insist,[6] I was concerned not to abolish transcendence (for without transcendence God becomes indistinguishable from the world, and so superfluous) but to find a way of *expressing* transcendence which would not tie God's reality to a supranaturalistic or mythological world-view which, if not actually falsifying, was largely meaningless for twentieth-century man. Nor was I saying that God is merely a function of human interpersonal relationships—that if there were no men to experience him he would not exist. On the contrary, I would want to say of God with the *I-Thou* philosophers, "Through *Thee, I* am": our existence as men is wholly dependent on his utterly gracious, prevenient reality.

Nor, incidentally, did I ever confine the awareness of God to relationships with persons—though I would, of course, agree that it comes to its highest articulation, as the Bible insists, through the neighbor (and ultimately through *the* son of man) rather than through anything subpersonal. But it is a common misunderstanding of Buber that in distinguishing the *I-Thou* from the *I-It* relationship he was differentiating our relationships to persons and to things. In fact, we can have both kinds of relationships to each, and the *Thou* of God is to be met as much through nature as through history.

[6] With particular explicitness on p. 44 (London, 1963).

14

The emphasis on persons that comes out in my writings (though I have sought to balance it in Chapter 5 of this book) reflects the fact that my world has been more that of human beings in society than, say, Teilhard de Chardin's world of rocks and fossils and organisms in the laboratory.

This reference to human beings in society may serve to introduce a final disclaimer that this language of the *Thou* means a focusing on the *individual,* in morals or in anything else. Personality is essentially a corporate, social phenomenon. Indeed, it was because of this emphasis that I was drawn into New Testament study through the insights of St. Paul on "the body" (the nearest equivalent Biblical concept to our "personality"), which stands for man, and for all life, in the solidarities both of sin and of redemption. And in the introduction to my study of that theme I made it clear that my interest in the subject was as much social and political as it was theological.[7] The same concern for the personal only within the structural nexus of a largely depersonalized society runs through the essays in *On Being the Church in the World,* which came out of the time when I was primarily a Biblical theologian. It also underlies my political engagement and explains why I found myself responding instinctively to men like Reinhold Niebuhr and William Temple, to James Burnham's *Managerial Revolution* (another of the seminal books in my history), and more recently to socially oriented theologians like Peter Berger, Gibson Winter, and Harvey Cox.

To round off this account, I should perhaps add something to say what it was that spoke to me in the authors I mainly

[7] *The Body* (London, 1952), pp. 7–8.

15

drew upon in *Honest to God,* who have not come into view so far. They entered during the "tunnel period" in which the stream I am here attempting to trace went underground. But they were tributaries which together built up to produce something of a breakthrough, at any rate for me. Indeed, I am inclined to think after the event that the most original thing about *Honest to God* (which I called the least original book I had written) was precisely the bringing together of three authors who were in fact very different. I have never claimed that they were saying the same thing or that they could be harmonized without injustice. But at least Tillich, Bultmann, and, on Bonhoeffer's behalf, Eberhard Bethge, his correspondent and biographer, were all gracious enough to say that I had interpreted them aright. What I was doing was quite deliberately to isolate aspects of the thinking of each which together, it seemed to me, posed the same question from different angles. Let me say briefly what in each caused me to respond, and what did not.

In Tillich it was the possibility of a third option between supranaturalism and naturalism, theism and atheism. He offered a way of speaking about God without dependence on the increasingly problematic notion of a supreme Being, an almighty Person. Yet his awareness of the reality of God was personal through and through. Particularly in his sermons, he spoke of the *Thou,* as heard by Prophet and Apostle, in grace and demand, in a manner which made his profoundly simple words heavy with spiritual power. And this was independent of the Platonic ontology through which he sought to give expression to his more systematic thought and to which I have never found myself particularly drawn.

In Bultmann I found a way of interpreting, in terms that

16

were existentially real, ways of speaking about God and Christ that were in danger of becoming meaningless to an age like ours which can no longer regard myth as in any sense an objective description of what the world is like or how it works. He enabled the personalistic language of the God who acts, and of beings from another world intervening in the affairs of this one, to be understood still in terms of genuinely personal relationship, without dependence on an antique cosmology. Yet there were many things in Bultmann to which I had no wish to be committed—his undue historical skepticism (as it seemed to me) as a New Testament critic, his heavy reliance on Heideggerian existentialism, and, at least in his more extreme left-wing followers, a tendency not merely to locate the meaning of God in statements about man but to equate the two.

In the case of Bonhoeffer, there was one of those immediate recognitions, when I first read extracts from his *Letters and Papers from Prison,* that here was an insight of tremendous potency and consequence. This was his detachment of Christian faith from what he called "the religious *a priori*." In all previous ages and societies there has been a way in for "God" through the presupposition that all men everywhere, if the opening could be found, were at some point religious. There was a sector in the life of the tribe, the village, the individual, which could never be closed by human explanation or control, in which the priest or "minister of religion" operated. But suppose that gap in the circle is closed, or is fast being closed? For such appears to be the effect of the modern phenomenon of secularization. Suppose completely secularized man (if there ever is such an animal) is not going to be religious at all—and we appear to be well on the way there already? Does

17

this mean the end of God, or prayer, or the Church? Bonhoeffer was convinced the answer was "No"; and he began to wrestle in his prison cell with the question "How do we speak in a secular way about God?"[8]

This question is fundamental, as I see it, to all contemporary "exploration into God." It does not in the least mean capitulation to secularism—to the "ism" which would interpret everything in terms of the age or *saeculum* that now is, which is only another form of naturalism, excluding all reference to God and the transcendent. But it does mean taking seriously the phenomenon of secularization, the rapidly increasing autonomy of one department of life after another from religious or metaphysical control. Secular man, "come of age," is no longer dependent as he once was—and it is futile, as well as immoral, to try to subject him to a God whose strength depends on man's weakness and ignorance. The Christian gospel is rather that man is responsible—terrifyingly responsible—in freedom to a God whose strength is made perfect in weakness and suffering.

Bonhoeffer was horrified at the idea of "cheap grace," and no one could have been further from selling the Gospel short to "modern man" if this made it palatable to his presuppositions. And this is a charge that I personally find it difficult to take too seriously. To adapt some words of William Temple I have used before: "I am not asking, 'What will secular man swallow?' I am secular man asking what there is to eat." There has been a pastoral passion running through all my concern with the theology of the personal. And, if there is a defect among those who rely on Bonhoeffer to the exclusion,

[8] *Letters and Papers from Prison*, p. 153. The references here and elsewhere are to the revised English translation (London, 1967).

say, of Tillich, it is in a curving in upon itself of evangelistic interest and missionary motive.[9]

But the point I am concerned to make here is that what attracted me to the three writers upon whom I chiefly drew in *Honest to God* was that they were all men whose roots were in Biblical personalism and who were prepared to explore its expression in radically changing circumstances without abandoning its presuppositions. Tillich was one who, to quote one of his titles, could never divorce "Biblical religion" from "the search for ultimate reality."[10] Bultmann was a man so steeped in the world of the New Testament as to feel the full force of its distance from our own, and hence the stumbling block to modern man of many things which are no true part of the offense of the Gospel at all. Bonhoeffer was astringently, perhaps too exclusively, Biblical in his thinking. And long before I personally became a Biblical theologian by specialism my dominating interest was in what Pascal distinguished as the living God, "the God of Abraham, Isaac, and Jacob," in contrast to "the God of the philosophers," the still-life deity, as Brunner put it, who only allows himself to be looked at. One of the formative influences at an early stage of my philosophical research was some almost verbatim notes, derived from an Oxford friend, of lectures given by O. C. Quick on the fundamental contrast between the Hebraic thinking about God in terms of will and personality and the Hellenic attempt to define his essence in the categories of being and perfection.[11] I now realize that this contrast was

[9] This comes out rather clearly in Paul van Buren's book, *The Secular Meaning of the Gospel* (London, 1963), pp. 190–92.

[10] *Biblical Religion and the Search for Ultimate Reality.*

[11] I think the nearest any of this material came to publication was in parts of his book *The Gospel of the New World.*

19

overdrawn. But there was no doubt on which side I found myself.[12]

I would agree with the great New Testament scholar Joachim Jeremias that one of the central and distinctive features of the Christian gospel is the utterly intimate, personal relationship which is summed up in Jesus' word *Abba* (Father or Daddy).[13] It is this relationship at the heart of the universe, at the very core of reality, for which Christian theology has to find expression—in such a way that it *is* made central to everything else that coheres in it. The problem is that so much traditional God-language, so far from making it the most real thing in the world, seems to many of one's contemporaries, and to so much of oneself, to add nothing—and even to detract from the reality it exists to express. This is the problem to which I have tried to address myself afresh in what follows.

[12] My "Hebraic" bias came out very strongly in *In the End, God . . . .*
[13] *The Central Message of the New Testament* (London, 1965), chap. 1.

CHAPTER ONE

The Displacement Effect of Theism

There are fashions in theology as in everything else. In each decade or so some area comes into the sharp focus of concern and debate. In the nineteen-twenties and early thirties, under the impact of historical criticism and liberal theology, it was the doctrine of the *person of Christ*. The most influential book of popular theology in Britain was T. R. Glover's *The Jesus of History,* and the report, for instance, of the Doctrinal Commission of the Church of England, which sat during the years 1922–38, was much preoccupied with what could be believed in the twentieth century about the life and person of Jesus Christ.[1] In the late thirties and forties, under the menacing cloud of strange and rival ideologies, attention had become focused on the doctrine of *man.* Illuminated in all its greatness and tragedy by Reinhold Niebuhr's Gifford Lectures, *The Nature and Destiny of Man,* it was chosen, almost inevitably, as the theological issue of the Lambeth Conference of 1948. Then, in the early fifties, as men's minds turned amid the anxieties of the nuclear age to the hope of a new world, came a reminder of the central place in the Christian procla-

---

[1] *Doctrine in the Church of England* (London, 1938).

mation of *eschatology,* or the doctrine of the end. "Jesus Christ the hope of the world" was the natural theme of the 1954 Assembly of the World Council of Churches. By the time the Council met again, at New Delhi in 1961, the focus of ferment and renewal was the doctrine of *the Church* itself. The most lasting outcome of that Assembly was its setting up of the Commission on "the missionary structure of the congregation," just as, subsequently, the central Decree of the second Vatican Council was that on the nature of the Church. And now we are agitated, most deeply of all, by a thoroughgoing reappraisal of the doctrine of *God.* Already this has reached the stage of throwing up its own Baedeker: David Jenkins' *Guide to the Debate about God.*[2]

And yet I detect a difference this time. All the previous debates (with the partial exception of that on *man,* which engaged Christians in dialogue with Marxists and scientific humanists) took place within the Church, which alone is usually interested in matters of theology. Now, however, the debate has broken through. Indeed, though it began with questions raised by Christian theologians, they were not questions arising directly from Church circles. In fact in Church circles they were not being asked, which explains both the relief and the resentment when they were. The interest and response has flowed right across the usual lines which bound the circles both of professional theology and of popular religion; and for the first time the debate has been overheard and entered by representatives of the non-Christian world-religions. "God" is news. Hardly a week passes without articles

[2] It is really a guide to the *background* of the debate. It is very lucid and illuminating on the theologians who lie behind it, but hardly touches on many themes of the debate itself, e.g., secularization, supranaturalism, God-language, the "death of God" theology.

and interviews in the secular journals and the mass media. As Alasdair MacIntyre has said, "When not only the *Observer* but also the *New Yorker,* and not only the *New Yorker* but also *Playboy,* finds that theology, even theology in so rapid a form as this, is what their readers will be titillated by, this casts an interesting and not wholly expected light on the situation. God may be dead, but he is also and most certainly making the scene."[3]

And yet this very considerable "revival of interest," as it was designated by a leading British newspaper, is a strange thing. It has coincided at any rate in England, though not in England alone, with a dramatic decline in the number of baptisms, confirmations, ordinations, etc. which set in, I should judge, some two years earlier[4] and certainly cannot simply be attributed to the "damage" done by the debate. Interest in these questions by no means indicates acceptance of the Church's answer to them. Indeed, one has the impression that people are interested in them despite rather than because of organized religion. They feel there is "something there," but are convinced it cannot be what the Church appears to offer them. And the interest is nothing transient or superficial. God —or, just as much, the absence of God—exercises a continuing fascination, like a candle to the moth. Even atheists cannot leave the subject alone. And if the whole debate were about nothing I cannot believe that it would have cut so deep. There is a reality here "soul size," which demands the new and wider chartings of which Christopher Fry speaks. The enterprise is one that engages the novelist, the dramatist, the film

[3] In a review of Ved Mehta's *The New Theologian, Encounter,* March 1967.

[4] See my contribution to the symposium "...And What Next...?" *Prism,* September 1965, pp. 9–17.

producer, the artist and the poet, the philosopher and the psychiatrist, as much as the professional theologian. And if the answer is to be in distinctively Christian terms at all, it must be in terms of a Christ who is inclusive rather than exclusive.

Indeed, a major part of the irrelevance of the churches appears to be their very posing of the question of God. As this has traditionally come to be stated, it signally fails to formulate the real issue. Hence the confusion, which the opinion polls reveal. It has been said that "the creed of the English is that there is no God and that it is wise to pray to him from time to time."[5] But ostensibly at any rate the creed of the English is emphatically that there *is* a God (the latest poll[6] gave 84 per cent[7]—the latest American figure being 97 per cent[8]) and that it is wise to pray to him from time to time (43 per cent, incredibly, said "regularly"). But most of their other answers indicate that in terms of that God they are practical atheists. The percentages of "Yes" and "No" could almost as well be reversed.

The polls merely reflect the fact that somehow the traditional question has ceased to be the right one to ask. People say "Yes" because there is something they do not want to be put in the position of denying. Yet the truer answer might

[5] Alasdair MacIntyre, *Encounter*, September 1963; reprinted in J. A. T. Robinson and D. L. Edwards, eds., *The Honest to God Debate* (London, 1963), p. 228.

[6] *Television and Religion: A Report Prepared by Social Surveys (Gallup Poll) Ltd. on Behalf of ABC Television, 1964.*

[7] This includes both belief in "a personal God" and in "some sort of Spirit or Vital Force." But the distinction between these two is itself in serious need of clearing up. Cardinal Heenan, for instance, in a television comment specifically mentioned me in the latter category. Would he also include Teilhard de Chardin?

[8] Lou Harris Survey, 1965.

24

be "No." Conversely, I who find the reality of God inescapable would doubtless be recorded among the 16 per cent who could not return a straight affirmative. I was reminded recently of the story of the American magazine which sent a telegram to Einstein: "DO YOU BELIEVE IN GOD STOP PREPAID FIFTY WORDS." For I was asked by a secular journal for one half of a double article on "Do We Need a God?"[9] My immediate reaction was to reply on a postcard (since a telegram was not prepaid): "To the question as put like that, No." But since mine was the half expected to provide the answer "Yes," and I proposed to accept the invitation, the editor might well have wondered what was happening.

Just what *is* happening? I tried to put my finger on it, as I see it, in the opening chapters of *Honest to God,* and in particular in that called "The End of Theism?" I should like to take up the argument from there.

No one can easily deny that there is at any rate a crisis in theism, that is, in the traditional case for belief in the existence of a personal God. Until recently the issue was relatively simple. It was summed up in the title of the book by A. E. Taylor (author of the justly praised article on "Theism" in the *Encyclopaedia of Religion and Ethics*)—*Does God Exist?* To that the theist said "Yes," the atheist "No"—and the Christian, of course, was on the side of the theist. The answer might be in doubt, but not the question. Now, however, the situation is more complicated.

This is not because the Christian has any more inclination toward the classic alternatives to theism, deism on the one hand and pantheism on the other. Deism started from the transcendence of God, his otherness from the world, but failed

[9] Since reprinted in *But That I Can't Believe!,* chap. 13.

to do justice to his immanence: it produced a remote, artificer Deity standing in a less than truly personal relationship to his creatures. Pantheism, on the contrary, started from the immanence of God, his oneness with the world, and failed to do justice to his transcendence. And again it conceived the universe in subpersonal terms, with human freedom and personal identity absorbed in an all-pervasive Divinity.

The reality that theism sought to safeguard and enshrine is not at issue, nor has it changed—the reality of the God-relationship as utterly personal and utterly central. There are, indeed, plenty of questions about the status of this reality— whether it describes anything outside us or merely our way of looking at the world, whether the word "God" is any longer meaningful or necessary, whether for many indeed the reality itself may not finally have gone dead, and so on. I propose to look at these questions in later chapters. But for the time being I am taking for granted the spiritual reality or dimension of experience for which men have used the name "God" and which Jesus defined for his followers in terms of *"Abba,"* Father. The immediate question is how that intensely personal, experienced reality can be represented and given expression in a view of the universe that truly makes it central.

The task of theology may be seen as a form of map making —trying to represent the mystery of *theos* (the incommunicable spiritual reality) by a *logos* or word-picture which can be used for the purposes of communication. It involves a translation or transposition from one dimension to another. And to make a map it is necessary to employ what the geographer calls a "projection." In physical geography the most familiar of these is Mercator's projection, named after the famous sixteenth-century Flemish geographer, which per-

26

forms the not inconsiderable task of transferring a spherical earth onto the oblong pages of an atlas (a name he also invented). There are, of course, many alternatives, which depict the earth as two flat circles or hemispheres, as strung-out segments like slices of a lemon, in cloverleaf form, or in other still more peculiar shapes. Each is as artificial as the other. This in theory we recognize. Yet we still need to be convinced that the shortest distance between two points on the real earth is not always a straight line on our maps. And we have got so used to visualizing the relation of the continents according to Mercator's projection that we forget that they are not "really" thus. It is difficult to believe, for instance, that Moscow is not much further from San Francisco than London, whereas in fact the two capitals are virtually equidistant from the Pacific coast. For most practical purposes until recently the projection was adequate—the distortion only seriously affected countries on the edge of beyond like Baffin Land and Greenland. But to plan an early warning radar system, or even airline schedules, on Mercator's projection is clearly asking for trouble.

But to return to the maps constructed by theology. Any *logos* about *theos* must also employ some projection to depict or represent the spiritual reality with which it is dealing. Usually we are no more conscious of it than we are when looking at an atlas. Indeed, there is one that has so dominated the tradition in which most of us have grown up that we almost forget that the map is not a direct transcript of reality itself. It has the same effect as the Authorized or King James Version in making people think it *is* the Bible. To question it is to question God. Yet we must question it and look at it for what it is.

Theism, like deism (but unlike pantheism), employs what, for want of a better name, may be called the supranaturalist projection. I am inclined, in this context, to retain Tillich's usage and use the term "supranatural" rather than "supernatural." Of course both words mean the same. But "the supernatural" is used so loosely to mean the same as "the divine" (when it does not mean "the spooky") that the more unfamiliar word may serve to pull us up and remind us that what is at issue here is not the reality of God as such but a particular way of representing or describing it.[10] This projection represents the reality of God in human experience by the *existence* of *a* God or gods in some realm above or beyond that of everyday relationships. So the question of God comes out in the form "Do you believe in the existence of a personal God?" or quite simply "Does God exist?"

So familiar are we with this form of the question that the transition is barely observed. It is a help therefore to look at its use in a tradition other than our own.

From time immemorial men have projected their religious convictions onto the heavens and there visualized beings who embodied them. This is a process we recognize readily enough in the gods and goddesses of ancient Greece and Rome. No one seriously believes these beings "existed" on top of Olympus or anywhere else. The realities of Greek and Roman religion, however, remain—insights into the deepest things of life from which we can still learn as we can from the art or

---

[10] Apart from its somewhat misleading title, it is a defect of Jenkins' otherwise excellent *Guide to the Debate about God* that he does not sufficiently distinguish at this point. For him "the end of theism" is equivalent to the end of belief in God, whereas I used the phrase to mean that a particular way of representing the personal reality of God has reached the end of its usefulness. Whether it has or not is another matter, and this is why I put a question mark after my chapter title.

philosophy of the same cultures. The projection[11] or description of these insights as beings inhabiting another, separate world of their own is now accepted for what it is, a personification in terms of superhuman entities of the profoundest realities of spiritual experience. We can acknowledge this without questioning the perception of the realities they sought to portray.

Similarly, the conception of God as *a* Being, a Person—like ourselves but supremely above or beyond ourselves—will, I believe, come to be seen as a human projection. (Most people already recognize this in the case of the Devil.) It is a way of making real and vivid to the imagination, by personification, the conviction that reality at its deepest is to be interpreted not simply at the level of its impersonal, mathematical regularities but in categories like love and trust, freedom, responsibility, and purpose. The real question of God is not the *existence* of a Being whom we visualize as embodying these in his Person. It is whether this conviction about the ultimate nature and meaning of things is true.

I would interject, in passing, that I am not here simply advocating the same position as that taken by Feuerbach in the last century. Feuerbach accused religion of filching *human* values and projecting them as attributes onto an imaginary subject in the heavens. He wanted to restore them to man and reduce theology to anthropology. I believe, on the contrary, that the reality encountered as personal rather than

---

[11] There is, I am aware, a blurring of the line here between the geographer's and the psychologist's use of the term "projection." But they have this in common: they both involve the throwing of the experienced reality, as it were, onto a screen. To recognize the mechanism at work is not in any way to imply that God is merely a projection, that there is no divine reality apart from the projection. It is simply to describe the human process by which the reality comes to be represented as a supranatural figure.

impersonal is indeed of God and not simply of man. My sole question is whether this conviction about the nature of the ultimate must necessarily be framed in terms of the existence of a divine Being.

Until now it has not been necessary for practical purposes to make much distinction between the religious reality and the projection by which it is represented. We have been able, for instance, to dismiss the spiritual inadequacy of the Olympian religion on the grounds that its gods did not "exist." But we are being forced to be more discriminating. For it is beginning to look as if we should be preparing if necessary to detach our own faith from this projection. It is possible that we may *not* need *a* God (hence part of my reluctance to answer "Yes" to the editor's question),[12] just as a Devil is not essential to the spiritual life of most Christians today. In fact, the projection may actually diminish the reality rather than express it.

Such a supranatural Person has hitherto been regarded by most of us as an indispensable focus for the imagination. But then, in the West, we have done our thinking and living, if not in a three-decker universe, at any rate in one divided mentally into two realms, a natural and a supernatural. In India and China and the East generally, men have not. And Eastern religions have not, for the most part, felt the need of this projection. To be sure, this is partly because they have seen the spiritual reality in less dynamic and personalistic terms than Judaism, Christianity, and Islam. But that is a separate issue. It does not of itself explain the phenomenon of the absence of

[12] The other part was a refusal to test the truth or falsity of God by whether or not he can be shown to be an object of human *need*. He may be "intellectually superfluous" and "emotionally dispensable" and yet an inescapable reality. See "Can a Truly Contemporary Person *Not* Be an Atheist?" *The New Reformation?* pp. 106–22.

"a God" at all in early Hinduism, Taoism, and Buddhism, especially when the perception of reality in the last is so close at many points to the Christian. A non-theistic religion seems almost a contradiction in terms to the Western mind; but, equally, the presentation of reality as a personified Being appears to trivialize it for the Oriental. There are indeed fundamental differences between these religions, which I have no desire to minimize, but their failure to share a common projection has added unnecessary misunderstanding to the spiritual dialogue between East and West.

But the attachment of Christianity to the supranaturalist projection is becoming less and less obvious. For many purposes we still find it virtually impossible to conceive of "God" except as a separate, personified Being. And there is nothing wrong with this projection, any more than there is with Mercator's. But I am convinced that to represent the spiritual reality (in its transcendent aspect) as a Being in another realm is to make it unreal and remote for vast numbers of people today. Not only do they take the projection for the reality and demand "evidence" for the existence of such a Being (often as crudely as Khrushchev's astronauts), but, more importantly, it has the effect of rendering God marginal and peripheral. Men cannot recognize the reality of God in the experienced relationship, because the image which should help to make it vivid locates him in an area in which they no longer *live*. This is the real point I was trying to make in *Honest to God* about the placing of God "up there" or "out there." It is not that people literally believe this and that this is somehow bad.[13] It is that these are "dead" areas. God is banished

[13] Ultimately, of course, all spatial terms in relation to God are interchangeable. Cf. *The Cloud of Unknowing*: "In these matters height, depth, length, and breadth all mean the same" (chap. 37); "We have got to take

31

to the edges of life—to the uncanny (about the only remaining significance for most people of "the supernatural"), to what men still cannot understand or control (so-styled "acts of God"), or to what is revealingly called the "after-life." At the end of their tether men may still turn to the One above—to pray to or to blame; but in the ordinary course of affairs he comes in, if at all, only after the vital connections have been made. Life is completed, for some, by the addition of God. Most others wonder why they should include this extra storey. In any case, the effect is a displacement of him as God. He has ceased by definition to be the *ens realissimum,* the most real thing in the world. He is on or off the edge of the map. No wonder that it is scarcely significant whether 84 per cent say they believe in him or 16 per cent. For the question is no longer in any real sense the question of God. The projection has distorted the reality it was there to express.

This is not a process confined to the secularized West. John Taylor, the author of that remarkable book on African religion *The Primal Vision,* says that Christianity and Islam with their supranaturalist projection have merely confirmed for Africans the irrelevance of the Sky-God Creator. "It seems," he writes, "that Africa endorses the conviction which is growing in almost every part of the world that if God has his being in some realm of the spirit, distinct from, and external to, the processes and relationships of the here and now, then that God and that realm are to all intents non-existent."[14] And it is in this sense that men in the Bible say, "There is no

particular care with those two words 'in' and 'up' "—i.e. not to be misled into interpreting them literally (chap. 51). However, psychologically, I am convinced that they can powerfully affect how real we feel God to be.

[14] *C.M.S. News-Letter,* April 1965.

God": he is not operative, he does not function, he is not real. And this lies behind, though it does not exhaust, the current proclamation by *Christian* theologians of "the death of God." Drained gradually but irrevocably of reality, he has become a shadow. Other things are more real—and that not simply visible, material things. Other spiritual distinctions—the difference, for instance, within human relationships, between *I-Thou* and *I-It*—mean much more than the difference between the world and God, the natural and the supernatural. Consequently, the Church, which seems to men to be framing the issue in an unreal way and asking men for commitments they do not find meaningful, appears increasingly irrelevant.

In the past the question of God's existence as a Being has been in practice indistinguishable from his reality for human experience. In what has been called the most Greek phrase in the Bible, the author of the Epistle to the Hebrews writes that "whoever would draw near to God must believe that he exists."[15] Today belief in his existence bears very little relationship to his reality, as the opinion polls show. The identification no longer holds, and I believe, with Tillich, that we should give up speaking of "the existence" of God.[16]

[15] Hebrews 11.6.
[16] See his *Systematic Theology,* I (Welwyn, Eng., 1953), 227: "The scholastics were right when they asserted that in God there is no difference between essence and existence. But they perverted their insight when in spite of this assertion they spoke of the existence of God and tried to argue in favor of it. Actually they did not mean 'existence.' They meant the reality, the validity, the truth of the idea of God, an idea which did not carry the connotation of some*thing* or some*one* who might or might not exist. Yet this is the way in which the idea of God is understood today in scholarly as well as in popular discussions about the 'existence of God.' It would be a great victory for Christian apologetics if the words 'God' and 'existence' were very definitely separated except in the paradox of God becoming manifest under the conditions of existence, that is, in the Christo-

For it belongs to a way of thinking that is rapidly ceasing to be ours.

In a thumbnail sketch called "Man and Reality—The History of Human Thought"[17] the Dutch philosopher C. A. van Peursen notes three main ways, so far, in which men have sought to represent and communicate what is real. First, there is the period of "myth," in which the inner and outer worlds are not yet understood as separate entities but continuously interpenetrate. It is a world before any division between science and religion or physics and metaphysics. Second, there is the period of "ontology," when the supernatural becomes disentangled from the natural, subject stands over against object, man separates to the city and the divine forces to the heavens. "Gods and ethical values are given a status as ontological beings, eternal substances, or essences." And books are written "on the nature of the gods." "What is a god?" comments Van Peursen; "that is an interesting subject for a book!" Third, there is the period of "functional" thinking. Substances and supernatural entities are eliminated as unreal. Things are what they do or what can be done with them. Van Peursen illustrates the change to functional thinking by comparing the way medieval man viewed the soul with the way modern man thinks of the I.Q. "An I.Q. is nothing in itself; it is not a hidden entity in our heads: it is merely the result of certain tests." In this

---

logical paradox. God does not exist. He is being-itself beyond essence and existence. Therefore, to argue that God exists is to deny him." See also J. Macquarrie, *Principles of Christian Theology* (London, 1967), pp. 108–9, and L. Dewart, *The Future of Belief* (London, 1967), pp. 176–80.

[17] *Student World,* 56 (1963), 13–21; reprinted in J. Bowden and J. Richmond, eds., *A Reader in Contemporary Theology* (London, 1967), pp. 115–26.

new world, he concludes, "the word 'God' can no longer function as a metaphysical entity."

In the ontological period the way to make God real was to give him an essence and existence of his own, *a se* and *per se*. In a functional age it is to show how he "comes in," how he "works"—*in* the processes of nature and history, rather than behind them or between them. It hardly needs saying that this is a way of thinking very congenial to the outlook of the Bible, which describes reality much more readily in terms of verbs than substantives. But the "ontologist" in us dies hard, and we are convinced that God cannot get on (or is it that *we* cannot get on?) unless he has an established substance and existence of his own, somewhere. If we cease to believe this he must become a nonentity. But in fact precisely the opposite is true. Unless we can represent him in functional rather than ontological terms, he will rapidly lose all reality. As a Being he has no future.

The point can be reinforced by further comparison with God's "opposite number," the Devil, where we may see the consequences of this process a stage further on. Of course, there is a genuine difference between the two in reality-status. In the Christian world-view, what is embodied in the person of the Devil is less than ultimate. As Edward Caird, the Scottish philosopher, put it, "What ought to be rests on a deeper 'is' than what ought not to be." Nevertheless, the process of giving expression to the reality, which is all that here concerns us, is the same in both cases.

The Devil represents that element in human experience which Jung speaks of as the dark side or the shadow. It is profoundly and inescapably real. In former times, to personify it had the effect of making it more real and more

35

vivid. To see Satan as a Person gave him objectivity, substance, "power of being." But gradually the Devil has suffered a severe loss of reality, which by now has become almost total. He has turned into a semi-comic figure. Only a minority of educated Christians today believe in the Devil except as a mythological expression for evil. And in order to make people take the reality of the dark side seriously the least effective way is to insist on the existence of the personification. For this has the opposite effect. The way to bring evil home is to demythologize. Or, rather, it is to show the reality in human experience which the myths have been describing. One may then remythologize, as the psychologists do, though without any suggestion that these figures and archetypes "exist" in the psyche or elsewhere. The irony is that by insisting on the ontological status of the Devil churchmen have powerfully contributed to the reality's being dismissed along with the supernatural figure. In an earlier part of this century an entire generation tried to forget or to suppress "the shadow," in theology as well as in politics.

But though many can now see this with regard to the Devil, few are yet ready to recognize it of the reality of God. A recent book, *The Existence of God as Confessed by Faith*, by the German theologian Helmut Gollwitzer, represents the forceful reaction of traditional orthodoxy to the undermining of what he regards as the objective existence of God as a supernatural Person. And most churchmen would regard him as valiant for the Faith. One can understand this, as the abandonment of the traditional projection does indeed seem, to those of us brought up within an ontological worldview, to threaten a serious loss. But if we wish to communicate with men in a functional age, and indeed with our real selves, we must recognize that faith has no more necessary commitment to this phase of human thought than to the mythological one before it. This is *not* to "give in" to secularism, that is to say, to a closed view of the universe seeking to comprehend life without reference to anything transcendental. It is to recognize the purely neutral process of secularization (another way of describing the transition to functional thinking); and, having taken this into account, to start our thinking about God once again from what, within that way of thinking, is most real for men rather than from what is unreal.

Indeed, not to do this is precisely to invite secularism and precipitate a view of life in which the entire dimension of God and the spirit plays no part at all. It is to court repetition of what happened previously when deism reached the end of the line. For from one point of view the mechanistic materialism of the nineteenth century represents the residue of eighteenth-century deism. When the *deus ex machina,* the God of the gaps, became squeezed out of his universe, the machine without God was the result. Because there were no gaps, there could, on this view, no longer be any place for God. A self-sufficient naturalism took over from supranaturalism.

In the same way, in this century, a God who is presented as the enemy of secularization, who depends on ontological existence for his reality, is merely inviting secularism. If he can no longer "work" in functional society, if he can survive only as a meta-physical[18] entity like "the soul," then

---

[18] The word "metaphysical" is a source of such confusion that I have decided to use it here only of reality conceived, as in this ontological way of thinking, as somehow behind or beyond the scene of sensible phenomena.

place will not be left for him and society will go on without him. Secularism is the direct result of clinging to a God
edged out: he cannot be born again at the center of the new
world-view.

How this *can* happen, how we may find a projection that
expresses rather than destroys his reality for us, is a vitally
important question, to which I shall be returning in Chapter 4.

But a word in retrospect about what I have said so far. It
may appear to have been somewhat academic and destructive. But my concern has been positive—removing that which
removes God. So many people have been prevented from
recognizing that what most deeply concerned them had anything to do with God, because their inherited map located
him in some *terra ignota* they had not explored and had no
urge to explore. Time and again this has come through in
the letters I have received, such as are excerpted in *The
Honest to God Debate*.[19]

But I am under no illusion that merely stripping away
what, for some, has become a misleading image will of itself expose the reality. Bringing men to God is much more
than a process of demythologizing. No changes on the map,

Originally meta-physics was simply the name for what came *after* "the
Physics" in Aristotle's works. From this it came to signify that which was
beyond or behind the physical, whether this was natural (like the soul) or
supernatural (like spirits or angels). Of course, it can be used more widely
for what is truly real, for "how things really are." In this sense, I shall go
on to argue, God-language has a metaphysical reference. But in the present
confusion it seems to me better to reserve the word "metaphysics" for its
traditional use. In an age of functional thinking it is likely to create as many
difficulties as it solves, at any rate until we are over the period of transition.
Later, of course, we may again be able to use it more freely.

[19] In particular I would draw attention to the letter on pp. 59–62.

in the *logos* or language about God, will in themselves deliver the reality. Indeed, it may well be that the very word "God" is so invincibly linked in men's minds with the supranaturalist projection that whatever we say they will *hear* it as speaking of something peripheral. For them it belongs to another world. As Harvey Cox puts it, "It is heard, often with deference and usually with courtesy, as a word referring to the linchpin of the era of Christendom (past) or as the totem of one of the tribal subcultures (irrelevant)."[20] He quotes Kierkegaard's story of the clown who went around the village shouting that the circus was on fire and pleading for help to put it out, but who was hailed with merriment as an ingenious advertisement to attract men to it. And Cox goes on:

The sociological problem of speaking about God is that the roles of the people who try to do so places them immediately in a perceptual context where what they say can be safely ignored. Of course there remain some people who can still understand what theologians mean when they use the word *God* and other religious terms. These include not only "religious" people but also people whose occupations or family histories have given them a visitor's pass, if not a membership card, to the meaning-world in which theologians and preachers live. Such people can often be found in church laymen's organizations. Academically trained people who specialize in the humanities also qualify.[21]

In circles predominantly composed of such people we should not forget how artificially we are isolated from the vast mass of our contemporaries who have no entrée to this meaning-world. "God" for them may be as dead a word as

[20] *The Secular City* (London, 1965), p. 246.
[21] *Ibid.*, p. 247.

"the Devil." For them, "to speak in a secular fashion of God," as Bonhoeffer demanded, may be not to use the term at all. It may, for instance, mean, like Jeremiah,[22] buying a plot of land in an apparently hopeless situation, witnessing to the "beyond" of faith by an act of political courage, going on caring when others give up, testifying to the openness of any human condition to the possibilities of God's future and the power of the new creation. It may involve, like Jesus in the parable of the sheep and the goats, translating, transubstantiating the encounter with God into service of the homeless and the hungry.[23] This, for most ordinary people, is likely to be how metaphysics, transcendence, eschatology "come out" in functional terms. It is only thus that the Word of God, or the word "God," is made flesh.

But this does not, as I see it, excuse us the intellectual task of constructing new maps. Without maps we cannot move far without losing direction. If they are absent or defective, exploration, even into God, will go round in circles. But before returning, as it were, to the drawing board, I propose to look more closely at that which the maps are meant to be reproducing.

[22] Jeremiah 32.6–44.
[23] Matthew 25.31–46; cf. Mark 9.37: "Whoever receives one such child in my name receives me; and whoever receives me, receives not me but him who sent me"; and Jeremiah 22.16: "He judged the cause of the poor and needy.... Is not this to know me?, says the Lord."

CHAPTER TWO

God—Dead or Alive?

In the previous chapter I began from the map which theology constructs in order to represent or depict the reality of God. Any map employs a projection, and my point was that the traditional supranaturalist projection which has been used by theism now has a serious displacement effect. What was intended to locate this utterly personal reality as the central fact of life now succeeds, for so many people, in banishing it to its margin. Personifying the reality of God in human experience as the existence of a supranatural Being, far from strengthening and sustaining the reality, has the effect in this age of evacuating it of power. It has contributed much to the "death of God" in our day by removing him spiritually to an area in which people no longer live with any significant part of their lives.

But so far we have *assumed* the reality we are trying to map: our attention has been on the *logos,* the word-picture, rather than on the *theos,* the spiritual reality. But just what is this reality, and how are we to put our finger on it? It is here that the map-making analogy fails us. In constructing a map at least what we are mapping is a known geographical location, which stays put. London is there and not here, and once we have plotted its latitude and longitude, the problem is simply how to represent this point in relation to other points.

But the reality of God is not a point within the world. One cannot pin it down like that. Indeed, the word "God" is so slippery and the reality so intangible that many today are questioning whether they have reference to anything that can usefully or meaningfully be talked about. What is it that has got displaced, and what is it that we have to try to re-center? To what reality does the word "God" refer?

But before we go further we must stop to face the challenge whether this is any longer the right question. Should we not rather ask to what reality *has* the word "God" referred, or even to what reality *did* it refer? For there are those who would tell us that "God is dead," and that it is futile to seek the dead among the living.

Before accepting his obituary as final, however, it is necessary to discover just what it is that is being asserted by his "death." And the meaning of this assertion is almost as elusive as God himself. As I see it, there are two main positions, within each of which there are differences of degree. The first is primarily concerned with what has happened to the word, the second with what has happened to the reality.

For the first, it is the word "God" that in our generation has died or is dying. It is a word that has ceased to function, or is burdened with such misunderstanding or misleading associations, or is confined to such a limited meaning-world, as to be obsolescent. If we cannot find a new word, then we must get by without it, at any rate for the time being. This is the position adopted by Harvey Cox in the final chapter of *The Secular City,* from which I quoted previously. But in the body of the book he continues to use the word.

A more extreme version of this is represented by Paul van Buren, the author of *The Secular Meaning of the Gospel.* For him the word "God" belongs irretrievably to the past. It has no future as a way of speaking about "how things are." There will still be those who find it natural to go on talking in this fashion in order to give expression to certain convictions and commitments. But increasingly we shall have to find other ways to express that dimension in human existence to which the word "God" has traditionally drawn attention.

For those who take this position it is primarily the word rather than the reality that has gone dead, and both the writers I have mentioned would in fact wish to dissociate themselves from talk of "the death of God."[1]

It is those in the second position who embrace, and indeed glory in, this slogan. For them it is the reality, not simply the word, from which the life has departed. But within this position too there are important differences. In his earlier book *The New Essence of Christianity,* William Hamilton saw ours as a period of the death of God insofar as a whole generation and not merely an individual seems to be suffering from a sort of dark night of the soul. The "death" of God on this view is really an extension of the absence, or silence,

---

[1] See further Harvey Cox, "The Death of God and the Future of Theology" in W. R. Miller, ed., *The New Christianity* (New York, 1967). There he distinguishes his own position from Van Buren's as follows: "It is not that the word ['God'] means nothing to 'modern man'. . . but that it means so many different things to different people that it blurs communication rather than facilitating it" (p. 381).

43

or eclipse of God. It may not be final. And one must go on waiting in hope—living before God, as Bonhoeffer said, *etsi non daretur,* even if he is not "there" for us.

But Hamilton has since moved beyond this position.[2] There has, he believes, been a real and permanent loss of any genuine sense of transcendence. There is no God-shaped blank in modern man: he is not in search of a soul. Some hearts may be restless till they find their rest in God—but this is not necessarily so, and is increasingly less so. There is no point in waiting for God, for God will never come. Yet this need not mean despair or moral dissolution. It is not true that anything goes. Man must create his own meaning, and for this Christ can still provide the key.

This death of the God-reality, which Hamilton sees fundamentally as a modern phenomenon, though with its origins in the past,[3] Thomas Altizer wishes to locate in the first century and to celebrate as the heart of the Gospel. In his significantly titled book *The Gospel of Christian Atheism,* the good news of Christianity for him is that the transcendent God emptied, evacuated himself totally in Jesus Christ, in whom he quite literally "died." Since then he has been wholly immanent in history, becoming progressively incarnate in the universal body of humanity. Yet ironically in this extreme form, by the *coincidentia oppositorum* to which Altizer is always appealing, it appears that God is not really dead after all. Only a form of God has died. He still goes marching on, no longer as "an existent Being" but as "a dia-

[2] T. J. J. Altizer and W. Hamilton, *Radical Theology and the Death of God.*

[3] "The coming and death of Jesus makes God's death possible; the 19th Century makes it real. And today, it is our turn to understand and accept" ("The Death of God," *Playboy,* August 1966, p. 137).

lectical process."[4] "God moves forward in history," says Altizer, "by negating his present and previous modes of Being. ... Nevertheless, it is crucial to maintain that God remains God or the divine process remains itself even while in a state of self-estrangement."[5]

It is important to distinguish all these positions from classical atheism as expounded, say, by Lucretius or Freud. For this the word "God" does not refer, and never has referred, to any reality. The whole thing is an illusion. God cannot "die" because he has never been alive. For Altizer, on the contrary, "the God who became Christ was once manifest and real as Creator and Lord. Otherwise, it is not possible to speak of ... the self-annihilation of God."[6] Indeed, he goes so far as to say that "only the Christian can truly speak of the death of God."[7] For the Jew, who knows nothing of his self-negation in Christ, God is still very much alive.[8]

In assessment, I should have thought that "the death of God" label was an unfortunate one. I can see its shock value. As Hamilton has put it, "It is just not something that conventional religious people or bishops or officials can pick up and use in their own way, saying, 'Why, we've been saying that all along.' ... The phrase is, you might say, nonsoluble in holy water, even when uttered with extreme unction."[9]

[4] *The Gospel of Christian Atheism* (Philadelphia, 1966), p. 89.
[5] *Ibid.,* p. 88. Cf. p. 91: "God is a forward-moving process of kenotic metamorphosis who remains himself even while passing through a movement of absolute self-negation."
[6] *Ibid.,* p. 90.
[7] *Ibid.,* p. 102.
[8] For a Jewish response to the debate, see R. L. Rubenstein, "Death of God Theology and Judaism" in *After Auschwitz: Radical Theology and Contemporary Judaism* (Indianapolis, 1966), pp. 243–64.
[9] *Playboy,* August 1966, p. 84.

45

But as a phrase I would agree with Van Buren that in any strict sense it is "logically absurd": "That about which theology has spoken doesn't fall into a category in which being dead and alive seem to apply."[10] As Rubenstein says: "It is more precise to assert that *we live in the time of the death of God* than to declare 'God is dead.' "[11] In fact, only Altizer really says that *God* dies, as opposed to men's apprehension of God. And on inspection the God who died turns out for him to be the "infinitely distant, absolutely alien, and wholly other" Being whom Blake inveighed against as Nobodaddy. And, though release from this Being is indeed good news, I cannot think that it was particularly "ingenious" of Blake, as Altizer claims,[12] to sense that "the God of deism and the God of orthodoxy are identical." That is far too simple an equation. Nor in order to "kill" this God does it appear to me necessary to repudiate the entire dimension of transcendence, and with it the whole witness of the Bible as interpreted by the Christian Church. For Altizer, transcendence and immanence have become polarized as violently exclusive alternatives, instead of being held together in creative tension.

But I have no wish to become involved in an extended assessment of a particular group of writers. This has to my mind been done with real sensitivity and fairness by Thomas Ogletree in his book *The "Death of God" Controversy,* and with his judgments I would almost wholly concur. The controversy could easily prove to be transient,[13] and there are

[10] In an interview for *Forum* (Garrett Theological Seminary, Evanston, Illinois), 1965–66, No. 1, p. 13a.

[11] "Death of God Theology and Judaism," p. 246.

[12] *The Gospel of Christian Atheism,* p. 91.

[13] Indeed, Hamilton himself wrote to me expressing this view even before the end of 1966 (the year in which the controversy "broke") in a private

46

plenty of signs of the inevitable risks concomitant upon doing theology by journalism. The bubble may well collapse upon itself by lack of what it takes to sustain it from within; or it may be swamped by sheer reaction from the theological right. I believe it would be a pity if either of these things happened. For there is a real issue at the heart of this protest which must be worked through.

The "death of God" is no doubt an unhappy slogan—certainly if it is taken as in any sense referring to a metaphysical event. Yet it has had its value in drawing attention to a phenomenon which I believe *is* more than the absence, silence, or eclipse of God. It is registering the fact that for millions today the living God has been replaced, not by atheism in the sense of a positive denial of God, nor by agnosticism in the nineteenth-century sense, but precisely by a dead God. The reality of God has simply gone dead on contemporary man in a way that has never quite happened before. This is not a matter of people being argued out of one conviction into another; nor does it involve the discrediting

letter, from which I quote with permission: " 'The death of God' can now be decently retired, I think. Not because it is false or offensive. But because we do not have the conceptual tools at hand to give it clarity. It is a myth, of course (and we probably need fewer, not more of these), a metaphor, a language event. I am increasingly persuaded that the real issue can be stated thus: Of course, the old god, the old theism, has gone. Even the center knows this. What do you do with that fact? Do you point to some newly perceived reality and give it the name of God? Or do you try to face the religious realities we share in today without the name of God, on the grounds that there are rules by which the name of the Christian God is ascribed to something, and not everything may be so named?" As will become clear, that for which I want to retain at any rate the freedom to use the word "God" is, as I see it, the old reality (constantly indeed having to be re-perceived in a new way) which the God of theism now fails to represent or communicate. Cf. the perceptive survey by W. R. Comstock, "Theology after the 'Death of God,' " *Cross Currents,* 56 (1966), 265–305.

of one intellectual position. To those for whom God has not "died" in any existential way there appears to be no particular problem and no case to answer. Indeed, they genuinely wonder why the old language will not do: for them, and for a part of many others (among whom I would willingly include myself), it continues to serve. But for increasing numbers God is simply not available as a live option.

It may be said that availability was never among the attributes of God anyhow. An available God, a God who is there to be used, is no God. And there is an important sense in which the God that died is the God that never was. The end of God as a stopgap for intellectual laziness or emotional immaturity is the end of an idol. There is much in the atheist critique which is entirely salutary. But I am convinced that there is more to the "death of God" phenomenon than this. For the new situation is that for so many the category of "God" is not available even for a non-idolatrous response. Moreover, more is meant by all this than saying that one particular way of thinking about God, *an* image or projection of God, is dead—though this certainly, as we have seen, has been a potent factor in the decay of living faith. It is simply that "God" is a dead word. It does not *do* anything. It does not signify, or add anything, or bring any illumination. It retains a certain reflected light and residual glory. But from having been the sun of the universe it is now more like the moon. It is still around, somewhere in most people's consciousness, but fundamentally as dead matter.

The first thing to recognize is that, like the moon, it is not alone in this class. There are other realities which have suffered the same change—the Devil, the angels, the supernatural generally, heaven and hell. If one wants to speak of the realities to which these words have referred, the best way may be not to use these words at all. And there are other words that are deeply affected by the same process—for instance, "miracle," "sin," "eternity." The realities to which they refer may be as valid as ever, and there are almost certainly no direct replacements for the old words. Nevertheless, these words belong to a universe of discourse in which any living exchange becomes increasingly restricted. They cannot be used without too much explanation: they are burdened with associations which lie heavy on them.

The death of these words is something which is as true for Christians as for non-Christians. Hence the phenomenon of "Christian atheism"—an apparently total contradiction, which would have been unimaginable to a previous age. I believe, indeed, that it *is* a contradiction, and that "atheism" is the wrong word to describe the new situation. Nevertheless, it must, I think, be recognized that there is a genuinely new situation.

For instance, however confusing it may be to an older generation, it probably now means something quite different to say of a student at a seminary or theological college that he does not know whether he could say he believes in God. In a previous age, and indeed till very recently, it would have been a sure sign that he had "lost his faith." Now it is likely to mean that he is not convinced that the word "God" is a definition that brings his Christian commitment to a point or adds anything to it. He would feel exactly the same about the Devil or the supernatural. These are part of a currency which he doubts whether he can still use with his secular friends or indeed with himself. They belong to a Church ghetto-world—identification with which, through, say, ordination, becomes increasingly problematic. And this is not simply for the reasons that have always made men stumble at the empirical Church and which could be dismissed as lack of humility. It is that to identify with this "currency area" is automatically to render questionable one's ability to do business outside it. For outside it—that is in any part of the human city except the old religious sector—to bring in "God" to give backing or definition to one's deepest commitments appears unnatural, meaningless, or positively falsifying.

But it is not merely that the category is not available to describe the reality. It is also that the reality is no longer available in the way that it was. There has undoubtedly been a change of consciousness, though it is very difficult to define. Time was when God or the gods, the saints or the Virgin Mary, according to the religious idiom, came into every event that we should now look at in an entirely secular way. There was an immediate sense, through the pores and surface of everything, of the numinous, of *mana,* of a presence, which induced a ready feeling of dependence and contingency and of man's evanescence in face of the eternal. The power of religion over *homo religiosus* was something that we can only dimly imagine today. The strength and security of the religious sector, the place of the priest in the life of the village, is something whose loss we scarcely realize until we find ourselves in a culture where it is still presupposed. The demise of all this under the impact of secularization is almost certainly irreversible. However God is available for modern man, it will not be as the power-center of a sacral world-view in which life cannot be organized without him.

Thus far Bonhoeffer, who was certainly no "death of God" theologian. Hamilton and others have gone on to question whether *any* sense of transcendence, of God-dimension, will in future mark the consciousness of ordinary men and women. It is partly that some experiences which men have in the past instinctively associated with God—like awe, wonder, mystery, tragedy, the "sacredness" connected with birth, sex, and death—simply no longer carry such a reference. But it is also that some of the experiences which previously pointed men to God are not available in the same way today. Thus Hamilton writes:

The other night I was out in the back yard with one of my children, who had to identify some constellations for his science homework. When I was young and used to stand under the starry sky, I recall being filled with all the things you were supposed to be filled with: awe, a sense of my own smallness, dependence. But my son is a full citizen of the modern world, and said to me, after he had located the required constellations, "Which are the ones we put up there, Dad?" He was more interested in what he could do up there than in what he could feel down here. He had become a technological man, and this means something religiously. . . . The death of God lives in this kind of world.[14]

It is difficult to judge whether this is simply the first brash effect of the impact of technology, crowding out the poetic, the imaginative, the mystical element from human life. In so far as it is, I have no doubt that there will be, and indeed already is, a full and proper reaction to this starving of the human psyche. But I think we should be foolish to imagine that nothing decisive has happened or that we shall be able to go on appealing to the sense of the transcendent in the same old way. And the Christian is affected by this change of climate like everyone else. The contribution of the "death

[14] *Playboy*, August 1966, p. 138.

of God theologians" is that they have seen this, and, paradoxically, insisted on continuing to call themselves "theologians." For despite what they sometimes say, and even glory in, theirs is *not* the same position as that of the pure humanist and atheist. And in this paradox lies the point at which I should wish to put my question to them.

For I believe that the situation is more complicated than saying simply that, whereas previously we said "Yes" to God, now we say "No" to him. The very lingering of the term "theologian" betrays the recognition that in the old language there is a pointer to something that we cannot simply deny or eliminate. To reduce is, finally, to falsify. Talk about God cannot be translated into talk about man without loss or remainder. And it is not enough to say, with Van Buren, that it is a poetic, imaginative way of talking about man, without which life in the secular city will be sadly impoverished.[15]

There is a sense in which the new crisis is simply driving theology back to what it has always known and witnessed to, namely, that God is "ineffable," that there is literally nothing that can be said about him without falsification—except that something must be said. All language, all definition is impossible: yet it is necessary that something be said, as Augustine put it of the Trinity, *ne taceretur*—lest by silence the reality should appear to be denied and therefore equally falsified. From one point of view, the meaningless monosyllable "God" simply stands for an "*x*," an asterisk over all human language, signifying that which cannot be expressed yet cannot be eliminated. It is what is represented by the "*neti, neti*" of Hindu theology: "Not this! Not this!" Of any-

---

[15] "The God of Imagination" [An unpublished lecture].

52

thing we know we can only say with confidence that God is not that: yet we have to say it. The same is expressed in the saying of Lao Tzu, "The *tao* that can be spoken is not the eternal *tao*."[16] Yet this is not an atheist or a humanist statement, asserting that there is nothing beyond. Precisely the opposite. There *is* a beyond—beyond *everything* of which we can speak. It is the same with the Buddhist affirmation of reality. It is arrived at by negation: yet it is certainly not atheist in the sense in which that word is used by atheistic humanism of the West. The reverence of aposiopesis, of speechlessness, is anything but reductionist.

Christian theology, alike in the apophatic (or "disclaiming") tradition of the Eastern Church and in Aquinas' refusal to say anything "univocally" of God,[17] as well as in the *via negativa* of the mystics, has been equally strong on this "No, no." And yet in the Christian community of faith it has always been balanced by an insistence that while it is impossible to define God it is always possible to point to him. While the theologian says of God constantly, "Not this, not this," in the sense that God cannot be identified with anything, the Bible as constantly says, "There is God ... there ... there, and supremely THERE—in the face and in the following of Jesus the Christ." Even in Christ, the Christian theologian is careful to say that God is not defined or contained, in the sense that Jesus *is* God or *vice versa*. Nevertheless, the entire fullness of the Godhead was there bodily; he was the Word, the incarnation, of God. God is not for the Christian simply an "*x*" or an asterisk: the unconditional *is* met here, and from here we can recognize him in all else with which he cannot be equated.

16 *Tao Teh Ching*, I.   17 *Summa Theologiae* Ia. 13.5.

Ogletree points out how Van Buren, Hamilton, and Altizer all replace the centrality of God by the centrality of Christ. Yet, as he says,

Unconditional loyalty simply cannot be given to a particular historical figure unless something unconditional is disclosed in that figure. Yet when we begin to use such language, we are already moving in the direction of formulating a doctrine of God in order to attest the Reality disclosed in and through the person of Jesus.[18]

Or again,

By acknowledging decisive significance in the person of Jesus, we confess that we discern in him that which both transcends and shapes the totality of experience, which is meant by the word "God."[19]

Any talk of the "lordship" of Christ entails, implicitly or explicitly, a doctrine of God. The "death of God" theology has made a real contribution in drawing attention to changes that cannot be ignored or reversed. Nevertheless, I am convinced that God-language, however little it may be able to say compared with what it used to be able to say (or may say again), stands for that which by its very nature cannot finally be reduced or translated without remainder into anything else. It stands guard against every attempt to persuade us that this is a closed universe, that the beyond, the unconditional, the radically other—all that Jesus represented by the kingdom of heaven or eternal life—is not as real as, or more real than, that for which we are always prepared to settle.

I do not see how Christians without this dimension (how-

---

[18] *The "Death of God" Controversy* (London, 1966), p. 36.
[19] *Ibid.*, p. 59.

ever they express it) can be Christians at all. That is why Bonhoeffer's question remains, I believe, an inescapable one: "How do we speak in a 'secular' way about 'God'?" For we must speak of God. We cannot simply let this reality go by default, without witness. And yet to speak of "God" is so often today to fail to communicate the reality at all: indeed, it communicates a dead rather than a living reality. To speak of God in a secular way may be not to use the word at all. This was something Bonhoeffer himself recognized: "Perhaps we cannot now even 'speak' as we used to."[20] The reality may have to be witnessed to much more indirectly, obliquely, parabolically, brokenly—in action, in suffering, rather than in words.

But this for anyone in the Biblical tradition is nothing new or alarming. For the Bible, while attaching great significance to the "name" of God, testifies to an equal reluctance to use it. Nothing hangs on words. Indeed, the name for God changes several times within the Pentateuchal tradition, and the one that has become "God" for us (*Elohim*) belongs to its latest strand. The Bible should teach us that we may be free in this matter of language.

And this freedom has been characteristic of the best tradition of Christian theology. In his pioneering book, *The Future of Belief: Theism in a World Come of Age,* the Roman Catholic philosopher Leslie Dewart quotes St. Thomas Aquinas' observation that "wise people do not worry about names"; and he goes on:

Precisely as name, God's name matters little. It is not truly a Holy Name, and we may please ourselves whether we retain it or not.

[20] *Letters and Papers from Prison,* p. 153.

It is our own invention, not God's, and what we have invented we may improve upon. All that matters for the development of the Christian faith is whether we stand ready to discard whatever might come between man and God. For we should not believe in God's name, any more than we should believe in faith: we should believe only in God.[21]

To use the famous image of Lao Tzu, it is the hole in the middle that makes the wheel.[22] The word "God" is useful, not because it fills in what is in the middle, but precisely because it witnesses to that which can never be filled in. In itself the word is expendable, it "says" nothing. But *something like it* is an indispensable necessity if we are to refer to the hole at all. Since there is in fact nothing quite like it—no word that can replace it as a direct substitute—I am convinced that we must be able to go on using it, if only as shorthand. And this means that we must try to redeem it.

It is obviously relatively easy to say that the word "God" is so completely identified with, or fossilized in, one particular image (of *a Being*) that it must either mean this or nothing at all. Such an identification will please both traditionalist Christians and atheist humanists, and it will have the advantage of equating the word with what has come to seem, through familiarity, what Descartes called "a clear and distinct idea." It is more difficult to defend the position that the word has no necessary equation with this image, and to continue using it to safeguard a reality which must be pointed to somehow. The reality is, inevitably, less distinct than one particular image of it, whose function is precisely to simplify, to clarify it for the imagination. But I am persuaded that such a

[21] P. 213.
[22] *Tao Teh Ching*, 11.

56

position should be defended. I believe that we cannot responsibly jettison the word "God" (while freely recognizing that many will not find themselves able or wanting to use it) if we are to explore the territory over which it has traditionally stood guard, even if this territory is represented on our maps by nothing more than the enigmatic warning: "Here be mystery."

I return, therefore, to the question raised at the beginning of this chapter. I am convinced that it is still relevant, and indeed indispensable, to ask in the present tense, and not merely in the past, what is the reality in experience to which the language of "God" has reference. The task of radical theology, as Humphrey Palmer has well put it, is not one of reduction but of location.[23] Where are we to "place" God-language? What, for instance, is the reference of such an affirmation as "Jesus is Lord"? Does such a statement (and by implication all God-talk) tell us something about reality, about how things are? Or does it merely tell us something about the commitment of the person who makes it? If we cannot escape God-language, if it cannot simply be translated into language about man or the world, what is its point of reference?

[23] "To Reduce and to Locate": Two B.B.C. broadcasts reprinted in *The Listener*, April 28 and May 5, 1966.

CHAPTER THREE

Locating the Reality of God

"From one point of view," we said earlier, "the meaningless monosyllable 'God' simply stands for an *'x,'* an asterisk." From this it might well be asked whether the word represents something worth arguing about at all. Has God not become merely a cipher, a wraith, the smile on the face, as Julian Huxley has put it, of a cosmic Cheshire cat?

It is important here to recognize a difference. From the point of view of what the word connotes, I believe this is true. Or, rather, it is even less than the truth. For in itself the word "God" *is* a strictly meaningless monosyllable. Even in St. Thomas Aquinas' day men had trouble with it.[1] For, as he points out, "nouns are either abstract or concrete"—there are common nouns and proper nouns—and "God" seems to fall into neither category. Indeed, the trouble so often in the past is precisely that it has come to connote too much. It has immediately signified and been equated with a particular image or object. This or that is what "God" has *meant,* only too clearly and unequivocally. To that extent the sifting process of linguistic analysis has been one of stripping down an idol.

[1] *Summa Theologiae* Ia. 13.1.

For God cannot be so identified without ceasing to be God. We cannot say that the word "God" means anything, in the ordinary dictionary sense of being the verbal equivalent of. This is why it cannot be replaced or dispensed with. Any ways of speaking about him that are suggested in order to fill the word with content for a particular age or culture are not substitutes for it. None of these can be made into God without becoming idols. And God is what compels us to use the word "idol."

Yet, as St. Thomas recognized, this does not mean that we cannot say anything about God. For while it is true that of none of these—and indeed of nothing—can we say "This is what 'God' connotes," of all of them—and indeed potentially of anything—we can say, at some time or for some person, "This is what 'God' denotes." One may say, "Here is God," or "This is God," not in the sense that this or that is an exhaustive definition but in the sense that here, existentially, one is compelled to say: "Surely the Lord is in this place."[2] This is one of the classic confessions of those who know that somehow they must speak of God. In any place, at any moment, it may be necessary to acknowledge the *Thou* that addresses one through all things. In that sense God appears to be much more everywhere than nowhere. The ineffable is omnipresent.

Nevertheless, one must still ask, what is this elusive reality that God-language is trying, not to capture (because it knows it cannot), but to point to? Can we locate God, not in the sense of pinning him down here but not there, but in the sense of designating the kind of reality we are talking about?

[2] Genesis 28.16.

59

To what in human experience does such language have reference?

The first, and traditional, answer to this question, as has already been indicated, is that the word "God" describes an objective, metaphysical, self-existent Being. Theological statements are statements about this Being, his existence, attributes, and activities. Propositions such as "God is almighty" or "God made the world" have objective reference to this Person behind the phenomena, inaccessible to direct human experience but deducible from his effects. Thus, to take an extreme example, when theologians debated among themselves—and split the Church east and west—on whether the Holy Ghost proceeded from the Father and the Son or from the Father through the Son, they may or may not have been arguing about words, but they had no doubt as to what these words referred—the eternal generation and procession of the Persons of the Trinity understood as metaphysical entities, existing prior to, beyond, and apart from any finite apprehension of them. But even the simplest believer who says "God loves me" takes the language to have the same reference. "Is there a God or isn't there?" means, as we have seen, "Does such a Being exist?"

It is this universally held reference of the word "God" among all unsophisticated folk (and until recently among the sophisticated) that has been under fire from the linguistic philosophers. Do such metaphysical statements really mean anything? Precisely what are we saying by such a simple proposition as "God loves me"? What could verify it, or what would finally count against it? And as for the generation and procession of the Persons, how do we know that we are not talking about celestial mermaids, divine figments of the human imagination?

If this is the reality—outside and beyond our experience—to which the language of God refers, then I for one am prepared to concede the force of the attack. It does not in the least follow that God is an illusion or that all the people who have spoken like this have been mistaken. It is simply that if this is the reality, then I do not think we can make statements about it that will finally stand scrutiny. Under pressure, theologians have been compelled to recognize that God-statements cannot have this naïve objective metaphysical reference. Previously they have not been under pressure, and they did not need to discriminate with such rigor. I believe it is thoroughly healthy that they have been made to. Perhaps the critical narrows through which we are passing are temporary (there are already signs that they have been drawn too strait), but I cannot believe that the situation will ever be quite the same again—any more than theological language about Adam and Eve can return to the simplicities of the pre-Darwinian age.

Under this pressure those who want to talk about "God" have been forced to ask themselves what then is the reference of the word if not to such supra-sensible metaphysical entities. The conclusion has been drawn that statements of Christian theology describe not "how things are" in any objective sense, but "how things are for . . . a man who sees a certain piece of history in a certain way": they characterize the particular perspective on life of a man who acknowledges "Jesus as Lord." In other words, the reality they describe is the reality of a man's own conviction, the ultimacy for him of a cer-

tain way of viewing life, his fundamental resolve to think or
behave in a certain manner. Paul van Buren, who has given
sustained and brilliant expression to this position in his book
The Secular Meaning of the Gospel, takes over Richard
Hare's word "blik" to characterize this fundamental perspective or frame of commitment. God-language, says Van Buren,
functions as a way of indicating the finality, grounded in the
irreducible reality of "I'm I," of this perspective for the person concerned.

A few illustrations will show how he carries this through:

> In saying that *God* raised up Jesus, the disciples indicated that
> what had happened to them was fundamental to their life and
> thought.[3]

> The doctrine of Providence is significant as an assertion of the
> strength of the grasp that the Christian's perspective has on him.
> This is the meaning of the Christian's assertion that nothing can
> separate him from the love of God in Christ.[4]

In other words, it tells us nothing about "things" but much
about "him." Similarly, to call a hope "eschatological" is to
make no assertion about the final state of man or the world:
it is "to say that one would die rather than abandon it. It indicates the unqualified, undebatable aspect of the Christian's
historical perspective."[5] Finally, he reverses the traditional
statement that "because ... the Christian believes in the Incarnation, he is therefore impelled to take this world, men,
and history seriously."[6] Instead, he says, the doctrine of the
Incarnation "*expresses* the believer's deep concern with history, the world of men, and the world which man investi-

---

[3] P. 133.   [4] P. 178.   [5] Pp. 154–55.   [6] P. 160.

gates; it indicates that his attitude toward men and their activities is related to his attitude toward a particular piece of history."[7] This is based on the premise that what verifies a person's faith (i.e., his attitude of concern) "gives the meaning of his faith"—a criterion which comes out very explicitly in the following: "If love for the neighbor is the test of 'love for God,' then by the verification principle it is the meaning of 'love for God.'" To be fair to Van Buren, he has a theological, as well as a purely linguistic, basis for this equation:

If the Logos, which is God, has really been made flesh, then we have no need to speak about anything other than this "flesh" which dwelt among us. The command to love God first and the command to love the neighbor, when taken together, *can only mean* that we are to love the neighbor on the model of Jesus and in his freedom.[8]

But it is clear that for Van Buren "God" is fast on the way to becoming an unnecessary category. And indeed he would be content to be called an atheist (though he would not think this very significant). In his judgment, the reality to which "God" refers still exists, but the concept is semantically superfluous: the reality can less misleadingly be described without it.

This conclusion does not disturb me, and if I were convinced that Van Buren's analysis of theological language was adequate, I should follow him. At any rate, the reality—of a man's final perspective on life—to which he says the word "God" is a pointer, is one that is open to inspection and argument. I am not so sure about his confidence that what he is saying is the same as what was intended by classical Christian

<hr>

[7] *Ibid.* Italics mine.　　[8] P. 183. Italics mine.

theology and Christology. And this links with my doubt as to whether, by swinging over from a completely objective, metaphysical answer to the question of the reality indicated by the word "God" to a completely subjective, experiential one, he has really given a sufficient account of what theological language is trying to describe.

I would share his concern with the "cash value" of God-statements. What is involved in the way of ultimacy of commitment, is, I would agree, an essential element in deciding the meaning of any supposed affirmation about what is finally real. But I am not happy about the *equation* of "test" and "meaning." To ask "What is the 'payoff'?" as the sole question about the truth or meaning of a statement is to adopt a philosophy of "so what?" which seems to me to leave out other perfectly legitimate questions. For a man to say, "Here stand I: I can no other," may indicate how the truth registers for him: it may show that for him this is a God-statement, which "he would die rather than abandon."[9] But to determine everything by the quality of the commitment is to say nothing of what has evoked that commitment. Luther certainly, if he uttered these words, believed himself to be up against something to which his unqualifiable reaction was the *response*. It said something to him of "how things are" and *therefore* of how things must be for him.

Van Buren would of course agree that the Christian "blik" is not subjective in the sense that the Christian chooses or thinks it up for himself: he is under the constraint of what he

---

[9] This suggests, incidentally, how inadequate this is as a *definition* of "eschatological" statements. These surely, if the word is to have any useful or distinctive meaning, are affirmations of what the believer is convinced *will be true,* not his convictions about anything and everything if only he holds them strongly enough.

"sees" in Christ. Following Ian Ramsey, Van Buren speaks of disclosure situations or occasions of discernment. He allows for the objective element of being convicted by, as well as for the subjective element of being convinced of. But, on inspection, the "given" factor always turns out to be the human, historical occasion of belief—"this piece of history" or some similar phrase.[10] What traditionally would have been described as the divine element of unconditionality confronting the believer *through* the history—that which for Van Buren gives the "blik" its finality—is grounded in the "I'm I" of the subject, not in any *Thou* by which the subject is addressed. It is failure to do justice to the givenness or objectivity of this *Thou* which I believe renders his translation of religious statements less than adequate.

Consider, for instance, the following characteristic affirmations of faith:

Speak, Lord, for thy servant heareth
Thus saith the Lord
Abba, Father
It seemed good to the Holy Ghost and to us
Herein is love, not that we loved God but that he first loved us

and, from Brigham Young arriving with the Mormons at Salt Lake City,

This is the place.

What sort of judgment is being made in these statements? Obviously there is a strong existentialist element of personal conviction. The payoff is there, evidenced by the unshakable commitment of prophet, apostle, and leader. But even more obvious is the testimony to being convicted by something to

---

[10] See *ibid.,* pp. 113–14, 140–41, 155, and 197.

65

which any commitment is but response. It compels the acknowledgment, "This is it. At this point I have struck bedrock reality, in face of which I can but reply 'Here am I; send me.' " Integral to any God-statement, at any rate in the Judaeo-Christian tradition, is the consciousness of being encountered, seized, held by a prevenient reality, undeniable in its objectivity, which seeks one out in grace and demand and under the constraint of which a man finds himself judged and accepted for what he truly is. In traditional categories, while the reality is immanent, in that it speaks to him from within his own deepest being, it is also transcendent, in that it is not his to command: it comes, as it were, from beyond him with an unconditional claim upon his life. The fact that life is conceived as a relationship of openness, response, obedience to this overmastering reality is what distinguishes the man who is constrained to use the word "God" from the non-believing humanist.

I am not concerned at this moment with whether this relationship is veridical or illusory. I am simply trying to describe the reality to which the Biblical writers and subsequent Christians would testify. It is a relationship in which a man knows himself bound, in which he is not his own, and yet in which alone he knows that his true freedom is to be found. It is this ineluctable relatedness, this being held by something to which one's whole life is *response*, this "answerability" (Brunner), that is the reality, I suggest, to which the language of "God" points. To speak of "God" is to refer neither on the one hand to an existence outside one's experience nor on the other simply to one's own way of looking at the world. It is to acknowledge a relationship, a confrontation at the heart of one's very constitution as a human being, of which one is

66

compelled to say, in existential terms, "This is it. This is the *ens realissimum,* that which is ultimately and inescapably true."

God-statements are statements about the reality of this relationship. Of what lies outside it or beyond it we can say nothing meaningful. Hence the reticence of the Bible even to utter the name of God, as though one were presuming to fill in the hole at the center of the wheel. One can only describe the spokes of relationship, the reality which is God-for-us. One can speak only, as Schleiermacher put it, of "the whence" of my life, of my creatureliness rather than of the Creator in himself.[11] That is why, as Jeremias points out in his book *The Parables of Jesus,* the action of God is so often described, as it were, from our end, in the passive tense: "Knock and *it shall be opened* unto you." That is the side of the door we can see.

The question of God is not a question of describing or defining what or who exists on the other side of the door, outside the relationship. It is the question of whether this relationship is veridical, of whether reality is of such a nature as to "answer" to this sort of knock, not to confound this sort of trust. To affirm belief in God is indeed to assert a faith in "how things are." But it is to make an affirmation not of something beyond our experience or in another world, but of something given in our relationships in this world. It is to say that "deepest down things" (in Gerard Manley Hopkins' phrase)

---

[11] *The Christian Faith,* 4.4. For a sympathetic interpretation of Schleiermacher's position, see R. R. Niebuhr, *Schleiermacher on Christ and Religion* (London, 1965), pp. 181–96. Cf. Herbert Braun: "God is the whence of my being taken care of and of my being obliged, which comes to me from my fellow men" ("The Problem of New Testament Theology" in J. M. Robinson, ed., *The Bultmann School of Biblical Interpretation: New Directions* [New York, 1965], p. 183).

67

we can trust the universe not only at the level of certain mathematical regularities but at the level of utterly personal reliability that Jesus indicated by the word *"Abba,* Father!" It is the faith that this is as true and objective a picture of reality as that described by the natural sciences, and more fundamental. The "promise to pay" which it presupposes is not only that of my own commitment. Faith is the trust that what is unconditional for my life, namely (in Christian terms), "the love of God in Christ Jesus our Lord," cannot be conditioned by anything, that nothing in all creation is able to separate from it.

God-statements are statements about the veracity of this relationship. They cannot finally be proved or disproved, any more than human trust or love can finally be proved or disproved. In that sense there is nothing that might occur, as Antony Flew has demanded there should be,[12] which would show conclusively that there is no God. The believer may still say with Job: "Though he slay me, yet will I trust him." Nevertheless, his trust may not be irrational, nor his use of the word "God" meaningless or redundant.

To say of this or that situation, as the Biblical writers do, that "God" is in it is not to start making statements about some supposed metaphysical entity outside it or beyond it; nor is it to say simply "This piece of history is of fundamental importance for my life." It is to say that in and through this event or person there meets me a claim, a mystery, a grace, whose overriding, transcendent, unconditional character can only be expressed by responding, with the prophet, "Thus saith the Lord." Naturally the man who says this may be mistaken (and there were certain tests of the false prophet in

---

[12] A. G. N. Flew and A. C. MacIntyre, eds., *New Essays in Philosophical Theology* (London, 1965), p. 99.

Israel, though not, of course, final proofs). But it is this dimension of events, this accent of unconditionality attaching to perfectly ordinary relationships, to which the word "God" is the pointer and the sign.

It is impossible, once again, to say what the word "God" connotes (hence the reticence about the "name" or essential being of Yahveh). It is possible only to say, when one recognizes it, "Yes, this is it again." For, in the words of Van Peursen, "The word 'God' in the Bible has no meaning as such. But we too often give it a false, supernatural meaning. Then our interpretation stands between us and the Bible itself. In the Bible the word 'God' takes on a meaning."[13] As the presence is sensed again and again, men reply: "Surely the Lord is in this place"; or "God is among you indeed"; or, supremely, "God was in Christ." Indeed, for the Christian, what he sees in Christ—not only in the historical Jesus, but in all that led up to him and in all that has flowed from him—is such as to make him say: "Yes, this is it, completely. I still cannot say what 'God' connotes, but I now know what he denotes—as fully as human flesh and blood can contain it."

Words, images, or descriptions can but try to catch and express this reality—either, as it were, in terms of "so what" or in terms of "as if." And both forms of translation fail if offered as adequate accounts of what God is. The former says, in effect, that what "God" means is a certain way of life. But God does not *mean* this. Rather, God-relationships *express* themselves as this; they "come out" like this in terms of commitment. The latter way of speaking, on the other hand, says that God *is* a Person and that God-statements describe this Person. But they do not describe this Person: they describe

[13] "Man and Reality—The History of Human Thought," *Student World,* 56 (1963), 20.

a relationship, of which the nearest human analogy is to be found in the intimacy and the ultimacy of human personal relationship. Traditional theology may often, particularly in popular form, have spoken as though the "as if" could be dropped and its statements directly designated this Being. At its most careful it has not done this. But now it is vitally necessary to be careful—just as in another field it is vitally necessary, in a way that it was not before, to distinguish "history" and "myth."

We live, as Van Buren says, "in an age in which statements about 'how things are' are expected to have some sort of relationship to men's experience of each other and of things."[14] This is a test which I believe theology should welcome. For its statements are not about realities outside our experience of each other and of things. They are statements about our experience of each other and of things in depth, as these relationships are shot through with an unconditional graciousness and demand for which men have found themselves driven to that brief and pregnant word "God." This dimension of reality may be an illusion; but I am not persuaded that, if this is what the word "God" is seeking to designate, it can be dismissed either as meaningless or as superfluous.

I have preferred to speak of the "reality" of God in preference either to the existence or to the experience of God.[15] For "reality" contains within it both the idea of objectivity and that of subjectivity: for what is real must always be real for someone. One can certainly sympathize with Gollwitzer

[14] *The Secular Meaning of the Gospel*, p. 195.
[15] So also S. Ogden, *The Reality of God and Other Essays*, and P. R. Baelz, "Is God Real?" in C. F. D. Moule, ed., *Faith, Fact and Fantasy* (London, 1964), pp. 45–78.

when he warns against the danger he detects in the existential-
ists' reduction of God to a mere function of human existence,
to a determinate of my being.[16] For as such God has ceased
in any meaningful way to be *God*. But such writers as Bultmann and Braun,[17] whom he attacks, are not, as I see it, concerned to deny the genuine awareness of being confronted
by a grace and a demand transcendentally other than myself.
What they are concerned with is the cash value, in empirical
terms, of the "objective" affirmations of traditional Christian
theology.

What *we* can speak of, from our human situation, is the
awareness of being addressed, claimed, and sustained. We can
testify to the relationship, utterly personal in its demand and
succor, in which we know ourselves held. We can say that
however much this awareness seems to come from within,
from the ground of our very being, it confronts us also with
an otherness to which we can only respond as *I* to *Thou*. But
we take the *I-Thou* character of the relationship seriously
when we recognize that of God we can only say *Thou*, not *I*.
Buber speaks of God as "the *Thou* that by its nature cannot
become *It*."[18] But we might say equally that he is the *Thou*
that by its nature cannot become an *I*. We can never put ourselves on the other side of the relationship, as we can with
human beings. Of course we *can*, and do, speak of God both
as "He" and as "I," as though he were another self, a superhuman Person like, but infinitely above, ourselves. But at this
point he has become *a* Being in the subject-object schema.

---

[16] *The Existence of God as Confessed by Faith.*

[17] Braun has answered Gollwitzer in "Gottes Existenz und meine Ges-
chichtlichkeit im Neuen Testament" in the *Festschrift* for Bultmann's
eightieth birthday, *Zeit und Geschichte* (Tübingen, 1964), pp. 399-421.

[18] *I and Thou* (Edinburgh, 1937), p. 75.

Immediately we translate or project the *Thou* of God as another *I*; then we start putting ourselves on the other side of the relationship. We make God finite by encompassing him in our categories of our own selfhood.

The personification of God, inevitable as it may be for creating an image of him (albeit the very thing against which the Second Commandment warns), falls into a further danger, that of the animist or panpsychist, who identifies the *Thou* of every claim upon his life with another "soul." He indeed takes seriously the *I-Thou* quality of *all* relationships—not only those with other human beings but those with nature and with what Buber calls the world of spiritual realities.[19] But he does this by peopling the world with innumerable centers of consciousness like himself—spirits and daemons indwelling everything. The polytheist makes these (or rather a selection of these) into "gods," behind or above the phenomena, each responsible for ordering some aspect of the world. The theist sees a single personal Being at work (with or without subordinate spirits) unifying all experience. Such a personification or hypostatization of the God-reality in any form is a perfectly legitimate projection, an entirely possible "as if," as long as we recognize it for what it is. But it represents a transcript from experience, not the experience itself. All *we* can describe or designate is the grace and claim of the *Thou* from the side of the relationship in which we find ourselves held. In this reserve of utterance the believer is not being subjectivist in the sense of regarding God merely as a function of human existence. On the contrary, he knows that human existence is but a function of this utterly gracious,

[19] *"Die geistigen Wesenheiten,"* somewhat misleadingly rendered in the English translation "intelligible forms" (*ibid.,* p. 6).

disturbing, all-encompassing reality to which his life is the response—or this reality cannot properly be given the name of "God" at all.

To conclude, therefore, God-language does not describe a Thing-in-Itself or even a Person-in-Himself. And yet it does more than register our commitments. It points to an ultimate relatedness in the very structure of our being from which we cannot get away. It is a way of keeping guard over the irreducible, ineffable mystery at the heart of all experience. Traditionally, theology—our map of this mystery—has depicted God at the frontier of human existence. But this has come to mean for most people today something at the periphery of their experience or beyond it. Can we work toward a projection that re-centers this reality—not at the boundaries of life where human powers fail but, as Bonhoeffer demanded, at its center and strength, as "the beyond *in the midst*"?

CHAPTER FOUR

An Exercise in Re-centering

In the previous chapter I sought to identify the reality for which men have found themselves constrained to use the name "God" and to determine what is meant by calling this reality "personal." It is not because he is conceived as a Being with personal attributes that God is properly described as personal. That is a secondary phenomenon. It is rather because at the deepest level men have experienced reality as encountering them with the sort of graciousness and claim that we recognize at its highest in the love of another human being (though not of course only there). That is why the New Testament says that "God is love." For in pure personal relationship we have the nearest clue to the nature of ultimate reality. "No man has ever seen God"; but "if we love one another, God abides in us . . . . He who abides in love abides in God."[1] And the corollary is that a man without love, who is closed to the claim of the *Thou,* cannot know God.

If this then is the central reality, how can we represent it as such on our maps? A defect of the supranaturalist projection is that it has never really succeeded in putting God at the center. It has taken various forms according to men's succes-

[1] See I John 4.7–21.

sive cosmologies. In primitive times God was conceived as "above" a flat earth. In the geocentric Ptolemaic universe, reproduced spiritually in Dante, the center of the circle is occupied, not by God, but by the point furthest from God, hell. In the theological version of the Copernican cosmology, the deism and theism of the eighteenth and nineteenth centuries, God is indeed the Supreme Being, the sun of his universe, around whom all revolves. But like the sun he is still "out there" from the point of view of human life. Transcendence continues to be represented as distance from man. Immanent though he may also be, God is very much of a separate Being, standing over against his creation.

Can we find a projection whereby he is represented as the center, radiating out—as "the within of things," rather than as a Being external to them? Is not perhaps the cry of this generation summed up in the famous passage of St. Augustine's *Confessions*: "Late have I loved thee! For behold thou wert within me, and I outside; and I sought thee outside"?[2] If, to revert to our map-making analogy, God is the pole, the point around which all our existence pivots, should we not use a projection that represents this point at the center rather than off the edge of the map, as in Mercator's projection? To be sure, it is primarily a difference of mapping—of theography, if you like, rather than theology, of how you represent God rather than of what you believe about him. But we are learning in our generation what a fresh appreciation of realities this can introduce. Exploration *into* God is only a change of spatial metaphor, but I believe it may be an illuminating and suggestive one.

How then shall we begin on this venture into the interior? There are, I believe, two tracks in contemporary theology

[2] 10.27.

which promise advance. But at first sight they lead in opposite directions. Leslie Paul has put the matter like this, and I cannot better his summary:

Two considerable theories of history clamor for the loyalty of Christians just now: they are Teilhard de Chardin's evolutionary theories on the one side, and a kind of Christian positivism on the other. De Chardin sees the whole cosmos as in the grip of a great expansive force rolling all things, including men, on towards some cosmic appointment with God. It is Bergson baptized, evolution sacralized. The other, very new Christian-wise, is the opposite doctrine of *secularization,* that men are in charge and rolling away from God. It is associated with such notions as "man's coming of age" and "religionless Christianity." The elements of this doctrine are familiar: man in the modern world becomes more self-reliant and responsible: he looks to his own resources and not to God's: his ways of thinking are pragmatic and functional and exclude the dimensions of the religious and metaphysical. If Christianity is to speak in that world it must demythologize itself and strip itself of metaphysics too.[3]

The contrast is unmistakable, and I have no wish to make out that the two are saying the same thing. Nevertheless I would urge that we should not be compelled to an either-or. Improbable as it may seem, I believe there is a creative tension in a both-and. It is the same combination which I attempted in *Honest to God* between ideas derived from Tillich and those derived from Bonhoeffer. Apparently the two men could not be more different: for the one everything is religious, for the other nothing is religious; the one focuses on ultimate concern, the other on what he called the penultimate questions; the one is a systematizer, the other an anti-systematizer—and so one could go on dividing them into separate

[3] In a review of Harvey Cox, *The Secular City, Prism,* September 1965, p. 97.

camps, philosophical and theological. They do not indeed seem to have felt much in common themselves. There is only one, rather depreciatory, reference to the early Tillich in Bonhoeffer's *Letters and Papers From Prison,*[4] and I have not noticed any serious response to Bonhoeffer's ideas in Tillich's published work—not even in his latest dialogues with students, *Ultimate Concern,* though he was specifically questioned about him. Moreover, the disciples of each tend to find the other's ideas unsympathetic, particularly the disciples of Bonhoeffer with regard to Tillich. Indeed, I have often been faced with incredulity in theological discussion as to how I could hold the two together. William Hamilton, in a colloquium he chaired for me at Cornell University in 1964, described my capacity to bless and sanction both (with Bultmann thrown in as a third) as a piece of "wizardry." But when this reaction comes up I always recognize the voice of the professional theologian, particularly the Protestant theologian. To laymen the two seem to lie together quite easily. At first my response was to say naïvely that both "rang bells" for me and that I refused to have to choose between them. But I am coming to believe that the holding of them together may, as I suggested earlier, be the distinctive contribution of *Honest to God.* And perhaps this is also the characteristically Anglican contribution to the present theological debate—to refuse the logical either-or and to attempt a creative synthesis.[5]

[4] P. 180.
[5] The same spirit is characteristic of the Archbishop of Canterbury's most recent book—A. M. Ramsey, *The Sacred and the Secular.* It is not accidental that it is really impossible to place the Anglican contributors to the debate about God in either camp. These include Werner and Lotte Pelz (*God is No More* and *True Deceivers*), H. A. Williams ("Theology and Self-awareness" in *Soundings,* edited by A. R. Vidler, *The True Wilderness,* and an essay in *The God I Want,* edited by J. Mitchell), and John Wren-Lewis

At any rate I believe it is worth someone pointing out how much there is in *common* between the two most lively approaches to the question of God in our current discussion.

Purely for the purposes of an identification parade, let me simply line up representatives of the two main ways of thinking (without implying that they would by any means agree among themselves).

First, the "secularizers," whose inspiration tends to go back to Bonhoeffer and who, as Leslie Paul said, represent a much more recent phenomenon and are mostly younger men. To begin with, I would cite, from Scotland, Ronald Gregor Smith, whose book *The New Man,* published in 1956, must be recognized as a genuine harbinger, since followed by his *Secular Christianity*. From America come authors whom we have already had considerable occasion to quote: William Hamilton, Paul van Buren, and Harvey Cox.[6] If only to indicate that this is not merely a Protestant procession, one should mention Michael Novak's *Belief and Unbelief* and Charles Davis' *God's Grace in History*. Many others could be added, from Germany[7] and elsewhere. But I would particu-

---

(*God in a Technological Age* and numerous articles). And though Leslie Paul in the review quoted above justifiably sees *The New Reformation?* as putting me with the secularizers, with whom indeed I have the greatest sympathy, I suspect the balance of *Honest to God* and of this book is the other way. I simply do not wish to be forced into what I regard as a false choice.

[6] In his "Afterword" to D. Callahan, ed., *The Secular City Debate* (New York, 1966), pp. 197–203, Cox also proposes a synthesis by bringing together Teilhard de Chardin and the secular atheist Ernst Bloch as the most suggestive "leads" for the future of theology.

[7] Notably, already in 1953, F. Gogarten, *Verhängnis und Hoffnung der Neuzeit*; also G. Ebeling, *Word and Faith* (London, 1965), especially "The Non-religious Interpretation of Biblical Concepts," pp. 98–161, and "Worldly Talk of God," pp. 354–62.

larly like to draw attention to the considerable Dutch contribution, made by such men as A. T. van Leeuwen, C. A. van Peursen, J. C. Hoekendijk, and Albert van den Heuvel.[8] Colin Williams' *Faith in a Secular Age* well summarizes this whole movement of thought.

In the other camp are a much more loosely associated group of thinkers whose spiritual affinity is with the cast of mind associated with Tillich. It would be possible to extend this list widely both backwards into time and well beyond the edge of distinctively Christian theology. Apart from Teilhard de Chardin, one might mention Nicolas Berdyaev, Martin Buber, Charles Hartshorne (with disciples such as John Cobb, Schubert Ogden, and Charles Birch), Carl Jung, Alan Watts, and, most recently, Leslie Dewart.[9] Behind several of these (particularly Buber, Berdyaev, and Watts) lies a long tradition of mystical theology, Jewish, Eastern Orthodox, Catholic, and Protestant, and they all of course have roots in much earlier dogmatic and philosophical theology, eastern and western.

[8] Van Leeuwen, *Christianity in World History*; Van Peursen, "Man and Reality—The History of Human Thought," *Student World*, 56 (1963), 13–21; Hoekendijk, *The Church Inside Out*; Van den Heuvel, *These Rebellious Powers* and *The Humiliation of the Church*.

[9] De Chardin, especially *The Phenomenon of Man, Le Milieu Divin, The Future of Man,* and *Hymn of the Universe*; Berdyaev, especially *Freedom and the Spirit, The Destiny of Man,* and *Spirit and Reality*; Buber, *I and Thou* and *Between Man and Man* (the English translations are by R. Gregor Smith, who thus has a foot in both camps); Hartshorne, *The Divine Relativity: A Social Conception of God* and, with William L. Reese, *Philosophers Speak of God*; Cobb, *A Christian Natural Theology, Based on the Thought of Alfred North Whitehead*; Ogden, *The Reality of God and Other Essays*; Birch, *Nature and God*; Jung, especially *Psychology and Religion: West and East* (*Collected Works,* Vol. XI); Watts, especially *Behold the Spirit* and *Beyond Theology: The Art of Godmanship*; Dewart, *The Future of Belief: Theism in a World Come of Age* (the subtitle indicates his debt to the Bonhoeffer tradition as well).

Although the two groups are so different, they are both equally suspicious of and suspected by what might be called main-line Western supranaturalism, whether in popular religion or professional theology.

The difference between them is one of starting point. Bonhoeffer once remarked that for the Bible "man lives just as much from 'outwards' to 'inwards' as from 'inwards' to 'outwards.' "[10] And this could stand for the difference of approach of the two groups. The latter begin from the inside out (the more traditional approach for theology), the former, in an age when so many doubt whether there even is an inside, from the outside in. But their points of convergence are, I believe, more significant. These I would list under four heads. Together they seem to me to constitute a base from which a contemporary exploration into God could proceed with some hope.

1. The first point of agreement is that a dualistic model of the universe is out. Whether looked at from the outside or the inside, reality for us is all of a piece. As Van Peursen puts it, "There is no supernatural reality, high and lofty, above us. There is only that reality which concerns us directly and concretely."[11] There is no second storey to the universe, no realm of the divine over and above or behind the processes of nature and history which perforates this world or breaks it by supranatural intervention. The traditional divisions with which theology has worked—body and soul, earth and heaven, this world and the other world, the secular and the sacred, the two natures human and divine, and so forth—are decreasingly viable or useful. They are categories which have ceased to

[10] *Letters and Papers From Prison*, p. 192.
[11] "Man and Reality . . . ," p. 16.

speak to the consciousness of modern man, who no longer does his thinking in them. He lives in "one world," in every sense. But it is more appropriate to speak in this connection of non-duality (as the Eastern religions also do) than of monism, a word which Teilhard de Chardin, for instance, would repudiate for all his emphasis on unification and which the secularists would reject in favor of pluralism.

2. The implication of this is not the abolition of the transcendent in pure naturalism: it is an apprehension of the transcendent as given in, with, and under the immanent. "The beyond" is to be found always and only "in the midst," as a function and dimension of it. This is a shot-silk universe, spirit and matter, inside and outside, divine and human, shimmering like aspects of one reality which cannot be separated or divided. As Teilhard de Chardin puts it, "In all things there is a within, coextensive with their without."[12] It is what Tillich is appealing to in speaking of God as the ground of being or the depth of existence, and what he tried to catch in calling his system "ecstatic naturalism."[13] For Dewart, God is not an omnipotent Being overruling nature and history: rather, "in God nature can do *anything*,"[14] and "*with* God . . . all things, all history, is possible to man."[15] This same conviction lies behind the refusal to see any final discontinuity between the

[12] *The Phenomenon of Man* (London, 1961), p. 56. I have quoted the translation given in the *pensées* in *Hymn of the Universe* (London, 1965), p. 83.
[13] In C. W. Kegley and R. W. Bretall, eds., *The Theology of Paul Tillich* (New York, 1961), p. 341.
[14] *The Future of Belief*, p. 193.
[15] *Ibid.*, p. 197. Cf. Harvey Cox, following Teilhard de Chardin and Karl Rahner: "Man, seen as the steersman of the cosmos, is the only starting point we have for a viable doctrine of God" (D. Callahan, ed., *The Secular City Debate*, p. 199).

81

depths of the spirit of man and the spirit of God, which in-spired Harry Williams' *Soundings* essay, "Theology and Self-Awareness," and the religious writings of C. G. Jung,[16] as well as the miscalled "reduction" of theology to anthropology in Bultmann and his school. It is this open frontier between God and man that fascinated mystics like Meister Eckhart, Jacob Boehme, and Angelus Silesius, who made such an appeal to Berdyaev.[17] It is what Buber points to when he sees every finite *Thou* as a "glimpse through" to the eternal *Thou,* and God as met "between" man and man.

But this refusal to separate what God has joined together is the basis also of the holy worldliness and the secular sanc-tity inspired by Bonhoeffer. Gregor Smith, for instance, is struggling to represent transcendence not in terms of some sacred super-history over the head of ordinary history but as "God's historicity"—this world shot through for faith with his unconditionality.[18] Similarly Harvey Cox is concerned to disclose the frontiers of social change as the locus of the Kingdom of God: God is to be found where "the action" is, in and through the obedience of what Gregor Smith calls an "authentic secularity."[19] And this comes out in the very "earthed" and often shocking spirituality of this school both Catholic and Protestant, to which I shall be returning in Chapter 6.

3. The other side of this coin is a strong insistence that we can say *nothing* of God *apart* from these relationships. "We cannot speak of God in himself.... We cannot put any con-tent into the concept of God's being. We can only speak in

[16] See also P. W. Martin, *Experiment in Depth.*
[17] As also to Tillich, who wrote the preface to J. J. Stoudt's study of Boehme, *Sunrise to Eternity.*
[18] *Secular Christianity* (London, 1966), especially pp. 110–24.
[19] *Ibid.,* p. 174.

terms of the ways in which we actually encounter otherness."
So Gregor Smith again, who talks of "falling back into the
trusting silence of negative theology."[20] And he is, of course,
echoing Bonhoeffer's theme: "As to the boundaries, it seems
to me better to be silent."[21] This reticence about what theology
can claim or presume to know is characteristic of the "style,"
as William Hamilton calls it,[22] in which any exploration or
soundings[23] can be done today. This is partly conditioned by
the linguistic rigor with which we have to learn to speak, and
which comes out in the use made by Van Buren and others
of the text "He who has seen me has seen the Father." It is
useless, Van Buren says, to ask with Philip, "Show us the
Father": all *theological* speculation must come to rest in this
man.[24]

But from the opposite point of view there is the same tendency toward an apophatic, or dis-claiming, theology. It is
profoundly characteristic of Berdyaev's whole approach, who
insists that it has "no relation to agnosticism."[25] Tillich refuses to say that any statement about God, except that he is
being-itself, is more than "symbolic"[26]—even the affirmation
that he is love. Teilhard de Chardin says remarkably little
about God: his real theology is of the *milieu divin*. Dewart
sees the future lying with greater silence, greater circum-

---

[20] *Ibid.,* p. 123.

[21] *Letters and Papers From Prison,* p. 155.

[22] *The New Essence of Christianity* (New York, 1961), chap. 1.

[23] See especially the preface to A. R. Vidler, ed., *Soundings* (Cambridge, 1962).

[24] *The Secular Meaning of the Gospel,* pp. 146–48.

[25] *Spirit and Reality* (London, 1939), p. 137 and the whole of chap. 6.

[26] *Systematic Theology,* I, 265. Subsequently he goes so far as to say that the only non-symbolic assertion about God is that "everything we say about God is symbolic" (*Systematic Theology,* II [London, 1957], 10). See J. Macquarrie, *God-Talk* (London, 1967), pp. 50–53.

spection, about any names or images of God. And, of course, this *via negativa,* this way of unknowing, has always been a mark of the mystics, as of Jewish theology, Eastern Orthodox spirituality, and Oriental wisdom: "He who knows does not speak. He who speaks does not know."[27] The recovery of this reticence has led to a humility before the truth which shows itself, finally, in the fourth point of convergence.

4. This is the growing conviction that the old dividing lines are not the real ones, which has led to a reassessment of former antitheses and exclusivisms. In the past there was a clear division between theist and atheist. The issue was belief in the existence of a supreme Being, and to that one either said "Yes" or "No" or remained agnostic. Now there is a much more subtle line between those who believe and those who cannot.[28] The problem is wrestled with by Michael Novak in his book *Belief and Unbelief.* "Many a believer," he writes, "feels out of step with others in his generation. He neither believes with the believers, nor disbelieves with the atheists." Nor is he an agnostic: "it is not fear or hesitation that inhibits him." In this situation "he feels spiritually far closer to men like Albert Camus than to many a bishop and theologian." What Christians and humanists have in common is a shared concern, commitment, intention, and this is frequently more significant than how they articulate or define it. "It appears to be this unity in intentionality," Novak goes on, "that leads believers to 'baptize' non-believers, and non-believers to say that believers, are, underneath it all, non-believers."[29]

[27] Lao Tzu, *Tao Teh Ching,* 56.
[28] See Dewart, *The Future of Belief,* chap. 2 and pp. 184f.
[29] (London, 1966), pp. 19, 20.

This is *not* to make out that there is no difference—there are very real differences—but to draw attention to the fact that to all the writers we are looking at, of both schools, the old demarcations appear falsifying and trivial. In his search for the new essence of Christianity, William Hamilton finds himself drawing indiscriminately on Christian and non-Christian novelists, poets, and dramatists. Tillich speaks of the Spiritual Community, both in its latent and manifest forms, as constituting a unity more significant than the division between "insiders" and "outsiders" to the Church. Bonhoeffer spoke of his greater natural sympathy with the non-religious[30] and insisted that "to be a Christian does not mean to be religious in a particular way ... but to be a man."[31] The mystical tradition notoriously flows over all ecclesiastical frontiers. And one of the notable features of our time—as characteristic of the ideal of "Christian presence"[32] associated with Charles de Foucauld and Bonhoeffer as of the writings of men like Tillich[33] and Alan Watts[34]—has been a new openness to and humility before other world faiths. It has become evident that the supranaturalistic projection has bedevilled dialogue especially with the East. Because Buddhism is non-theistic it does not mean that it is atheistic in the Western sense,[35] and its understanding of Reality must be viewed sympathetically

[30] *Letters and Papers from Prison*, p. 154.

[31] *Ibid.*, p. 198.

[32] See *The Christian Presence* series edited by M. A. C. Warren. For a definition of the concept see also Colin W. Williams, *Faith in a Secular Age* (London, 1966), p. 12.

[33] Especially *Christianity and the Encounter of the World Religions*.

[34] Besides those already mentioned, see, among his many other books, *The Way of Zen*.

[35] See D. T. Suzuki, *Mysticism: Christian and Buddhist*, and G. Appleton, *On the Eightfold Path: Christian Presence amid Buddhism*.

85

alongside the more dynamic Christian view. Or again, because Hinduism has rejected the personification of God, that does not of itself close the possibility of discussion with Christianity:[36] the question is whether or not Hinduism is finally incompatible with what Teilhard de Chardin calls a personalizing universe.

So much for the common points, despite the diversity of expression and accent. What do they all add up to? Here is a summary of a position taken from a non-Christian which I do not think is too wide of the mark. He speaks of "the metaphysic that recognizes a divine Reality substantial to the world of things and lives and minds; the psychology that finds in the soul something similiar to, or even identical with, divine Reality; the ethic that places man's final end in the knowledge of the immanent and transcendent Ground of all being." That, to be sure, is very much in the idiom of those whose movement is from the inside out rather than from the outside in, as one would expect from Aldous Huxley.[37] And it would need restatement in terms of a more personalist, historical world-view. But is there anything in the *projection* which is basically unchristian?

If one had to find a label to replace that of traditional "theism," I would fall back on one that has a respectable pedigree but has never quite succeeded in establishing itself in orthodox Christian circles—namely, "panentheism." This is defined by *The Oxford Dictionary of the Christian Church*[38] as "the belief that the Being of God includes and penetrates the whole

---

[36] See G. Parrinder, *The Christian Debate: Light from the East,* and R. Panikkar, *The Unknown Christ of Hinduism.*

[37] *The Perennial Philosophy* (London, 1958), p. 1.

[38] F. L. Cross, ed. (1957). It notes that the word was coined by K. C. F. Krause (1781–1832) for his own system. The term was used by Baron F. von Hügel (*Essays and Addresses on the Philosophy of Religion,* I, 162f.;

universe, so that every part of it exists in him, but (as against pantheism) that his Being is more than, and is not exhausted by, the universe." It is the view that God is in everything and everything is in God. In the words of the anonymous author of *The Cloud of Unknowing,* "He is the being of all."[39]

In this way of thinking there is a co-inherence between God and the universe which overcomes the duality without denying the diversity.[40] Often indeed, especially in the mystics, one gets expressions of *identity* between the creature and the Creator, the soul and God, which, if taken as dogmatic generalizations, are clearly heretical. But they are no more than attempts to affirm, at a given focus of time or space, an experience of total identification: "For me, this *is* God and God *is* this"; "Here and now I am one with him and he with me." But there is no transference of divine attributes to the subject, and no denying the difference between the self and God. As the author of *The Cloud of Unknowing* puts it in the same passage, "He is thy being but thou art not his."

Similarly, from the "secular" camp one finds the same identification of God or Christ with the "least of his brethren," which created such a furor, for example, when the *Litany for the Ghetto,* to which I shall be returning in Chapter 6 below, was reported in the public press:

> O God, who hangs on street corners, who
> tastes the grace of cheap wine and the sting
> of the needle,
>
> Help us to touch you....

II, 39) and has been adopted extensively by Hartshorne (see especially *The Divine Relativity* [New Haven, 1964], pp. 88–90, and, with W. L. Reese, *Philosophers Speak of God* [Chicago, 1953], Introduction and Epilogue).

[39] *The Epistle of Privy Counsel,* chap. 1.

[40] See at this point particularly A. Watts, *Behold the Spirit* (New York, 1947), pp. 121–54.

O God, whose name is spick, black-nigger,
bastard, guinea and kike,

Help us to know you.

The heavy-handed way in which orthodox churchmen and theologians laid into this as pantheism showed that they evidently failed to distinguish what the linguists would call the language-game being played. As Berdyaev puts it,

Mystics are always suspected of pantheistic leanings and indeed, when an attempt is made to understand them rationally and to translate their experience into the terms of theology or metaphysics, they certainly come very near to pantheism. Yet, while pantheism is in reality a highly rationalistic doctrine, mysticism uses paradoxical and apparently contradictory expressions, because for the mystics both the identity between the creature and the Creator and the gulf which separates them are equally facts of existence. *Mysticism cannot be expressed either in terms of pantheistic monism or of theistic dualism.*[41]

It is the quest for a third alternative between these two which I believe is being pressed upon us so creatively from such different angles today, secular as well as religious. Nowhere does it come to more sensitive expression than in the worldly mysticism of Teilhard de Chardin. For him God veritably "fills" the universe, as Jeremiah put it,[42] permeating all things from within with the luminosity of his diaphanous presence. And this "diaphany of the Divine at the heart of the universe,"[43] "shining forth from the depths of every event, every element,"[44] is characterized by the utter indissolubility

[41] *Freedom and the Spirit* (London, 1935), p. 242 (italics mine); cf. *Spirit and Reality*, pp. 132–37; also Watts, *Behold the Spirit*, p. 129.
[42] Jeremiah 23.23.
[43] *Le Milieu Divin* (London, 1960), p. 15, n. 1.
[44] "The Mass on the World," *Hymn of the Universe*, p. 28.

of transcendence and immanence on which the panentheist (unlike the pantheist) is concerned to insist. Teilhard speaks of "that which in everything is above everything":[45] it *is* not everything, but it shines through everything, for those with the eyes to see it. In the poet's vivid words:

> The world is charged with the grandeur of God.
>   It will flame out, like shining from shook foil;
>   It gathers to a greatness, like the ooze of oil
> Crushed.[46]

And yet "the minute particular," as Blake called it, is not swallowed up in the all-embracing whole. Indeed, for the poet or the mystic the very "thusness" (to use the Buddhist term) of the particular takes on an infinite significance. He sees "a world in a grain of sand."[47] It is not, says Alan Watts, "because he is a pantheist, [that] the mystic apprehends all things as one with God. He does not see the reality of God behind the illusion of the creature; he sees God in the very reality, entity and uniqueness of the creature, in its very distinction from God."[48] In a truly personal panentheism there is no absorption of the individual in the Absolute. Even in the intensest moment of identification the distinctions of creature and Creator remain. As Jung put it in the closing words of his *Answer to Job,* "Even the enlightened person ... is never more than his own limited self before the One who dwells

---

[45] *Ibid.,* p. 30.
[46] Gerard Manley Hopkins, "God's Grandeur."
[47] W. Blake, "Auguries of Innocence." Cf. his words:
   Seest thou the little winged fly, smaller than a grain of sand?
   It has a heart like thee, a brain open to heaven and hell,
   Withinside wondrous and expansive: its gates are not clos'd;
   I hope thine are not.
[48] *Behold the Spirit,* p. 148.

within him, whose form has no knowable boundaries, who encompasses him on all sides, fathomless as the abysms of the earth and vast as the sky."[49]

This, of course, is what traditional theism has always sought to represent. There is nothing new or unorthodox about it. The only question is whether the classic projection of theism can for most people today succeed in expressing it. In the *content* of what it is affirming panentheism stands nearer to theism. Part of the difficulty is that the *word* sounds very much nearer to pantheism. But instead of avoiding it for that reason it is worth asking *why* pantheism is suspect from the Christian point of view.[50]

In its familiar forms, whether of Eastern religion or of Western intellectualism, pantheism tends toward an aesthetic, impassive, impersonalistic view of life in which the individual loses his significance. It makes for an unhistorical quietism, without political cutting edge or involvement with the neighbor. And it plays down evil and suffering as partial or illusory. In sum, it depersonalizes and dehistoricizes.

Its *advantage* is that it sees God as the inner truth, depth, and center of all being. And this surely is a more promising

---

[49] *The Collected Works,* XI, 470.

[50] Teilhard de Chardin, indeed, while desiring in the last paragraph of *The Phenomenon of Man* "to put an end once and for all to the fears of 'pantheism' " by insisting that "the universal center of unification . . . must be conceived as pre-existing and transcendent," nevertheless boldly seeks to redeem the word: "A very real 'pan-theism' if you like (in the etymological meaning of the word) but an absolutely legitimate pantheism—for if, in the last resort, the reflective centers of the world are effectively no more than 'one with God,' this state is obtained not by identification (God becoming all) but by the differentiating and communicating action of love (God all *in everyone*). And that is essentially orthodox and Christian." For a careful assessment of Teilhard's position in relation to pantheism, see H. de Lubac, *The Religion of Teilhard de Chardin* (London, 1967), chap. 14.

projection than visualizing God and the world as existences with separate centers. Theism rejected the depersonalization of God in deism but retained its projection. Can we reject the depersonalization of God in pantheism but retain its projection? Can we, in fact, depersonify but not depersonalize?

I believe that the attempt must be made. It will involve looking in particular at that whole area of doctrine which deals with the relation between God and the world, and seeing how it "comes out" in the new projection.[51]

But, first, I want to end this chapter by trying to bring panentheism out of the world of abstract theological "isms" into that of real life. For the purpose of trying to "re-center" the idea of God is not one of intellectual satisfaction. It is to undo the displacement effect of traditional theism. If it does not in fact achieve this, and relate God to what *is* most real and central, then the exercise is purely academic. I should like therefore to illustrate what a way of life lived radically from this panentheistic perspective could look like. And for this I go to a novel, by the ex-Communist Rumanian writer Petru Dumitriu, called *Incognito*, which in fact stimulated me to pursue this particular line of exploration into God as much as any of the more purely theological influences to which I have found myself responding.[52]

It illustrates beautifully all the four points of convergence I previously mentioned. Profoundly steeped in Eastern European spirituality, it nevertheless speaks straight to the condi-

[51] James A. Pike alludes to this same massive task in an extended footnote in *What Is This Treasure?* (New York, 1966), pp. 45–47.

[52] In what follows I have reproduced some material from an article in which I first tried to set down its significance for the contemporary theological debate: *New Christian*, October 7, 1965, reprinted in *But That I Can't Believe!*, chap. 14.

tion of Western, Bonhoefferian man. It would be impossible to say whether it should be placed in the "mystical" or in the "secularizing" camp, and it well shows up the falsity of any either-or. It is an account of secular sainthood, and makes no pretensions to be avowedly Christian. It speaks of the God dwelling incognito at the heart of all things, disclosing himself in and through and despite the corruptions and inhumanities of life in our generation.

Its theology is unashamedly panentheistic, though it never uses the term. God is in everything and everything is in God—literally everything material and spiritual, evil as well as good. Yet nothing could be further from the typical world of pantheism described earlier, in which the individual loses his significance in an impassive, unhistorical quietism, without political involvement and without any real entry into the depths of suffering and sin.

Here we are in an intensely personalistic world, in which everything depends upon the utterly individual response of love. Indeed it is this that gives the world its meaning and makes it possible to speak in terms of God at all. I quote from the passage in which this first breaks through:

This was it, the sense and meaning of the universe: it was love. This was where all the turns of my life had been leading me. And now everything was truly simple, revealed with a limpid clarity to my eyes as though in a flash of light *illuminating the world from end to end,* but after which the darkness could never return. Why had I needed to search so long? Why had I expected a teaching that would come from outside myself? Why had I expected the world to justify itself to me, and prove its meaning and purity? It was for me to justify the world by loving and forgiving it, to discover its meaning through love, to purify it through forgiveness.[53]

---

[53] (London, 1964), p. 354.

And yet clearly it was not I imposing my meaning, my love on an alien universe. This love was essentially *response* welling up "from some unknown source that was not me but *thou*."

What name was I to use? "God," I murmured, "God." How else should I address Him. O Universe? O Heap? O Whole? as "Father" or "Mother"? I might as well call him "Uncle." As "Lord"? I might as well say, "Dear Sir," or "Dear Comrade." How could I say "Lord" to the air I breathed and my own lungs which breathed the air? "My child"? But He contained me, preceded me, created me. "Thou" is His name, to which "God" may be added. For "I" and "me" are no more than a pause between the immensity of the universe which is Him and the very depth of our self, which is also Him.[54]

This illumination of unspeakable meaningfulness at the heart of everything comes in the novel only after nearly three-quarters of it has elapsed, and at the moment of utter dehumanizing degradation and torture.

They went on beating me, but I learnt to pray while the screams issued mechanically from my ill-used body—wordless prayers to a universe that could be a person, a being, a multitude or something utterly strange, who could say? We say "Thou" to it, as though to a man or animal, but this is because of our own imperfection: we may no less say "Thou" to the forest or the sea. We say "Thou" to the universe and hear its voiceless answer in our hearts as though it were a person and had heard us. But it is He who prays within us and answers the prayer which is His gift.[55]

It is the ability to take up *evil* into God and transform it that is the most striking—and shocking—feature of this theology.

[54] *Ibid.*, p. 356.   [55] *Ibid.*, p. 358.

"But you're giving the world the name of God, which is monstrous!" cried Erasmus. I asked if it was monstrous of me to call him Erasmus. I used the name of God because it was a way of directing towards the world all the worship, veneration and prayer which our forebears had devoted to gods growing increasingly less circumscribed; until they became the God of the monotheistic religions, defined by the universe, or by evil, or by His own goodness and perfection, or by reason. Erasmus burst out: "You must be mad! Do you mean that this God of yours is not perfect?" "Yes. He is perfect, but He is also terrible and evil. He is both perfect and imperfect. He is all things, and He confines himself to none."[56]

God is in everything. All things, all events, all persons are the faces, the incognitos of God. This naturally brings protest.

"In fact, you're nothing but an atheist," he said. "You've no real religious feeling at all. To include evil and imperfection in the concept of God is outrageous and immoral." I answered that the idea of a single God had at one time been attacked in similar terms, and that I could not disregard what I had seen with my own eyes in the course of my life.[57]

This refusal to exclude any experience from the raw material of theology is courageous in its honesty if nothing else.

God is everything. He is also composed of volcanoes, cancerous growths and tapeworms. But if you think that justifies you in jumping into the crater of an active volcano, or wallowing in despair and crime and death, or inoculating yourself with a virus —well, go ahead. You're like a fish that asks, "Do you mean to say God isn't only water, He's dry land as well?" To which the answer is, "Yes, my dear fish, He's dry land as well, but if you go climbing on to dry land you'll be sorry."[58]

[56] *Ibid.*, pp. 403–4.   [57] *Ibid.*, p. 405.   [58] *Ibid.*, p. 407.

94

What is required is not to accept everything as it stands but to "vanquish lethargy" in the seemingly impossible response of love.

What is difficult is to love the world as it is now, while it is doing what it is doing to me, and causing those nearest to me to suffer, and so many others. What is difficult is to bless the material world which contains the Central Committee and the *Securisti*; to love and pardon them. Even to bless them, for they are one of the faces of God, terrifying and sad.[59]

Yet

If I love the world as it is, I am already changing it: a first fragment of the world has been changed, and that is my own heart. Through this first fragment the light of God, His goodness and His love penetrate into the midst of His anger and sorrow and darkness, dispelling them as the smile on a human face dispels the lowered brows and the frowning gaze.[60]

Nothing is outside God. I have sought to love in as far as may be. I have tried to keep within the radiance of God, as far away as possible from His face of terror. We were not created to live in evil, any more than we can live in the incandescence that is at the heart of every star. Every contact with evil is indissolubly linked with its own chastisement, and God suffers. It is for us to ease His sufferings, to increase His joy and enhance His ecstasy. I made friends in the crowd, at meetings, in the sports stadium and coming out of the cinema, as a rule only for a moment, linked with them by a friendly exchange of words, a smile, a look, even a moment of silence. And in closer contacts my discovery spread slowly but constantly from one person to another, in that dense and secret undergrowth which is wholly composed of personal events.[61]

[59] *Ibid.*, p. 458. [60] *Ibid.*, p. 459. [61] *Ibid.*, p. 432.

It is this fellowship of the "secret discipline" of love that constitutes the invisible leaven of the kingdom of God. For this, he is saying, no labels are necessary, and any structure kills it.

This is essentially a theology of the latent, rather than of the manifest, Church. And we should listen to it as that, rather than criticize it for what it is not. There is nothing specifically, let alone exclusively, Christian about it. But there is one explicit reference to Christ on which it is fitting to end:

It was in that cell, my legs sticky with filth, that I at last came to understand the divinity of Jesus Christ, the most divine of all men, the one who had most deeply and intensely loved, and who had conceived the parable of the lost sheep; the first of a future mankind wherein a mutation of human hearts will in the end cause the Kingdom of God—the Kingdom, Tao, Agarttha—to descend among men.[62]

Comment would be an anticlimax. But perhaps in the light of this "diaphany of the divine," penetrating the darkness and unintelligibility of things from within, we may see fresh significance in some words of St. Paul's: "The same God who said, '*Out of* darkness let light shine' has caused his light to shine *within* us, to give the light of revelation—the revelation of the glory of God in the *face* of Jesus Christ."[63]

[62] *Ibid.*, p. 383.
[63] II Corinthians 4.6 (N.E.B.). Italics mine.

CHAPTER FIVE

The Divine Field

The scope of this chapter is that vast area of theology which has sought to relate the reality of God to that of the world and which has traditionally included the doctrines of creation, providence, and miracle, of design in nature and purpose in history, together with the problems of evil and suffering. Clearly no attempt can be made in a single chapter, or even in a single book, to cover such a field. All that can or will be done is to show how the change of projection suggested in the last chapter could affect the *approach* and to illustrate from this crucial area of doctrine the kind of difference it could make.

I have not found it easy to find a title for the chapter that would indicate its scope and emphasis. By choosing the one I have I am attempting to signify the fact that for panentheism "the world" is not simply something that can be joined to "God" by the word "and," as in traditional theistic discourse, but that it is in God and God is in it in a way that perhaps enables one to talk of "the divine field" as a physicist might talk of a magnetic field. But all analogies, especially impersonal ones, are very hazardous. I shall come back to this suggestion in the final chapter.

Nowhere more than in this area of theology is the influence

to be felt of what has been called the "long shadow" of deism. The doctrine of creation has been rendered well-nigh incredible for many today by the hangover of what Alan Watts brilliantly caricatures as *deus faber,*[1] the artificer God, the master Potter, Planner, and Producer of the universe. Western tool-making man has allowed himself to become fixated by this mechanistic imagery, when hardly anything could be less appropriate to the processes of evolutionary growth —to what Sir Alister Hardy, the biologist-philosopher, in the title of his Gifford Lectures[2] calls "the living stream." But even where the imagery has been modified (Dorothy Sayers, for instance, proposed substituting that of the author or play-wright)[3] the presupposition has remained of *a* Creator, who was there before the world began and who will be there after it has finished, the starter and sustainer of the whole drama. The doctrine of creation has meant that the universe took its origin in, owes its continuance to, and will be brought to consummation by, a Person conceived on the model of a cosmic Supremo.

In the eighteenth century, indeed, this supreme Being was still regarded as necessary in the role of resident engineer. Newton, as Charles Birch reminds us, "was unable to account for the precise orbs of the planets in terms of his mechanics. So he supposed that God personally intervened when they went off their paths. The universe was like a self-winding clock that ran pretty well on the whole, but it could get out of time. Then it was necessary for God to return to regulate it."[4] Equally, for Kant, God was in the last analysis indispensable

---

[1] *Beyond Theology* (London, 1966), pp. 24–25, 62–63.
[2] *The Living Stream* with its sequel *The Divine Flame.*
[3] *The Mind of the Maker.*   [4] *Nature and God* (London, 1965), p. 16.

to the moral system. This system was self-validating, and yet God had to be there to ensure the final coincidence of virtue and happiness which otherwise nothing could guarantee. This was "the God of the gaps," concerning whom the nineteenth century was overwhelmingly to endorse Laplace's famous words to Napoleon: "I have no need of that hypothesis." But the effect was to render God still more of an outsider to the process. He had no place within the system nor right to intervene. The *deus ex machina* led to the *machina sine deo*.

Theism, in contrast, has always insisted upon an intimate, continuous, fatherly relationship between God and every part of his creation. He is indeed transcendent, yet he is also immanent in all his works. Nevertheless, classical theism failed to establish a genuine reciprocal relationship between this Being and the world. This is the point of criticism that is developed by Schubert Ogden,[5] following Hartshorne. For Aquinas, for example, while creatures are really related to God (in the sense that their relationship to God is part of their very being, which would disappear without him), God is not really related to his creatures: nothing would happen to him if they disappeared.[6] Ultimately he is in no way dependent on them or affected by them. They are not necessary to him—and that not merely in order for him to be what he is but even because he is what he is. There was no need for him to create—even out of love. In this as in everything else (as Karl Barth has reasserted so vehemently in our day) God is completely free. His being is wholly necessary: that of the world totally un-necessary and contingent.

[5] *The Reality of God* ... (London, 1967), p. 48; see the whole section "Toward a New Theism," pp. 44-70.

[6] *Summa Theologiae*, Ia. 13.7.

It is this doctrine of God—of a Being ultimately impassible (in the strict sense of not being able to be acted upon), eternally unaffected, for whom the world and all it stands for is finally expendable, that has proved so repugnant to atheists like Camus. And it is important to recognize that this protest is not made simply on the grounds of God's character—that, for instance, in face of the evident evil in creation such a God is morally intolerable. In this the atheist's critique is often penetrating, but it may be turned by the theist on the grounds that a God of this character is not the God he believes in. No; Camus' charge is against *any* God whose very existence makes the world we know un-necessary. Of course, he would agree that the world might not have been. But it *is*. And that is the only base from which we can start—the sheer givenness of what is. In this Camus stands solidly for a generation which believes that whatever else is real, this world at least is real. For this generation, no philosophy, no theology which does not take this conviction seriously is itself to be taken seriously. To that extent one must agree with Ogden that the God of traditional theism cannot be the God of secular man. This is not, again, to give in to secular*ism,* which holds that this world *alone* is real. But I believe that the contemporary protest against the God of theism is valid, because such theism does not start where we are.

Where "we" are can perhaps be caught best in a quotation:

If, as a result of some interior revolution, I were successively to lose my faith in Christ, my faith in a personal God, my faith in the Spirit, I think I would still continue to believe in the World. The World (the value, the infallibility, the goodness of the World): that, in the final analysis, is the first and last thing in which I believe.

These are the words not of a cosmic pantheist, nor of a Hux-
leyan humanist, but of a profound Christian believer of our
time—Teilhard de Chardin.[7] They reveal an approach, a
view of reality, which is very different from that, say, of
medieval man (or, indeed, of pre-secular man generally).
This does not mean that it is necessarily less Christian in any
way. But it must, I am convinced, profoundly affect the manner in which we can hope to make real the centrality of the
Thou—to ourselves or to anyone else.

Instead of postulating a necessary Being for whom the
world might or might not exist, we have to begin from the
sheer givenness, the isness, the thusness of the only reality
we can certainly know. This is the necessary starting point,
the knot in the thread, *for us,* in relation to which everything
else is contingent. All statements about God, if we make them,
are interpretations of this reality. We have to begin our thinking, even about transcendence, "from below."[8] This is *not* to
say that the world = God, or that God is dependent on the
world or is a mere function of it. On the contrary, the world
is entirely dependent on God, the *Thou* in whom it is grounded and of whose being and activity it is the field. It is this that
one is affirming when one says of everything: "In the beginning, God"—as also "in the middle, God" and "in the end,
God"—"for from him and through him and to him are all
things."[9] The doctrine of creation *ex nihilo* does not exist to

[7] *How I Believe*; quoted by H. de Lubac, *The Faith of Teilhard de Chardin* (London, 1965), p. 136, who devotes the whole of the second half of his
book to a defense of this passage.

[8] See the very perceptive comments in Colin W. Williams, *Faith in a
Secular Age,* pp. 39–42 and 75–89. He characterizes secular man as "concerned to understand life from within and to master life from below"
(p. 112).   [9] Romans 11.36.

assert that there was a time or a state in which a Being called God was there alone and that "out of nothing" he made the world—though he might not have done. That is to indulge in a tissue of mythopoeic speculation. What it asserts is that there is nothing in the whole range of experience which cannot be interpreted in terms of God or which requires any other ground. That is to say, there is no aspect of nature or history, however resistant to personal categories, that is not *ultimately* to be seen in terms of spirit, freedom, love. From the start, affirms the believer, this is a "personalizing" universe, in the sense that the whole is to be understood as a process making for personality and beyond. The "omega point," as Teilhard de Chardin calls it, is a suprapersonal communion in which "God is all and in all," in which everything is related to the source, ground, and goal of its being in a relationship not merely of physical dependence but of spiritual interdependence.

This involves the assertion that freedom and consciousness and personality are not simply accidental productions, emergent epiphenomena, toward the end of the evolutionary process. A non-dualistic doctrine of creation involves taking creativity seriously as of ultimate significance all the way through. Whatever *more* one may want to say by insisting on transcendence, *at least* one is asserting an immanent creativity, a purposive spontaneity on the "inside of things," continuously from the beginning—so that consciousness, freedom, and personality are but making explicit what was already implicit.

There is ultimately no proof of this: it is an act of interpretation. But it is one that is borne out rather than contradicted

by the direction in which biologists of very different convictions are moving—e.g. Julian Huxley, C. H. Waddington,
Alister Hardy, W. H. Thorpe, as well as Teilhard de Chardin.[10] Without what John Cobb, under the influence of Whitehead, calls some "appetition" running right through creation
it is difficult to explain the momentum of the process:

A stone is far more capable of survival than a plant or animal,
and on the whole the lower forms of life are more readily adapted
to survival than are the higher. Some other force seems to be at
work in nature besides random variation and the survival of the
fittest—some appetition toward more complex forms of order
more difficult to sustain but more valuable in their results.[11]

The argument about the evidence I must leave to the biologists, and it can never in itself be conclusive. My concern here
is rather to relate the Christian interpretation of creation to
the panentheistic rather than to the theistic projection.

First, I should like to attempt to rephrase the Biblical passage which above all is trying to express the conviction that
the entire process of nature and history is to be viewed not
only, to use Teilhard de Chardin's categories, in terms of
"hominization" but of "Christification." This will frankly
be a paraphrase, not a translation, and is not meant to be

[10] It is not of final consequence for our purposes what in Teilhard is the
vision of "the scientist" and what of "the seer" (to use the two categories of
C. E. Raven's title: *Teilhard de Chardin, Scientist and Seer*). Any man in
this area is speaking as more than a scientist, however important it may be
for other purposes to differentiate more rigorously. On this see Hardy, *The
Living Stream* (London, 1965), pp. 17-20; W. H. Thorpe, *Science, Man and
Morals* (London, 1965), pp. 56-58; and I. G. Barbour, *Issues in Science and
Religion* (London, 1966), pp. 403-8.
[11] *A Christian Natural Theology* (Philadelphia, 1965), p. 171.

taken as exegesis. But it may help to interpret what was intended to be a cosmic panorama in terms of modern evolutionary cosmology. The passage is, of course, the prologue to St. John's Gospel. Recast it might run something like this:[12]

The clue to the universe as personal was present from the beginning. It was to be found at the level of reality which we call God. Indeed, it was no other than God nor God than it. At that depth of reality the element of the personal was there from the start. Everything was drawn into existence through it, and there is nothing in the process that has come into being without it. Life owes its emergence to it, and life lights the path to man. It is that light which illumines the darkness of the subpersonal creation, and the darkness never succeeded in quenching it.

That light was the clue to reality—the light which comes to clarity in man. Even before that it was making its way in the universe. It was already in the universe, and the whole process depended upon it, although it was not conscious of it. It came to its own in the evolution of the personal; yet persons failed to grasp it. But, to those who did, who believed in what it represented, it gave the potential of a fully personal relationship to God. For these the meaning of life was seen to rest, not simply on its biological basis, nor on the impulses of nature or the drives of history, but on the reality of God. And this divine personal principle found embodiment in a man and took habitation in our midst. We saw its full glory, in all its utterly gracious reality—the wonderful sight of a person living in uniquely normal relationship to God, as son to father.

From this fulness of life we have all received, in gifts without measure. It was law that governed the less than fully personal rela-

---

[12] I have omitted the interrupting (and I am convinced, with many scholars, the originally independent) prose sections relating to John the Baptist. For the scholarly basis of this omission, see my article "The Relation of the Prologue to the Gospel of St. John," *New Testament Studies*, 9 (1963), 120–29, reprinted in S.P.C.K. Theological Collections 4, *The Authorship and Integrity of the New Testament* (London, 1965), pp. 61–72.

tionships even of man; the true, gracious reality came to expression in Jesus Christ. The ultimate reality of God no one has ever seen. But the one who has lived closest to it, in the unique relationship of son to father, he has laid it bare.

Everything was alive with his life, from the very beginning. Such is the Biblical interpretation of the creative process. The full reality was not visible in the process. Indeed, from the start and all the way through, it transcended the process: always it was "above" it, "beyond" it, drawing it upwards and onwards. In the vivid imagery of the Old Testament, the Spirit was moving or brooding over the face of the waters.[13] Even the inorganic is to be interpreted not simply in terms of life (*nephesh*) but in terms of spirit (*ruach*), of the Spirit of God drawing it out to freedom and love. For the divine action is seen not simply as an immanent purposiveness, but as a brooding over. The process is not self-activating but is always response to a Call, to a Beyond. The creative Ground is not identified with the process, like the emergent Deity in some forms of Bergsonian pantheism: the Creator is not created, God is not evolved.

It may indeed be difficult for us as men to picture the process as purposive except in the anthropomorphic myth of the *deus faber,* of the Person who plans and makes. It is incontrovertibly a Biblical image. Yet the potter and his pot (or any variation upon it) is clearly a subpersonal representation of the relationship, if not of the agent. It is not in fact how *persons* are brought into being, and we should never dream of using it as an analogy to explain to an individual how he came to be. Purely biologically, the image of fathering or begetting is obviously nearer the mark. Yet in the Christian tradition this

[13] Genesis 1.2.

language has been reserved for the second Person of the Trinity, who, in distinction from every creature, is "begotten not made." Yet this biological imagery does not in any case take us to the heart of the matter. A human infant does not become a *person* by the process of fathering, or as a result of any purely physical nexus. It might be nearer the truth to say it is by mothering, since it is normally with the mother that the relationship of love, which draws the child out to freedom and responsibility, first begins. I am not made a person by a super-Person casting me in his own image. That is a hopelessly limited metaphor. I am made a person as the *I* of the *I-Thou* relationship is drawn out to selfhood in response to the grace and claim of the *Thou*.

And what is true of the growth of an individual to personality is more likely to be a satisfactory analogy (though it is only an analogy) for representing the evolution of the whole cosmic process to the level of personal response. Left to itself, without the personal relationships surrounding it, the human infant would never come to personhood. Without the *Thou* of another, drawing it, as it were, from beyond, it would remain at the subpersonal, biological level. In the same way, for the Biblical world-view, the universe itself is seen not in terms of a purely immanent self-developing process but as "called" into being and drawn to the level of life, personality, and spirit by the evocative lure of a love that will not let it rest. The Bible thinks of creation not in terms of emanation, in Hindu fashion, as though it were being spun—or were spinning itself— out of the body of a spider, but in terms of evocation, of its responding to a call to ever higher life and freer relationship.

I know of no more vivid expression of this than a passage from the autobiography of the Cretan writer Nikos Kazantzakis, author of *Zorba the Greek*. The language is inevitably poetic rather than scientific.

Blowing through heaven and earth, and in our hearts and the heart of every living thing, is a gigantic breath—a great Cry—which we call God. Plant life wished to continue its motionless sleep next to stagnant waters, but the Cry leaped up within it and violently shook its roots: "Away, let go of the earth, walk!" Had the tree been able to think and judge, it would have cried, "I don't want to. What are you urging me to do? You are demanding the impossible!" But the Cry, without pity, kept shaking its roots and shouting, "Away, let go of the earth, walk!"

It shouted in this way for thousands of eons; and lo! as a result of desire and struggle, life escaped the motionless tree and was liberated.

Animals appeared—worms—making themselves at home in water and mud. "We're just fine," they said. "We have peace and security; we're not budging!"

But the terrible Cry hammered itself pitilessly into their loins. "Leave the mud, stand up, give birth to your betters!"

"We don't want to! We can't!"

"You can't, but I can. Stand up!"

And lo! after thousands of eons, man emerged, trembling on his still unsolid legs.

The human being is a centaur; his equine hoofs are planted in the ground, but his body from breast to head is worked on and tormented by the merciless Cry. He has been fighting, again for thousands of eons, to draw himself, like a sword, out of his animalistic scabbard. He is also fighting—this is his new struggle—to draw himself out of his human scabbard. Man calls in despair. "Where can I go? I have reached the pinnacle, beyond is the abyss." And the Cry answers, "I am beyond. Stand up!" All things are centaurs. If this were not the case, the world would rot into inertness and sterility.[14]

[14] *Report to Greco* (London, 1965), pp. 291-92.

"The Cry" is both immanent and transcendent. The call is of God and the response is of God. As in the great passage of St. Paul's on the same theme, the Spirit is on both sides of the relationship, taking up the sigh of creation for fulfilment and turning it into prayer.[15] God is "the beyond" yet "in the midst" —at the heart of the process from the beginning, yet ever ahead, going on before. His is the lure of the *Thou* drawing out all things to a level of life perpetually beyond the grasp of attainment. The "how," the "mechanism" (if that is the right word), of this process, is the particular concern of the scientist, not the theologian. But the fascinating picture of the evolutionary process drawn by Sir Alister Hardy in his Gifford Lectures, *The Living Stream,* gives the layman at any rate a glimpse of how, as it were, a carpet may look from its underside. He explores the evidence not only of external natural selection operating on the physical level but increasingly, as the story advances, of internal behavioral selection on what might be called the pre-psychic level. As the species reaches out to meet the challenge of new patterns of life and environment, this leads to the development (not by the inheritance of acquired characteristics, but by the selection of the gene-mutations favorable to this habit or environment) of structures, whether of lung, wing, eye, or brain, which enable the organism to live above its previous level.

But the Biblical writers are concerned not with the detail but with the interpretation of this entire process in terms of the evocative "word" of God "calling the generations from the beginning"[16] and coming in the fullness of time to definition in Christ. And it is this that gives unity to their understanding

[15] Romans 8.14–28.   [16] Isaiah 41.4.

of the whole, in the purpose of him who is both Beginning and End, Alpha and Omega. For the same pattern can be traced throughout what we separate as nature and history, though it is interesting that the Bible is close to modern science in stressing the unbroken continuity of the two. Man does not, as we should expect, have a separate "day" of creation to himself; he shares it with all the other land animals.[17] And in the second creation story, not only is man, like everything else, formed out of dust from the ground, but the link between nature and history is symbolized in God bringing every beast and bird to Adam to be given its *name,* that is, its significance in terms of personal purpose.[18]

The God who "calls the foundations of the earth and the heavens that they stand forth together"[19] and "calls for the corn and increases it"[20] is the same God who summons Adam to response and responsibility, and above all calls out a people to himself. It is this pattern that Harvey Cox fastens on in making the point that for the Biblical writers the characteristic "place" of God, if we must localize him, is not so much "out there" in space as "ahead" of man in history.[21] God is the one who goes on before; who challenges Abraham to set forth, not knowing where he is going; who calls to Moses out of the midst of the burning bush, summoning him through the mysticism of nature in the depths of the wilderness to the politics of history in industrial Egypt, and disclosing his "ultimate" reality in the name which is as much "I

---

[17] Genesis 1.24–31.   [18] Genesis 2.4–24.   [19] Isaiah 48.13.
[20] Ezekiel 36.29.
[21] See *The Secular City* (especially chaps. 5 and 6); D. Callahan, ed., *The Secular City Debate,* pp. 197–203; and "The Death of God and the Future of Theology" in W. R. Miller, ed., *The New Christianity,* pp. 379–89.

will be what I will be" as "I am what I am";[22] who teaches his people to live as men who must be on their way in the morning; who precedes them in the cloud by day and the pillar of fire by night; who draws them on as pilgrims that have here no abiding city; who puts eternity into man's heart and teases him with the hope of a Messianic age.

And when the Messiah does come, he still calls men out to a kingdom which within history is always "at hand," to a quality of living that always eludes their grasp. Constantly it is there before them,[23] just as he himself is on the road ahead,[24] urging them to follow. And even at what appears to be the end, he again goes on before them, first into Galilee, and then to the ends of the earth and the end of time.

Once more the process starts afresh in the apostolic Church. Its whole life is directed toward the *parousia,* or presence, of Christ, viewed not as a static, appropriated reality, but as a constant coming into the midst. And St. Paul's final testimony is typical of the craning hope on which the Bible closes: "I do not consider that I have made it my own; but one thing I do, forgetting what lies behind and straining forward to what lies ahead, I press on toward the goal for the prize of the upward call of God in Christ Jesus."[25] "I am not yet perfect," he says: yet the Christian's calling is to be *teleios,*[26] which means fundamentally not one who is morally perfect but one whose entire life is moulded by the *telos* or end of God in Christ.

This has led us from the God of nature to the God of history, from the doctrine of creation to the doctrine of God's dealing

[22] Exodus 3.14.
[23] The force of the verb in Matthew 12.28 = Luke 11.20.
[24] Mark 10.32.   [25] Philippians 3.13–14.   [26] Matthew 5.48.

with men in providence and miracle. The distinctive feature of the Biblical record is that he is indeed the God of history and not merely of nature, the God who acts, in contrast to the Baalim of the nature religions or the Brahman of Hinduism. And yet the *representation* of this indispensable personal quality in traditional theism has tended to discredit the very thing it is most concerned to safeguard. God has been pictured as a super-Self, deciding to act, intervene, or send this, that, or the other, including his own "Son." As anthropomorphic myth, this is easy on the human imagination, and of course those who use this language are readily prepared to admit the "as if." But the projection it employs has the effect of locating the action of God as a Being outside, behind, or between the processes of nature and history. It gives men today little help toward seeing him as the inside *of* these processes. In consequence it has the opposite result of confirming them in belief in a system of scientific humanism closed to such eternal interference. Somehow we must find a projection which enables us to represent the divine initiative as *in* the processes of nature rather than as acting on them from without, as exercised through the events of secular history rather than in some sacred super-history.

There is at this point a very real hangover of thinking to be overcome which goes back to the notion of God that received its classic expression in deism. This requires, psychologically, that the distinctive action of God be marked by at least an apparent suspension or overruling of what would otherwise happen "in the natural course of events." Teilhard de Chardin alludes to this in relation to the presumption that the appearance of the first man must represent a special, discontinuous

act of creation (although, as we have seen, the Bible does not
even give it a "day" to itself):

Many people suppose that the superiority of spirit would be "jeop-
ardized" if its first manifestation were not accompanied by some
interruption of the normal advance of the world. One ought
rather to say that precisely because it is spirit its appearance must
take the form of a crowning achievement, or a blossoming. But
leaving aside all thought of systematization, is it not true that
every day a multitude of human souls are created in the course
of an embryogenic process in which scientific observation will
never be able to detect any break however small in the chain of
biological phenomena? Thus we have daily before our eyes an
example of an act of creation which is absolutely imperceptible
to, and beyond the reach of, science as such. Why then make so
many difficulties when it is a question of the first man?[27]

One could naturally go on to ask the same question, to which
he might not have given so easy an answer, of the appearance
of "the Christ." Why should this require a discontinuity of
germ-plasm? I do not wish in this book to enter the field of
what are properly Christological questions. But the presupposition that the uniqueness of Christ, like the uniqueness of
man (whatever we may mean by each of these), *depends upon*
a special divine intervention is part of the doctrine of God, not
Christ. This is in no way to deny that there could have been
or was such a special act. What must be disputed is that the
theological truth of the Virgin Birth depends upon, or indeed
consists of, a belief in a biological discontinuity. It is possible
to believe that Jesus' entire life, from conception to death
and beyond, was indeed "of the Holy Spirit," and yet to regard
the culminating answer of sonship to which creation points as

[27] Quoted in the collection of *pensées* in *Hymn of the Universe*, pp. 100–1.

given *through* the nexus of heredity and environment rather than as possible only by their breach and supersession. Indeed, I believe that one of the most important functions of a contemporary doctrine of God is precisely to *safeguard this possibility*, not only in relation to the Virgin Birth, but also in relation to the miracles and resurrection of Jesus. I am convinced as any of the theological truth which these represent, and have no wish to depreciate or deny them. But I am equally convinced that, if this truth is made to depend on or is equated with suspension of the physical processes, then men are being asked to give assent to something different from the heart of the Biblical gospel. For faith for the New Testament is *not* belief in the occurrence of a physical miracle, but trust in the utterly gracious action and presence of God in Christ. This is the *miraculum*—the wonderful thing —the sheer, overwhelming sense of the *Thou* of God meeting us in particular events or particular persons. Nothing in the New Testament *requires* (though equally nothing excludes) the belief that these events or persons also represent a break or discontinuity in the stream of life. To speak as though it does is to confound the categories, to insist that the reality of the *Thou* can be represented only by certain configurations or lacunae in the world of *It*.

This, I would stress, is in no way to prejudge the evidence— for instance, with regard to the Empty Tomb (which I hold to be strong) or with regard to the Virgin Birth (which is considerably weaker). I am not discussing that here. I am solely concerned with the presumption, carried over from a particular (supranaturalistic) projection of the divine reality, that belief in the personal initiative of God in history necessarily demands a certain way of representing his action. But

one has only to use the phrase "personal initiative" to suggest
the idea of "intervention" or, conversely, to deny "intervention" to be assumed to have an impersonal doctrine of God.
Such is the long shadow of deism from which theism has
never quite escaped.

The same holds of the doctrine of providence, which is essentially the assertion that in, through, and under every event
there is to be seen the grace and claim of the *Thou,* the personal reality of God from whose love literally nothing can
separate. God is "in" everything from the hairs on a head to
the fall of a sparrow. Yet the very mention of "providence,"
let alone of "special providence" (which is only asserting the
utterly personal quality of this gracious presence for the sub-
ject-in-relationship), brings up the notion of some divine ma-
nipulator who disposes the mechanism of events to produce a
result that would otherwise not have occurred, or who dis-
penses blessings, or curses, in the lives of individuals or groups.
The concept of a "disposer supreme" who, like some celestial
Mikado, so works everything that all turns out for the best in
the best of all possible worlds (otherwise God could not be
both good and all-powerful) dies very hard. In its extreme
form this expresses itself in the conviction that somewhere
there is a Planner and Purposer who sees that every accident
is no accident and fits each effect to its cause to accomplish his
grand design. But it is widely—and not unjustifiably—believed that everything that happens to an individual is held by
the theist to be intended or "meant," and that to question this
is *ipso facto* to question belief in a personal God.

But this correlation between personal providence and
planned intent is, I believe, a consequence of the particular
projection (found in deism and theism) of God as a Father-

figure or Super-ego designing and directing the operation of the world from above. What essentially the Christian faith is asserting is that in and through all the processes of nature and history there is a personal outcome to be traced and a love to be met which nothing can finally defeat. It does not necessarily imply that these processes are themselves the deliberate expression of willed intention, any more than are the millions of physical and psychological reactions which in human beings form the raw material of personal purpose. It is not that "all things work together for good," or that God deliberately "works" all things thus, by some super-computerized design, but rather that "in everything . . . he [the Spirit] co-operates for good with those who love God"[28]—that is to say, for those who make the response of love, in every concatenation of circumstance, however pointless[29] and indeed intentionless, there is to be met the graciousness of a *Thou* capable of transforming and liberating even the most baffling and opaque into meaning and purpose.

All this is intimately connected, as in Romans 8, with the problem of evil. It is not my intention, at the end of a chapter, to launch into a full discussion of this inexhaustible theme. The classical treatments of the problem of evil in Christian theology have tended to push the answer either back to a primeval past or forward to an eschatological future. If this were the choice, I would side with John Hick in his *Evil and the God of Love* in preferring the latter. But I agree with H. A. Williams in feeling that neither is really any answer at all.[30] The problem lies in how we relate evil to our conception

---

[28] Romans 8.28 (N.E.B.).   [29] The "vanity" of Romans 8.20.
[30] *The God I Want,* edited by James Mitchell (London, 1967), pp. 183–90. Williams' own thinking moves in much the same direction as mine.

of God in the present. And once again it seems to me that here is an area in which there has been serious displacement in the theistic projection. All I can say is that the traditional presentation of the problem fails to locate it for me and that its attempt to justify the ways of God to men is strangely irrelevant, if not grotesque. Confronted by a personal tragedy or a large-scale disaster it never really occurs to me to regard it as the work of a Being who "allows" (let alone "sends") such terrible things. If, for instance, a person for whom I cared deeply were killed in a plane crash or were found to have an inoperable cancer, I should find it wholly unnatural to blame a divine Planner or to disbelieve in his existence because of it. For in these things there is not intentionality (apart from any possible human factor). They have not been willed or planned for the individual concerned. Nor are they *against* God's will, as if he were merely at their mercy and had been frustrated by blind factors or other wills. God is *in* the cancer as he is in the sunset, and is to be met and responded to in each. Both are among the faces of God, the one terrible, the other beautiful. Neither as such is the face of love, but, as in the Cross for the Christian, even the worst can be transformed and "vanquished." The "problem" of evil is not how God can will it (that is not even touched on in Romans 8), but its power to threaten meaninglessness and separation, to sever and to sour, and to darken our capacity to make the response of *Thou*.

If this is the case, then the first task for theology is to restate the problem rather than to look for a solution. So much of the conventional presentation of the problem of evil, both from the Christian and the anti-Christian side, assumes a Being who is "personally responsible" for directing the course of events so as to produce the distribution of suffering we see, or even "visiting" individuals with occurrences in which they should be able to detect "the hand of God." Such a Being is declared by the atheist to be morally intolerable, and I find myself concurring. Any human planner who foresaw, let alone designed, a flood or a landslide, would evacuate the area beforehand. I have no wish to defend such a conception of God, and presentations of the problem of evil, however poignant, which state it in this form, fail, in my experience, to engage. One senses the genuine agony that lies behind the discussion, say, of the innocent suffering of a child, but to define the problem in terms of how this can be "meant," and therefore justified, in terms of an almighty Being who permits it, is to distort the issue from the beginning. Yet such is the effect of traditional theism.

Once again, it seems to me, we have to start from the other end. The concatenation of events that produces earthquakes and accidents, the cruelties of natural selection and the indiscriminate sufferings of war, are not to be seen in terms of prevenient intention. That is to introduce categories of interpretation as foreign as those of the old teleologists who argued that fleas were made black so that men could see to swat them against white sheets. Taking the immanence, the incarnation, of God seriously as the form or field of his transcendence, as the panentheistic projection does, means that categories of intentionality and the like are relevant only when the Divine is operating through personality.[31] In the dense world of sub-personal relationships (which includes all but the self-conscious tip of human life, as well as the rest of nature), the purposiveness of love works itself out through "blinder" cate-

---

[31] Jung speaks of God's "unconsciousness" and reminds us that of the four "faces" of the living creatures round the throne of God in Ezekiel and Revelation only one is human (*The Collected Works*, XI, 416 and 383).

gories. There is no *intention* in an earthquake or an accident. But in and through it it is still possible to respond to the *Thou* that claims even this for meaning and personal purpose. Everything can be taken up and transformed rather than allowed to build up into a dark patch of loveless resentment and meaningless futility.

Such is the message of the remarkable passages from *Incognito* quoted earlier. God is in everything and not merely in the obviously good and meaningful. This is the significance of the words, "I form light and create darkness, I make weal and create woe, I am the Lord, who do all these things,"[32] which make God such a Devil if they are understood in terms of intentionality. In this, panentheism takes its stand against the dualism of theism, moral as well as metaphysical. But it does not side with the indifferentism of pantheism, which has to maintain that evil is in some way illusory or unreal. The evil in the world is indeed terrifyingly real, both at the subpersonal and at the personal level; but it is still part of the face of *God*.[33] That is to say, love is there to be met and to be created through it and out of it. It is not without purpose: meaning can be wrested from it even at the cost of crucifixion. It is not separate from the face of love, and therefore cannot separate from it. That is the saving grace: God is not outside evil any more than he is outside anything else, and the promise is that he "*will* be all in all" *as love*. And that, in Christ, is the ultimate truth of everything *now*, however hidden or obscured.

[32] Isaiah 45.7.
[33] This recognition receives moving, if at times perverse, expression in Jung's *Answer to Job* and at the end of his earlier work *A Psychological Approach to the Dogma of the Trinity.*

CHAPTER SIX

The Journey Inwards

*The longest journey
Is the journey inwards.*[1]

In the last analysis the way of exploration into God is the way
of prayer. It is not an exercise in theology. And yet theology
can have the effect of seriously distorting the map. And nowhere perhaps is the effect more powerful than in the area of
prayer itself.

This chapter is in no sense a treatise on the spiritual life, let
alone a conducted tour into the interior. It has a more modest
aim. It is concerned with the hindering of hindrances. For I
am coming to be convinced that in this area the very word
"prayer" may be suffering for large numbers of people the
same displacement and loss of reality as the word "God"—
and for the same reasons. For "prayer" is equated with making contact with this Being who has ceased to be anything
but peripheral to men's deepest sense of reality. Just as he is
no longer the *ens realissimum,* and, as God, is dead, so prayer
has become a dead area for vast numbers of our contemporaries.

Within the Church this is accompanied by a great sense of
largely unadmitted guilt. I am sure that large numbers both

[1] Dag Hammarskjöld, *Markings* (London, 1964), p. 65.

of clergy and laity have simply given up praying, in the sense in which they feel they have been taught to do so. They are consciously or unconsciously aware that they *ought* to be finding reality in something they are not. Equally, in the field of public worship they are going along with forms of service and patterns of address to the Almighty which have largely become emptied of reality but which tradition tells them are what worship is. And because, like those canvassed in the public opinion polls, they are clinging to some reality, they refuse to let go altogether.

But outside the Church I wonder how far the word "prayer" connects with what is most real, or is felt ought to be most real, at all. Just as there is an unbelievable percentage of people who say they still believe in God, so there is an astonishingly high number who still claim to pray "regularly." Again, this is testimony to something they will not let go, if only as a lifeline. But if one starts at the other end, from what *is* most real for them, one finds a rather different picture.

This was brought home to me by an experience from which it would be entirely unscientific to generalize, but which I instance simply as a pointer. I had been conducting a somewhat "offbeat" retreat for ordinands, which started not from addresses by me but from asking them to write down what they felt to be their deepest personal need. In this company and context it was accepted as natural that many, though by no means all, of the questions raised fell within the field of what would be called "spirituality." Indeed, what lay behind my intention in beginning this way was to discover what were the real questions about prayer that were exercising them, instead of imposing on them what I thought edifying.

As a result of this experiment I thought I would try it on

another group—this time of people who had written to me as a result of *Honest to God,* who were either "insiders" hanging on by the skin of their teeth or "outsiders" to the Church who wished they need not be. They had already been to a previous such gathering. So this gave the opportunity of going deeper, of trying to get down to the things that lay beneath the surface. I explained the purpose of the weekend to them in the invitation, quoting from the letter I had sent the ordinands, and speaking of it as a sort of experimental "secular retreat." At the end of the first evening I asked them to put down the questions they would most like to see tackled under the general headings of "What is my own deepest need?," "What is the deepest need of the world in which I move?," and "How are these related?" By the last session I ventured to remark that not one of the questions had touched on the subject of prayer or spirituality, nor had it once been introduced into the discussion. The reaction was interesting. It brought out that the very process of digging down into the things that *did* concern them most (and the discovery that it was possible in the freedom of such a fellowship to bare their need for communication at real depth) was to them a way into the spiritual life, or life at the level of spirit, which they refused to believe was not prayer. Indeed, because this was a genuine spiritual reality, its articulation in terms of a Communion service on the Sunday—particularly at the point of absolutely free and open intercession—obviously meant a very great deal. Yet both the word "prayer" and still more the prospect of a church service would have been a complete deterrent in advance. If I had phrased the invitation in terms of "How can we learn to pray?," rather than "What is your deepest need?," it would not, I think, have occurred to them that learning to pray was a need, any more than "their deepest need" had for them any association with "prayer." The two simply belonged to different worlds.

How is it possible to restore a link? Here again I believe it is largely a question of the projection which is used. The word "prayer" in popular usage is immediately connected with praying "to" a Being, who seems, if not to have nothing to do with the case, at any rate to be peripheral to the real issue, except perhaps *in extremis*. He does not seem to come into the question of living life to its fullest. Prayer is commended as a great "venture" or even "adventure," but because of the projection with which it is associated it does not appear to most people to beckon them in a direction in which they believe the exploration of reality lies. The invitation seems to take them out of life rather than more deeply into it. How do we reverse this?

The starting point, I am sure, is the recognition, common to all, that prayer has to do with life at its most personal—which means not simply with relationships between persons, but with response to all reality as *Thou*. It is the point at which all life (and the Bible has no hesitation in extending the attitude of "worship" to the whole of creation) responds to the claim of the Voice, the Cry, the *Thou*—the claim to live at the level of the spirit, to refuse to be content with the surface determinisms of the *It* world, but to be open to the "beyond," the creative "interior" of love, at the center of everything. Worship is the response to him who is "above all and through all and in all."[2] It is seeing all in God and God in all. Anything that discloses, or penetrates through to, this level of

[2] Ephesians 4.6.

reality, whether corporately or in solitude, whether in talk or action or silence, is prayer.

Prayer is opening oneself to the claim of the unconditional as it meets one in all the relationships of life. It is life at its most intimate, intense, and demanding, requiring the response of the whole person. "For the *I* of the primary-word *I-Thou* is a different *I* from that of the primary word *I-It*."[3] The pray-er is different from the user, the communer from the commuter. He is giving himself to reality at the level of ultimate rather than of proximate concern. Such a relationship can only be described in categories of *Thou,* not of *It.* And in human experience this is supremely defined in, though not confined to, response to another person.

Hence it is entirely natural that the reality of God should be *expressed as* the grace and claim of another Person. As a myth, as a projection, the description of God as *a Person,* encountered and addressed in prayer, is an entirely legitimate way of putting it. It is the simplest possible aid to the human imagination. Indeed, for most people most of the time (at any rate in the West) it is impossible to conceive of prayer except as talking to an invisible Person. Certainly this is a point at which the language of "as if" gets a great deal nearer to the heart of the reality than the language of "so what."[4] To analyze prayer, as Van Buren does,[5] simply in terms of what produces a comparable effect (e.g. supplying irrigation instead of praying for rain) is likely to kill it far more effectively than any dangers from the other side.

Nevertheless it is essential, if imagery is not to become

[3] Buber, *I and Thou,* p. 3.
[4] See above, pp. 69–70.
[5] *The Secular Meaning of the Gospel,* pp. 188–90.

idolatry, that the "as if" should not be forgotten—so that prayer becomes *defined* as "talking to God." And above all it is necessary to ask whether there may not be at least as much hindrance as help in this image, however inescapable.

I believe in fact that the theistic projection by which the reality of God is represented by the existence of "another" Person is the most powerful factor in prayer's going dead in the way that I have described. For the Christian it creates a conflict and sense of guilt because this is how he has been taught that God *ought* to be real to him. For the non-Christian, it makes prayer, so far from being a way *into* reality, seem—if anything—to be an escape from it. Prayer appears to be a means of leaving the world (even if only to return to it) in order to "be with God."

Moreover, however much one tries to avoid it, the theistic projection encourages the personalistic interventionist conception of the divine working described in the last chapter. The God who "answers" prayers or "makes" people well again is inevitably seen as disposing the events of nature and history or the lives of individuals in a way which envisages him as standing above the processes, manipulating them from the outside. What we need is a conception of prayer that organically relates the processes themselves to the depths of the divine creativity and love. As Alister Hardy puts it:

Instead of supposing that one great personal-like Deity is thinking out simultaneously the detailed answers to millions of different problems of all the individuals in the world, is it not more reasonable to suppose that some action is set in motion by prayer which draws the particular solution for each one of us from our own subconscious minds? In saying this I must again make clear that I am not implying that I believe this destroys our conception of the Divine. All the evidence of religious experience, I believe,

124

shows that man makes contact with this Power which appears partly transcendent, and is felt as the numinous beyond the self, and partly immanent within him. I also think it likely, however, that it may well be this uplifting power which does in fact activate the subconscious solution-providing mechanism in a way which would not otherwise be possible. In a similar way it may be the same power which assists in the healing of a sick person.[6]

But, above all, the highly personalistic theistic model of prayer and worship may subtly become an escape from the very personal reality it is designed to safeguard and express. The essence of prayer is opening ourselves to the grace and claim of the unconditional as it meets us in, through, and under the finite relationships of life. It is allowing ourselves to be met and addressed by the *Thou.* And common or corporate prayer, as the Christian understands it, is the *sharing* of this ultimate concern, exposing ourselves together to be sensitized, deepened, built up in the awareness of *agape* love as the ground of all our lives. It involves meeting, sharing at the deepest level, in the *koinonia* of Holy Spirit. It means listening and confessing to each other, making corporate response and commitment to that which encounters us in Christ. By its very nature it is a "face-to-face" activity in which evasion of the *Thou* is by definition impossible.

And yet, as we know only too well, worship can easily become the very opposite of this, a face-to-back activity, in which one can take part without really meeting or even speaking to anyone; and so-called "Holy" Communion can become a substitute for real communion. There are doubtless many reasons for this having to do with human fears and failings, but I think it has to be recognized that one of

[6] *The Divine Flame* (London, 1966), p. 236.

125

the most effective mechanisms of this evasion is precisely the bringing in of the unseen Person and the addressing of ourselves to *him* in the presence of the others. By thus "turning" to God in prayer, it is easy to substitute the *Thou* we cannot see for the *Thous* through whom the claim meets us. The special diction of prayer (in which we should never address *each other*) assists us to direct our response out and away, beyond the east wall, to the other end of each individual telephone wire—anywhere to avoid being confronted by the beyond in the midst "between man and man." And in intercession the "telstar" image of prayer, by which, as it were, messages for others are redirected off a heavenly Being, can make for effective escape from direct communication—or action. Concern for the everyday world of the newspapers is translated into "prayer" by the introduction of some such circumlocution as "O Lord, thou knowest . . ."; and it is when the *Thou* addressed in the ordinary responses of life *gives way* to the *Thou* of God that "worship" is usually held to begin.

These are not, of course, necessary implications of the theistic projection of God as a separate Person *to* whom prayer is addressed *from* the world. Indeed, they would properly be rejected, and probably resented, as distortions. But they are such common *accompaniments* as at least to raise the question whether this projection does not do as much harm as it undoubtedly does good.

But what of an alternative projection? In a real sense there is no need to look for one. For there is an already existing alternative in the mystical tradition, which, both inside and outside the Christian Church, has worked with a very different model. A useful conspectus of this tradition is readily accessible in F. C. Happold's anthology, *Mysticism*; and, except where I have indicated otherwise, the brief excerpts I have taken from original sources can all be checked in their context there. What, then, are the characteristics of this model of the spiritual life?

In the first place, there is no doubt that the mystics, without by any means being pure immanentists or pantheists, have worked with a projection which locates God at what St. John of the Cross calls "the deep center." "The journey inwards" is sufficiently indicated by Boehme's invitation: "Gather in all thy thoughts and by faith press into the Center"; for "God is more inward to us than we are to ourselves" (Ruysbroeck); "God is nearer to us than our own soul; for he is the ground in whom our soul standeth" (Mother Julian). Meister Eckhart employs the same analogy from cosmology that we used before:

Suppose one dropped a millstone from the sun to earth, the earth being pierced straight through the center, the millstone would stop falling at the center of the earth. Here is the heart of the earth, the stopping-place of everything on earth. So is the Trinity the stopping-place of creatures as a whole.

Yet even so extreme an immanentist as Eckhart never *identifies* God with the depths of the soul. While God can plumb to the bottom of the soul, the soul can never exhaust the depths of God. On the one hand,

God enters the ground of the soul. None can touch the ground of the soul but God only.

Yet, on the other hand,

Though she [the soul] sink all sinking in the oneness of divinity she never touches bottom. Wherefore God has left her one little point from which to get back to herself and find herself and know herself as creature. For it is of the very essence of the soul that she is powerless to plumb the depths of her creator.

The language of the mystics is that of "transcendence *within* immanence,"[7] of union without the abolition of distinction, of identification without identity, of a "coinherence" of the divine Spirit with the human, of "a presence ... far more deeply interfused."[8] It is the language of what Thomas R. Kelly, the American Quaker, in a modern classic, *A Testament of Devotion,* calls "infused prayer," with its "awareness of a more-than-ourselves, working persuadingly and powerfully at the roots of our own soul, and in the depths of all men." "We are joyfully *prayed through,*" he says, "by a Seeking Life that flows through us into the world of men."[9]

Yet though the projection is encouraging, what of the reality mapped? How far is it "the God and Father of our Lord Jesus Christ"? Certainly, it is hardly that in Wordsworth, valid as his vision may be. How far can mysticism be true to the personal, the historical, the incarnational element in the Christian awareness of God? And above all does it begin to satisfy the worldly, secular approach upon which we previously insisted with equal emphasis? It is the apparent absence of this from the mystical tradition which has caused many, including myself, to suspect it. Indeed, temperamentally I should have said that I was the least mystical of persons, just as I am the least musical and the least psychic. It is not that I am uninterested in these aspects of reality: I find them fascinating. But if, as has been suggested, there are two spiritual types, the mystical and the prophetic, then I should have to align myself with the prophetic.

[7] I take the phrase from A. C. Bouquet's "Numinous Uneasiness," *The Modern Churchman,* April 1966, p. 206; quoted by H. A. Williams in J. Mitchell, ed., *The God I Want,* p. 177.

[8] W. Wordsworth, "Tintern Abbey."

[9] (London, 1957), p. 39.

For there is far too strong an element to be fortuitous in the mystical tradition which is anti-historical, anti-temporal, acosmic. It involves a turning away from the multiplicity, the individuality, the flux of phenomena—all that the Hindu sums up as *maya* or the Buddhist as *samsara*. It tends to make for detachment rather than involvement, for indifference rather than commitment, and there is a strong emphasis on purgation, renunciation, mortification—on "forgetting all outward things" (Richard of St. Victor).

The following excerpts are far from atypical:

Three things prevent a man from knowing God at all. The first is time, the second corporality, and the third is multiplicity or number. As long as these three things are in me God is not in me nor is he working in me really (Eckhart).

Learn to turn from worldly things, and give yourself to spiritual things, and you will see the Kingdom of God come within you (Thomas à Kempis).

The soul does this [namely, has knowledge of itself, which is the prerequisite of all "knowledge of spiritual things"] when it is so recollected and detached from all earthly preoccupations and from the influence of the senses that it understands itself as it is in its own nature, taking no account of the body (Walter Hilton).

And, finally, there is the terrifying section on detachment in St. John of the Cross which includes the words:

Strive to go about seeking not the best of temporal things, but the worst. Strive thus to desire to enter into complete detachment and emptiness and poverty, with respect to everything that is in the world, for Christ's sake.[10]

---

[10] *The Ascent of Mount Carmel,* I.13.

It is hardly surprising that the mystics have had a limited appeal. Yet I am not convinced that this one-sided anti-world-liness is of the essence of their contribution. It belongs partly to a Manichean world-denying strain that entered Christian mysticism through Plotinus and Pseudo-Dionysius. It belongs also to a pre-scientific, pre-humanist, pre-industrial age in which, if one cannot master the world, the only thing to do is to forsake it or try to forget it. No mystic writing today in fact uses *that* language.

But all along there has also been another, cosmic mysticism in which "Creatures are a guide and a path unto God and Eternity. Thus this world is an outer court of Eternity, and therefore it may well be called a Paradise, for it is such in truth" (*Theologia Germanica*). It is a tradition, which like acosmic mysticism, spreads across the boundaries of all religions. It is represented by the *Bhagavad Gita* in Hinduism, by Zen in Buddhism, by the Sufis in Mohammedanism, and by the Chasidim in Judaism who so influenced Martin Buber. Within Christianity, W. H. Auden makes the interesting observation that it is characteristic of the northern rather than the Mediterranean countries,[11] and so it seems to be.[12] For all their differences, it is possible to recognize

---

[11] *The Protestant Mystics,* edited by Anne Fremantle (London, 1964), Introduction by W. H. Auden, pp. 15f.

[12] It would always be possible, of course, to find exceptions—e.g. the intense nature-spirit-mysticism of Kazantzakis: "I closed my eyes, soothed. A quiet, mysterious pleasure took possession of me—as if all that green miracle around me were paradise itself, as if all the freshness, airiness and sober rapture which I was feeling were God. God changes his appearance every second. Blessed is the man who can recognize him in all his disguises. At one moment he is a glass of fresh water, the next your son bouncing on your knees or an enchanting woman, or perhaps merely a morning walk.

Little by little, everything around me, without changing shape, became a common strain that links Mother Julian, Brother Lawrence, George Fox, Thomas Traherne, William Blake, William Wordsworth, Richard Jefferies, George Macdonald, Johannes Anker-Larsen,[13] and Pierre Teilhard de Chardin. Within this tradition one should mention also the long-standing contribution of Eastern Orthodox and Quaker spirituality, represented respectively in recent years by Nicolas Berdyaev and Petru Dumitriu[14] and by Rufus Jones and Thomas Kelly.[15] The difference from the previous type is sufficiently illustrated by two brief quotations:

Keep contact with the outer world of sense and meanings.... Walk and talk and work and laugh with your friends.[16]

The way to God lies through love of people, and there is no other way.[17]

Yet even here there are limitations to be overcome. There are two main forms of this more earthy spirituality, which are sometimes distinguished as nature-mysticism and love-mysticism. In the former there is a strong impersonal streak, represented so hauntingly in Wordsworth:

a dream. I was happy. Earth and paradise were one. A flower in the fields with a large drop of honey in its center: that was how life appeared to me. And my soul, a wild bee plundering" (*Zorba the Greek* [Oxford, 1959], p. 213).

[13] A Danish novelist, selections from whose writings appear in *The Protestant Mystics*, pp. 303–12.

[14] See also *Orthodox Spirituality*, by A Monk of the Eastern Church, and, for a moving practical outworking of it, Sergei Hackel, *One of Great Price: The Life of Mother Maria Skobtsova, Martyr of Ravensbrück*.

[15] See also *Christian Faith and Practice in the Experience of the Society of Friends* and H. Loukes, *The Quaker Contribution*.

[16] Kelly, *A Testament of Devotion*, p. 34.

[17] Hackel, *One of Great Price* (London, 1965), p. 29.

A motion and a spirit, that impels
All thinking things, all objects of all thoughts,
And rolls through all things. Therefore am I still
A lover of the meadows and the woods.[18]

In so far as human beings come into this mysticism, it is as part of the cycle of nature,

Rolled round in earth's diurnal course,
With rocks, and stones, and trees.[19]

Civilization and the city, with its "dark Satanic mills," are the enemy, as they were for Blake and later for D. H. Lawrence. And even in the personalizing mysticism of Teilhard de Chardin there is the honest admission that "other people" are much more like hell than heaven:

I find no difficulty in integrating into my inward life everything above me and beneath me ... in the universe—whether matter, plants, animals; and then powers, dominions and angels: these I can accept without difficulty.... But "the other man," my God— by which I do not mean "the poor, the halt, the lame and the sick," but "the other" quite simply as "other," the one who seems to exist independently of me because his universe seems closed to mine, and who seems to shatter the unity and the silence of the world for me—would I be sincere if I did not confess that my instinctive reaction is to rebuff him? and that the mere thought of entering into spiritual communication with him disgusts me?[20]

It is this relationship with "the other" simply as "other" which is in fact the foundation of the "love-mysticism" of which Buber is the towering representative. And it includes rather than excludes a rapport with nature, represented for

[18] "Tintern Abbey."
[19] "A Slumber Did My Spirit Steal."
[20] *Le Milieu Divin,* p. 138.

instance in the *I-Thou* relationship with a tree which Buber describes so memorably.[21] Yet even this love-mysticism has a tendency to limitation. It is not for nothing that the more recent "secular" theologians tend to depreciate, or at any rate to find themselves in the opposite camp to, the personalists and those who emphasize the centrality of the *I-Thou* relation. For there is always a tendency (more in some of his followers than in Buber himself)[22] to regard the entire "world of systems,"[23] with its inescapable translation of love into justice and the necessity for organization and politics, as the enemy of true, personal existence. It is fair to say that what Harvey Cox notes as some of the "saving" features of life in "the secular city,"[24] its very impersonality and anonymity and mobility, its pragmatism and profanity, are among the aspects of life which "love-mysticism" would instinctively regard as destructive of spirit. The "switchboard" and the "cloverleaf" taken by Cox as the city's symbols are, to say the least, not central to the "style" of the mystics. Cox is the first to admit that "well-intentioned forays against the 'depersonalization of urban life' " are fed by a *misunderstanding* of Buber's *I-Thou* philosophy; but he thinks Buber opened the door for this by neglecting a theology of the *I-You* relationship: "The danger with an *I-Thou* typology is that all relationships which are not deeply personal and significant tend to be swept or shoved into the *I-It* category."[25] In fact, as we saw earlier, John Macmurray has worked with a threefold classification—into the instrumental, the functional, and

---

[21] *I and Thou*, pp. 7–8.
[22] See some of the very social concerns treated in *Between Man and Man*.
[23] As Brunner calls it in his *Justice and the Social Order*.
[24] *The Secular City*, chaps. 2 and 3.
[25] *Ibid.*, pp. 44, 48–49.

the personal relationship[26]—and Berdyaev was acutely aware of the need for a way of thinking that saw the answer to the "they" not simply in terms of the individual but of the "we."

Berdyaev, in fact, probably comes as near as anyone to the theological synthesis we are seeking. He was already, before the last war, talking of the "new spirituality"[27] and Chapter 6 of *Spirit and Reality,* "Mysticism: Its Contradictions and Achievements," is a penetrating analysis of precisely the problem of whether mysticism can be a valid answer to the question of "a whole spirituality."[28] He ventures to affirm a "prophetic mysticism." This is not only a mysticism of love, which makes personality, freedom, and love central, but is almost a mysticism of justice, including within it an active engagement in the social, political, and economic order. Of this social mystery he writes: "There are two symbols, bread and money; and there are two mysteries, the eucharistic mystery of bread and the satanic mystery of money. We are faced with a great task: to overthrow the rule of money and to establish in its place the rule of bread."[29] The aim can be nothing less than "a spiritual permeation of the world in order to inspire and transfigure it."[30]

"This," he recognizes, "will involve the appearance of a new type of saint, who will take upon himself the burden of

[26] See especially *Interpreting the Universe.*
[27] The title of chap. 7 of *Spirit and Reality.*
[28] Cf. his earlier *Freedom and the Spirit,* chap. 7.
[29] *Spirit and Reality,* p. 178.
[30] *Ibid.,* p. 164. He must be one of the few mystics to make central the inescapably social category of the kingdom of God (pp. 165–66). Most confine themselves to citing the highly ambiguous text "The kingdom of heaven is within you" (Luke 17.21), which is just as likely to mean "among" or "between" you. In any case, the pronoun is plural.

the complex world."[31] This is exactly the type of sainthood that Petru Dumitriu is exploring in *Incognito* (and, less successfully, in his subsequent *Westward Lies Heaven*), and which is epitomized in the moving portrait of the modern suffering servant sketched in the closing paragraphs of Pierre Berton's *The Comfortable Pew*.[32] It is the spirituality which George McLeod pleads for in his chapter on prayer in *Only One Way Left*, and which is summed up in Dag Hammarskjöld's dictum: "In our era, the road to holiness necessarily passes through the world of action."[33]

At what *stage* it passes through the world of action is no doubt partly a matter of temperament. I quoted earlier the remark of Bonhoeffer's that man's life is lived as much from the outside in as from the inside out. It is probably true that most men's lives have always been lived more from the outside in than *vice versa*. And this is particularly true of secular man. Yet the mystic has tended to be the type who lives from the inside out, and therefore to be regarded as the exception who is "not for us." This contrast comes out explicitly in Ruysbroeck. After saying that "God is more inward to us than we are to ourselves," he goes on:

And therefore God works in us from within outwards; but all creatures work from without inwards. And thus it is that grace, and all the gifts of God, and the Voice of God, come from within, in the unity of our spirit; and not from without, into the imagination, by means of sensible images.

Happold makes the observation that "in the poets the movement is usually from the *without* to the *within*; in the

[31] *Ibid.*, p. 99.
[32] (London, 1966), pp. 143–44.
[33] *Markings*, p. 108.

contemplatives always from the *within* to the *without*."[34] I would question the "always." Or perhaps it is a matter of how one defines "contemplative." For I believe there is truth in George McLeod's suggestion that for our time it may be necessary for most people who are not "religious" in the technical, monastic sense, to *invert* the traditional stages of contemplative mysticism—the purgative, the illuminative, the unitive.[35] It is by "a deeper immersion in existence" (Kierkegaard), rather than by beginning with detachment, that most people today, I believe, are likely to experience the "pressure and the wounding" (Hamilton) of the presence of God. Caught up in the solidarities of involvement, they may then find themselves driven to what Berdyaev calls the "asceticism" of "action in the world,"[36] of stripping down, con-centration. The traditional approach has been to start at the center and then go out, to begin with prayer and "work it out" in politics. This approach may be reversed for our generation, with so many of its most articulate and responsible members heavily committed to such involvements as the Freedom Movement, the struggle against poverty, overpopulation, and war, and the revolution for "tomorrow's sun"[37] that lies so close beneath the horizon of the southern hemisphere. Perhaps today most things begin in politics and end in mysticism, rather than the other way round. At any

[34] F. C. Happold, *Mysticism, A Study and Anthology* (Harmondsworth, Eng., 1963), p. 93.
[35] *Ibid.*, pp. 154–62.   [36] *Spirit and Reality*, p. 168.
[37] The title of a remarkable book on the anti-apartheid struggle in South Africa by Helen Joseph. It is not irrelevant that this has been for her the way back into the life of the Spirit. In this she is, I suspect, representative of many in our age.

rate, for many, picketing and praying have become so assimilated that it is difficult to draw a line between them.

This has begun to show itself in what I believe is a new and significant form of contemporary spirituality. I tried to delineate it in an article I wrote for *New Christian*,[38] and I have adapted some material from it in the paragraphs that follow.

The essence of this spirituality is that it starts from life rather than works toward it. In distinction from the traditions I have previously mentioned, it seems so far to have flowered most in French-speaking Catholicism and American-speaking Protestantism. From the former, the classic is Michel Quoist's *Prayers of Life*. It begins from life just as it comes—the telephone, a five-pound note, the pornographic magazine, hunger, housing, a bald head—and turns it all not only into prayer but often poetry as well. "The Sea" is not only pure poetry but an example, by contrast rare in this genre, of equal sensitivity to nature and to that which "wears man's smudge and shares man's smell."[39]

Of the second, American, variety one may take Malcolm Boyd's collection *Are You Running with Me, Jesus?* This is Quoist in prose, prayer in the raw, with the last varnish gone. "All human life is there," as *The News of the World* advertisement claims, in all its warmth and all its lovelessness, laid bare before God. Malcolm Boyd, himself formerly in advertising, is an Episcopalian priest whose ministry has lain in state universities and civil rights. Section headings indicate the scope of this very worldly holiness: "Prayers for the Free Self," "Prayers for the Free Society," "Prayers in the City,"

[38] September 8, 1966; reprinted in *But That I Can't Believe!*, chap. 23.
[39] Gerard Manley Hopkins, "God's Grandeur."

"Meditations on Films," "Prayers for Sexual Freedom," and so on. What he calls in his introduction "the heretical gap" between the holy and the profane has quite disappeared. And he has followed this with a set of "secular meditations" called *Free to Live, Free to Die,* which is in many ways the best example yet of this prophetic spirituality.[40]

It was another Episcopalian priest, Robert Castle, who wrote the *Litany for the Ghetto* already referred to. Here there is such an identification between God and the city that grammar is strained to breaking-point in bringing together the *Thou* addressed and the third person indicative of those who *are* the city:

> O God, who lives in tenements, who goes to segregated schools, who is beaten in precincts, who is unemployed ...
>
> Help us to know you
>
> O God, who is cold in the slums of winter, whose playmates are rats—four-legged ones who live with you and two-legged ones who imprison you ...
>
> Help us to touch you

—and so on, ever nearer the bone.

If one were to try to sum up the marks of this mode, or mood, of prayer, certain things recur. Its controlling rubric

---

[40] See also Robert A. Raines, *Creative Brooding,* a collection of daily readings, each starting with an excerpt from a contemporary writer or journalist and leading through Biblical passages into prayer. Its method is to use the secular to "sharpen thought and provoke reflection." Alan Watts also speaks of "contemplation in its secular form" (*Behold the Spirit,* p. 233), which has always been one of the strengths of Zen.

might be the words of Coventry Patmore, "You may see the disc of Divinity quite clearly through the smoked glass of humanity, but not otherwise."[41] Indeed, its key preposition is "through." God is to be met in, with, and under, not apart from, response to the world and the neighbor. Its point of entry into God, the *ens realissimum,* is whatever *is* most real for the person concerned, however irreligious. Its form of the divine is more often than not the Son of Man incognito, whose presence is to be known obliquely, parabolically, brokenly—but always presently. Its style is that of a *secular mysticism,*[42] with each of these words equally stressed. There is—in Christ—no gulf, no difference even, between ordinary life and prayer. And, needless to say, any special holy language or devotional diction is out. The "thees" and the "thous" have gone without trace.

And yet it is saturated with awareness of the world as *Thou* —and with the meeting through it of "the eternal *Thou.*" As an art form it is liberally interspersed with vocatives— usually "Lord," in Boyd as often as not "Jesus." The Deity is invoked freely, even chummily. It reads like devotional Don Camillo, with "the Lord" always around, as a gnome on the shoulder or a friend at the side.

And this conversational tone is odd, because Malcolm Boyd says specifically that he has come to see prayer as "not so much talking to God" as "just sharing his presence." It appears indeed often more like Jesus sharing Boyd's presence and being conveniently at hand to compare notes with. But

[41] *The Rod, the Root, and the Flower* (London, 1895), p. 45.
[42] W. R. Comstock uses the same phrase, instancing as examples, among others, Ludwig Wittgenstein and Simone Weil ("Theology after the 'Death of God,' " *Cross Currents,* 56 [1966], 294–98).

even at its best, as in Quoist, there is the sense of talking to a third Person, apart from and invisible to the person whose concern engages one. Does this take the *Thou* of the other with real seriousness and do justice to the fact that the claim of the unconditional must be met *in him* and *through him* —even if it is not possible or natural to say "Lord, Lord"?

The inauthenticity of this somewhat embarrassing talk contrasts at times jarringly with the ruthless honesty and economy of the general "style." I suspect it is the residual influence of the supranaturalist projection that still requires this third Person if the exercise is to qualify as "prayer."[43] Is there a relic here of what I called the "telstar" image, of re-directing messages off a celestial Being? Has this been re-placed—instead of demythologized—by a three-cornered conversation? The current "pop" prayer idiom, with its stage asides, strikes me in fact as less truly incarnational than the (far more reserved) Quaker tradition of spirituality, which has its ambience much more *in* the Spirit and sees the Pres-ence rather in terms of that which lights up every man from *within*, or, as Buber would put it, is *"between* man and man."

The strength of this contemporary prayer-style is that it is inescapably personal. It knows God as given in response to the whole of life as *Thou*. Its weakness is that it is often arti-ficially personalistic—envisaging God as a separate *Thou*. Is "O Lord" the last remnant of the poetic diction of a by-gone age—or is it unavoidable? And if the latter, can we use rather than stumble at the "myth"?

[43] Toward the end of *Are You Running with Me, Jesus?* (e.g. in the "Meditations on Films" and the "Prayers for Sexual Freedom") it is notice-able that the interjections "Jesus" and "Lord" become increasingly inciden-tal. In *Free to Live, Free to Die* they have disappeared entirely, without the meditations ceasing to be prayers except in the purely formal sense.

The *Litany for the Ghetto* with its identification of God with the scene rather than the spectator here seems to me to have the advantage. It has provoked the inevitable charge of pantheism. But it is not asserting a metaphysical identity between God and the city; it is simply affirming that at the given moment for the subject in prayer this is where, and who, God is—and there is no turning aside, not even to Another.

In spirituality as in theology I find myself returning to the utterly personal panentheism of the God dwelling incognito at the heart of all things. Indeed, there is ultimately no line between a living theology and "a whole spirituality." So much is this the case that I will repeat in closing, to sum up what I have said on prayer, words that I originally wrote of the vocation held out to the theologian:

It is a call in the first place not to relevance in any slick sense but to exposure, to compassion, sensitivity, awareness and integrity. It is the call to bear reality, more reality than it is easy or indeed possible for a human being to bear unaided. It is to be with God in his world. And in each epoch or culture the place of the theologian is to stand as near as he may to the "creative center" of God's world in his day.[44]

That is also the place of the man of prayer. It is indeed "the longest journey" upon which a human being can embark.

The function of the map, whether in doctrinal or in ascetical theology, is, by the projection it uses, to assist rather than hinder that journey inwards. So, finally, let us return to the map, to see whether there is anything more adequate we can draw in order to represent the center and goal of the whole quest.

[44] *The New Reformation?*, p. 75.

CHAPTER SEVEN

Beyond the God of Theism

The God above or beyond God: such is the concept on which Tillich ends his psychological study *The Courage to Be.*[1] It is heady language, dangerous language. It is language from which one instinctively draws back. I sheered off it and deliberately refused to use it, among so much else from Tillich, in *Honest to God.* For it has a long theological history, strewn with many warnings. Those who have spoken about going above the God of theism have usually sunk below it; and those who have aimed at a suprapersonal Deity have ended more often than not with one that is less than fully personal. From Apostolic times onwards, Gnostics, Marcionites, Theosophists have sought to pass beyond the creator-God of Biblical faith only to lose themselves in airy speculation.

Yet, as constantly, the profoundest and greatest minds return to the theme. Above all has this been true of the mystics, and among them many of the giants—Eckhart, Boehme, Angelus Silesius, Ruysbroeck. Eckhart's distinction between *Gott* and *Gottheit,* the God of revelation and the ineffable mystery of the Godhead, like Boehme's *Ungrund* or abyss of Being, has been drawn upon by modern writers like Berdyaev

[1] (Welwyn, Eng., 1952), pp. 172–78.

and Tillich, who are certainly not unaware of the perils of such talk. One cannot simply dismiss a quest by such men. One is bound to ask what impels them to it.

Fundamentally, what impels them is an acute awareness of the limitations of any theology that describes God, the final reality behind and beyond all existence, in terms of *a* Person or indeed *a* God. That it has done this has been the strength as well as the weakness of popular theism (professional theology has always been more careful—and more remote). For it has presented God to men as a God they can visualize, a Being not too unlike themselves, who does things, who enters into real relationships with them, who can be prayed to and blamed. And the power of such a presentation is that it has done justice to the reality of encounter, of relationship, of over-againstness at the heart of the spiritual awareness. Personality implies a genuine frontier between *I* and *Thou* which preserves the freedom both of man and of God. Destroy this delimitation and both God and man are swallowed up in a boundless impersonal Absolute, in "the dark silence in which all lovers lose themselves" (Ruysbroeck).

Yet the price of this presentation is to depict God as a Being among beings, as a Person contrasted with the rest of reality, "as a self which has a world, as an ego which is related to a thou, as a cause which is separated from its effect."[2] Philosophically and spiritually this representation of the Divine has been under constant criticism from acute minds and sensitive souls who cannot be ignored. Such a God has been found inadequate to carry the spiritual quest. And this is becoming more, not less, evident as new dimensions in physics,

[2] *Ibid.,* p. 175.

in evolution, in psychology, in spirituality are constantly being opened up. The contemporary case for something that
breaks through the limitations of traditional Western personalism is well made in F. C. Happold's *Religious Faith and
Twentieth-Century Man*. Leslie Dewart also appeals to a
widespread popular sense of the insufficiency of traditional
categories:

> The typical experience of the disaffiliated religious person today
> is that "God could not possibly be a person. He must be some
> kind of cosmic force." This is surely a naive view to the degree
> that it implies that God is less than man. But this is not all that
> this common expression connotes. It also means that God is, rather
> than a center of being to which we are drawn, an expansive force
> which impels persons to go out from and beyond themselves. This
> expression represents an effort, born of understandable impatience,
> to transcend the primitive God-being, God-object and God-person
> of absolute theism. The truth that that crude expression so mistak-
> enly conceives may yet be redeemed in the future by Christian
> theism.[3]

Unfortunately this is his last word on the personality of God.
His book is more helpful for the fascinating trails it suggests
than for its follow-through. And this merely reflects the fact
that it is much easier to sense the constrictions than to pass
constructively beyond them.

Yet before attempting this I am concerned to try to avoid
the gaping pitfall of doing less than justice to the reality to
be represented in the illusion of doing more. "Absolute theism" or "Western personalism" may have its limitations, but
at least it has affirmed, in Feuerbach's words, that "to predi-
cate personality of God is ... to declare personality as the

---

[3] *The Future of Belief,* p. 189.

absolute essence."[4] In questioning the *way* it does this, it is very easy to question—and even more to appear to question —the central affirmation it is concerned to safeguard. Indeed, in trying to move out or on from even the most traditionally personalistic ways of speaking of God one is so constantly accused, both by churchmen and by humanists, of "no longer believing in a personal God" that, at the risk of some repetition, it may be desirable to preface any further exploration by going over again the ground that must not be surrendered.

In one sense, it is perfectly true that one *is* questioning belief in a personal God, if by that is meant that commitment to the personal as the central interpretative category of the whole of reality involves being tied to the particular image or projection that represents this as *a* divine Person. But to question the image is of much less significance than to abandon the reality. And therefore, though technically it may be correct to say that one "no longer believes in a personal God," it is far more false than true. What one is concerned to affirm is the conviction theism has always been concerned to make central. And, as we have sought to show, this conviction is given *in the first instance* not as belief in the existence of a Being but as apprehension of a relational reality.

Perhaps one can try to explicate this further by risking an analogy—though every analogy involves the danger of being as misleading as it is helpful. But at least this is a well-tried and Biblical analogy, as well as a personal one—that of mother-love. "Can a woman forget her sucking child, that she should have no compassion on the son of her womb?" asks Isaiah in the name of God. Yes, "even these may forget,

[4] *The Essence of Christianity* (New York, 1957), p. 99.

145

yet I will not forget you."[5] The primal experience of being human is to find oneself held in a relationship of sustaining, claiming love. This is the given, gracious context of all human life, and it is through this relationship of more than biological stimulus and response that the infant is gradually drawn out to distinctively personal existence and responsibility. The law of all life, that "through thee I am," is given additional significance in the case of human beings. For it is only through the grace and claim of the *Thou* that the individual comes to know himself as *I*. The umbilical cord of responsibility supersedes the purely physical connection between mother and child. This relationship is invisible, though it is mediated by the visible features, especially of the face. And it gradually broadens, or should broaden, into a fully adult, free relationship with society and the world at large, without however ever losing its fundamental structure of grace and claim, response and responsibility.

It is some such relatedness which the Judaeo-Christian tradition sees as supplying the context and structure of all life. Everything is held in being and given its distinctive character by the fact that it is essentially and inescapably response to a creative, evocative "word" of grace and claim, drawing it out and upwards to a love in which alone it can find its fulfillment and freedom. In man this response becomes conscious as responsibility.[6] The divine grace and claim is invisible, intangible—and indeed undefinable in and for itself —and yet is mediated through whatever "face" of God presents itself. It comes, in all its reassuring givenness and in all

[5] Isaiah 49.15.
[6] This theme receives classic statement in Brunner's great book *Man in Revolt*.

146

its disturbing power, through the whole of existence, impersonal and personal. But the *quality* of its graciousness and claim are sensed as *more like* those of a personal relationship than of an impersonal, of a free, spiritual communion which it is possible to reject than of a purely physical connection which can only be accepted.

Hence the picture of a Person behind the phenomena, a supreme Father-figure corresponding to the earthly mother-figure. Yet this is anthropomorphism, creating God in our own image. There is nothing wrong with it, as long as we recognize it for what it is. And the best way to recognize it is to switch to another metaphor, where anyone can see the difference.

"The Lord is my rock and my fortress," sings the Psalmist,[7] in language used by many Biblical writers. The "rock" is a symbol for the security which is also an essential element in mother-love. God is the foundation of life, the ground of being, the undergirding reality that prevents everything falling through into meaninglessness and dread. To affirm that "the Lord is my rock" is to affirm that there is a bottom, an utterly reliable and unshakable basis to living. It is the same trust that is expressed in more human terms by saying that "underneath are the everlasting arms."[8] Yet no one supposes that this means that there is in any sense a Rock, somewhere around, like a cosmic Rock of Gibraltar, which must "exist" if the whole experience is not to be an illusion.

"Father" is a much ampler and more adequate metaphor for this security. The security of a rock is impersonal, hard, unfeeling. It could not serve the Psalmist who wanted to

[7] Psalm 18.2.
[8] Deuteronomy 33.27.

affirm that "like as a father pitieth his own children, even so is the Lord merciful unto them that fear him."[9] Yet the metaphor of "father" by very reason of its greater adequacy contains the greater danger that its metaphorical character will be forgotten. Men can easily say that God *is* a father in a way that they can never seriously say that he *is* a rock. And they can go on to say that the reality to which the metaphor points can be true only if there *is* a Being who *does* exist, with these attributes, somewhere around. "Otherwise," they will ask, "what do you mean by talking about love as the ultimate reality, unless there is a Lover? What do you mean by talking of God in personal terms unless there is a Person? If that is what you believe in, then we can understand it (even if we cannot believe it). But if you do not accept that there is such a Person, then it is merely confusing and dishonest to go on speaking of 'God.' For the word must refer to this Being— or mean nothing."

So the familiar argument runs. But in fact the New Testament says that "God is love" (not that it means this literally or univocally, any more than when it says "God is light" or "God is spirit"): the proposition "God is a Being who loves" is a transposition (as is the familiar mistranslation "God is *a* Spirit"). The conviction that reality is reliable, not merely in a rock-like way, but in the kind of way in which a person can be trusted, is transposed into belief in an ultimate divine Person. It is a harmless and indeed a profoundly helpful symbol. The Bible, and the New Testament in particular, is full of language speaking of God in terms such as "Father!," "my Father," "like a father"—though it is noteworthy that it never says directly that God is a father, any more than it

[9] Psalm 103.13.

says that he is a rock. "My rock," "our rock" indicate the typically existential, rather than metaphysical, character of such affirmations. And the same applies to "father." But to talk of God *as though* he *were* an invisible father seated in heaven presented no difficulty—let alone stumbling-block— when the whole universe was peopled with invisible personal beings in a quite naïve way. In an age in which mythology was taken entirely naturally as description of how things are there was no need to differentiate or to stress the "as if." Jesus could use it quite freely as a way of making vivid the utterly personal relationship of trust and dependence in which his whole life was grounded. It caused no barrier to belief, and it made God immediately and obviously real—though the Bible is constantly warning against the danger of *all* images, and not merely of graven ones.

But now, as we have tried to indicate, the simplistic representation of God as a Person is the source or at any rate the occasion of great stumbling—as well as, still, of great comfort and faith. It produces in many sheer unbelief. Such beings, it is held, simply do not exist (or at least there is no evidence for them), and the reality of the God-relationship is quickly made to turn on quite extraneous arguments and proofs. In an age of science and technology the image of an invisible Superman personally creating phenomena as a potter makes a pot strikes more people as incredible than helpful. And in an age of planning a cosmic planner who cannot or does not prevent disasters merely appears supremely incompetent or grossly culpable.

On more and more occasions it is positively imperative to sit loose to the image—or even to discard it—if the truth it is intended to represent is to be maintained. And I am profoundly convinced that the truth does remain. For this reason I believe it is more important to insist on the continuity of belief in God as personal—and to retain the word "God" however loaded—than to give it up. The reality of being surrounded, sustained, claimed abides—even though there is a healthy process of detachment going on from certain childish notions of dependence which religion has often fostered[10] (contrary to everything in the New Testament's equation of "sonship" with the maturity and freedom of man come of age).[11] And the need to speak in some way of "God" represents the conviction that this encompassing reality, the element in which man lives and moves and has his being, is not merely materialistic or even humanistic. The question is *how* one gives expression to this conviction. Certainly it is not adequate to describe the reality in impersonal categories—though it reveals itself in many impersonal "faces." Yet to envisage it as embodied in a Person diminishes it and trivializes it. If the only alternative to a personal God is a less than personal Absolute, then let us by all means retain the former. Yet it is impossible to escape the fact that this is a serious obstacle to faith for modern secular man, as, indeed, it has always been for Oriental religious man. There are only too many today who do not think it possible to believe in God as personal *at all* unless it be in the old image. Can we get beyond this dilemma,

[10] Berdyaev writes: "Schleiermacher is wrong when he says that the religious feeling is a feeling of dependence. Dependence is an earthly thing. We might have better reason for saying it is a feeling of independence. We may speak of God only by analogy with what is revealed in the depths of spiritual experience" (*Truth and Revelation,* translated in Donald A. Lowrie's Berdyaev anthology *Christian Existentialism* [London, 1965], p. 45). I should prefer to substitute the word "interdependence."

[11] See especially John 8.31-38 and Galatians 4.1-7.

this false either-or, of having to be atheists or theists in the old sense? This is the question to which we must now return.

I should like to focus it by seeing it through the mind—the often strange, contorted, visionary mind—of one man. He is the relatively little known Victorian English naturalist and mystic Richard Jefferies.[12] Part of his fascination is that he was almost totally self-educated, with many of the oddities of judgment and perspective which this tends to produce,[13] but with a vision both into nature and, as it were, through nature that makes him a spiritual brother of writers whom he had not read nor probably even heard of. The reason for his particular interest as a mystic is that he was an atheist, in the sense of rejecting—often with vehemence—the only theism he knew, with, nevertheless, an intense sense of and insatiable openness to what he called "the Beyond."

At first sight he appears to be a typical nature-mystic with an overwhelming sense of the immanence of the spiritual in the natural:

Through every grass blade in the thousand, thousand grasses; through the million leaves, veined and edge-cut, on bush and tree; through the song-notes and the marked feathers of the birds; through the insects' hum and the color of the butterflies; through

---

[12] His most remarkable—and here most relevant—book is his spiritual autobiography, *The Story of My Heart,* of which it may be said, as Walt Whitman wrote of one of his own: "This is no book / Who touches this, touches a man." Of the many books on Jefferies see, for a contemporary verdict, W. Besant, *The Eulogy of Richard Jefferies*; for a modern biography using the evidence of unpublished notebooks, S. J. Looker and Crichton Porteous, *Richard Jefferies: Man of the Fields*; and for a literary criticism, W. J. Keith, *Richard Jefferies: A Critical Study.*

[13] E.g., his rejection of any notion of evolution and his naïve theory of the eventual capacity of man physically to live forever.

the soft warm air, the flecks of clouds dissolving—I used them all for prayer.[14]

He has an exquisite, almost excruciating, sense of the presence of the Beyond pressing upon him through earth, sky, and sea, and above all through the rays of the sun. Yet he has no sentimental illusions about nature. There is, he recognizes, "nothing human in nature," nothing, that is, that cares a jot for personal values. Indeed, it is anti-human. Nor is there any god in nature, no evidence of design or benevolent purpose. Like the Preacher of Ecclesiastes, he is forced to the conclusion that "time and chance happen to . . . all."[15] In this sense he is as skeptical as any nineteenth-century atheist.

And yet he is not, cannot be, content to leave things there. Indeed, his atheism is not negative or destructive. Rather, the idea of a God is, for him, totally inadequate for the reality which the soul touches but cannot hope to grasp. He sees it as "an invisible idol." "The mind goes on and requires more . . . something higher than a god,"[16] "something infinitely higher than deity."[17] And he links this with the need to press beyond the "three ideas" concerning the inner consciousness of man which have in the course of civilization so far been "wrested from the unknown"—"the existence of the soul, immortality, the deity."[18] The fashioning of these three ideas corresponds, we may say, to the stage in the description of reality that Van Peursen designates as the ontological.[19] The soul, immortality, and God are conceived in terms of sub-

---

[14] *The Story of My Heart* (Swan Library edition; London, 1933), p. 15.
[15] Ecclesiastes 9.11.   [16] *The Story of My Heart,* p. 198.
[17] *Ibid.,* p. 206.   [18] *Ibid.,* pp. 52–61 *passim.*
[19] See p. 34 above.

stantial existence, and men's intimations of the Beyond are given "objective," metaphysical reality in these imaginable entities. And Jefferies has no desire to go back on them: they are indeed pointers, "stepping-stones" to a "fourth idea" or, rather, to an illimitable series of ideas, "an immense ocean over which the mind can sail, upon which the vessel of thought has not yet been launched." "The mind of so many thousand years has worked round and round inside the circle of these three ideas as a boat on an island lake. Let us haul it over the belt of land, launch on the ocean, and sail onwards."

Meanwhile for Jefferies the God of theism must be transcended as far too small. It is this God that for him must die, and not simply the God of deism, of absolute transcendence, whom it seems Altizer is railing at. The God of theism is a legitimate protest against monism, in the name of a genuine relationship, a real duality of *I* and *Thou*, such as personality requires. And yet it is not able to transcend dualism. It polarizes God and the world *as though* they existed alongside each other in unresolved juxtaposition. This dualism runs through all the characteristic language of Western theism. It speaks of

> God *and* the world
> Heaven *and* earth
> Eternity *and* time
> The infinite *and* the finite
> Transcendence *and* immanence
> The one *and* the many
> Good *and* evil
> The divine nature *and* the human in Christ.

And so one could go on. Like Descartes' principles of thought and extension, neither can be reduced to the other. Yet neither has the power to unify the other with itself. God is on *one side* of each pair of opposites.

But there is a powerful and perennial tradition—in philosophy, in mysticism, in Oriental religion—which refuses to remain content with this situation, and constantly yearns to break through to a non-duality, to a *coincidence* of opposites, to a higher all-embracing unity. "By the Beyond," wrote Richard Jefferies in the notebooks of his last pain-wracked years, "I mean the Idea of the *whole:* that would fill the sky." It is the same vision as that of the thirteenth-century Umbrian mystic, Angela of Foligno:

The eyes of my soul were opened, and I beheld the plenitude of God, wherein I did comprehend the whole world, both here and beyond the sea, the abyss and the ocean and all things. In all these things I beheld naught save the divine power, in a manner assuredly indescribable; so that through excess of marvelling the soul cried with a loud voice, saying: "The whole world is full of God."[20]

There is the characteristic paradox that the whole world is *in* God and, at the same time, that the whole world is full *of* God. As Meister Eckhart puts it, "The more God is in all things, the more he is outside them. The more he is within, the more he is without."[21]

The overcoming of the duality which divides even Creator and creature is, of course, a commonplace not only in Hinduism but in the Christian mystics. The so-called "mystic copula," which says with the Hindu *tat tvam asi*—"Thou (the

[20] From her *Liber Visionum,* quoted by F. C. Happold, *Religious Faith and Twentieth Century Man* (Harmondsworth, Eng., 1966), p. 131. H. de Lubac notes the influence of this mystic on Teilhard de Chardin in *The Religion of Teilhard de Chardin,* p. 26.

[21] Quoted by Happold, *Religious Faith* ..., p. 130.

self) art That (God)"—or with Angelus Silesius, "He who seeks God must become God,"[22] is not asserting, as was said earlier,[23] a metaphysical equation, so that all the attributes of God are transferred to the finite self. It is affirming an identification which passes beyond what Nicholas of Cusa called "the door of the coincidence of opposites." And God for Nicholas is to be seen always "beyond the coincidence of contradictories..., and nowhere this side thereof."[24] In other words, God is not *one* of the poles of traditional theism, but transcends these inevitable finite distinctions. To express this within the logic of non-contradiction is of course finally impossible. But the same writer struggles with an answer when in this philosophical meditation he asks of God, "How then dost thou create things other than thyself—for thou wouldst seem to create thyself?" and goes on:

Yet this is no real difficulty, since with thee creation and existence are the same. And creating and being created alike are naught else than the sharing of thy Being among all, that thou mayest be All in all, and yet mayest abide freed from all. For to call into being things which are not is to make Nothing a sharer in Being: thus to call is to create, while to share is to be created. And beyond this coincidence of creating and being created art thou, Absolute and Infinite God, neither creating nor creatable, albeit all things are what they are because thou art.[25]

This may appear abstruse and rarified mystification—or, on the other hand, a commonplace of what many of the great-

---

[22] Quoted by Berdyaev, *Spirit and Reality*, p. 143, who also cites from the same source these other equally horrifying sayings: "I am as great as God, he is as little as I"; "When I with God into God am transformed"; "It is I must be the sun, to give color with my beams to the colorless sea of the Godhead entire."

[23] See p. 87 above.   [24] *The Vision of God*, chap. 9.

[25] *Ibid.*, chap. 12.

est minds and spirits have always been seeking to say. There is nothing new about it. What is new, I believe, is that in our generation its relevance is no longer confined to upper reaches of ascetic and philosophical theology. For a revolution is taking place which is exposing the inadequacies of the theistic image of God, which has hitherto served for ordinary "lay" thought and spirituality. Windows have been thrown open on a vastly larger world. There has been extensive—and intensive—popularization of insights into aspects of reality which threaten to break the thought-barriers of traditional Western theism. There has been a communications-explosion in psychology, in mysticism, in parapsychology, in the effects of psychedelic drugs, in a living awareness of Hindu, Buddhist, and Sufi spirituality, and so on and so on. One has only to mention the wide influence of deeply serious writers like Jung and Tillich, Aldous and Julian Huxley, Arnold Toynbee and Thomas Merton. This means that what were before marginal speculations have become frontier problems. The issues of this chapter—of how one thinks beyond the God of theism—are raised, for instance, quite explicitly and urgently in such books of popular "lay" theology as F. C. Happold's *Religious Faith and Twentieth Century Man,* Alan Watts' playful, perverse, or profound book (according to how one looks at it) *Beyond Theology: The Art of Godmanship,* and the Chicago journalist William Braden's study, *The Private Sea: An Inquiry into the Religious Implications of LSD.*

Moreover, in all this the effect must not be underrated of the revolutions that have taken place in the myths, models, and thought-patterns used to describe the purely physical world. Both matter and spirit present themselves very differently than they did even a generation ago. They are thought of as

156

far less divergent and as far less "substantial." And I would
basically agree with Happold when he predicts that

The religious thought-forms of twentieth-century man will represent a new fusion of religious and scientific "myths," mystically
(in the sense we are using the term) interpreted, accompanied,
particularly among the more sensitive types, by a growth in spirituality, and by a deeper sanctification of secular life, as the sacred
and the profane are more and more seen as one.[26]

Watts points out that the modern scientific way of *describing* the identity of things and events is much nearer the way
in which the mystic *feels* them.[27] Causes and effects are no
longer viewed as separate occurrences, bumping into each
other like billiard balls, but as aspects of a single event. What
anything *is* is seen to depend more and more on its relation
to the "system" of which it is a part. The behavior of things
and objects is viewed as the behavior of "fields"—spatial, grav-
itational, magnetic, or social. As he says, "these unitary, relational, and 'fieldish' ways of thinking give immense plausibility to non-dualist or pantheist (to be frightfully exact 'pan-
*en*theist') types of metaphysic."[28] And he makes the good
point that the defect of what he calls "theological monarch-
ism," or a Supreme Being type of theology, is not that it is
anthropomorphic but that it is (now) bad anthropomorphism:

To construct a God in the human image is objectionable only to
the extent that we have a poor image of ourselves, for example,
as egos in bags of skin. But as we can begin to visualize man as

[26] *Religious Faith and Twentieth-Century Man*, p. 122.
[27] *Beyond Theology*, pp. 226–27.   [28] *Ibid.*, p. 225.

the behavior of a unified field—immensely complex and compris-
ing the whole universe—there is less and less reason against con-
ceiving God in *that* image. To go deeper and deeper into oneself
is also to go farther and farther out into the universe, until, as the
physicist well knows, we reach the domain where three-dimen-
sional, sensory images are no longer valid.[29]

This convergence of the models appropriate to the scientific and the theological exploration is relevant also as an answer to one of the major traditional hazards of trying to push
"beyond" the God of theism. Historically this seems always
to have been associated with a movement to get further and
further *away* from the natural order. In Gnosticism, the God
"above" the Demiurge who created this world was to be found
by passing through and out the other side of all the spheres of
material existence. In Neo-platonism, which so powerfully
influenced Christian mysticism by way of Pseudo-Dionysius,
the One was to be gained at the expense of the many, by the
flight of the alone to the Alone. In Hinduism and in many
forms of Buddhism (though others are more incarnational),
salvation is to be attained by negation of the world of *maya*
and *samsara*. But today any relevant theology, like any relevant spirituality, must come through what Berdyaev calls the
"realization" (that is, the fuller incarnation or materialization) of spirit.

This applies to each of the "three ideas" which Jefferies saw
as needing to be transcended. "The soul" can no longer be
thought of (as in the period of ontology) as an individual,
nonmaterial, substance implanted in the body to which it in
no real sense belongs. Rather, if we are to go on using the
word, it must be related to the whole form of the personal in

[29] *Ibid.,* p. 222.

158

its spiritual aspect. Similarly, "immortality" cannot be seen (as Jefferies recognized) in terms of something in man which is not dissolved by physical death and which "goes on." Rather, it is a dimension to the whole of life as personal, represented more adequately by the New Testament phrase "eternal life." It is better described as "the life beyond myself" than merely "life beyond death," and it is given cosmic expression in the Jewish-Christian myth of the "resurrection" of the whole body of history.[30] In the same way, "God" is not to be understood as an Ego over against the world, *a* Spirit in contrast with created matter. Rather, if again we are to go on using the term, it must relate to that which compels us to speak of the whole of reality in terms of personal spirit, the transcendent source and goal of all being—in all things and through all things and above all things.

Ultimately in speaking of God all words are bound to fail. Yet rather than end in final aposiopesis, there is perhaps one more thing that can be said. One of the insights of our century is that the trans-personal character of God is better expressed not by envisaging him as a bigger and better Individual, nor as a sort of Hobbesian collective Personality incorporating all other persons, but in terms of the interpersonal. This is the result of applying "field" or relational thinking to persons as well as to things. For Buber has taught us that in the beginning—and in the end—is not the individual, the *I* or the *Thou,* but the nexus *I-Thou.* And the whole of reality too must ultimately be seen in terms, not of a God, a monarchical Being supreme among individual entities, but of a divine "field" in which the finite *Thous* are constituted what they

[30] See *In the End, God* (2d ed.), chaps. 8 and 9.

are in the freedom of a wholly personalizing love. In the same vein, Berdyaev, summing up what he calls "the pivotal idea" of his *Spirit and Reality,* says that the only justification of anthropomorphism is that "God is like a *whole humanity* rather than like nature, society, or concept."[31] The pledge of ultimate Reality within this world, the sign of the Kingdom, is what Dumitriu describes as "that dense and secret undergrowth which is wholly composed of personal events." But it is Teilhard de Chardin who has taken this idea to its most daring limits in the vision which closes *The Phenomenon of Man.* He sees the universe as pointing to "the hyperpersonal, beyond the collective," in which God is "the Center of centers" in an interlocking web of free spiritual relationship in which the All and the Personal are no longer exclusive.

This is the vision, too, to which the New Testament points, of God as "all in all."[32] This passage is the charter of Christian panentheism. Yet it is, as its context in I Corinthians 15 makes abundantly clear, an eschatological panentheism. This does not mean, for the New Testament, that it is something that will only be true *after* everything else.[33] It is the truth "in Christ" now. As the Epistle to the Hebrews puts it, "We do not yet see everything in subjection" to man—that is, to personal purpose. "But we see Jesus ... crowned with glory and honor."[34] And it is this, symbolically, that the Christian sees as the first fruits and guarantee of the whole cosmic process. The God who was *in* Christ is the God who is and must be

---

[31] P. 187. Italics mine.
[32] I Corinthians 15.28.
[33] For this I must again refer to my *In the End, God.*
[34] Hebrews 2.8–9.

in all. The model of panentheism is essentially an incarnational one. That is why I believe it is fundamentally appropriate to Christianity—in a way that deism or pantheism or even theism is not—without being exclusively Christian. And, *per contra,* I also believe that the most appropriate model—perhaps the only appropriate model today—for a satisfactory theology of the Incarnation is a panentheistic one.

But that is another book.

Index

these relate to the spiritual pilgrim who senses an inward need not met by conventional faith.

The second part of Ellwood's book explores the impact and meaning of unconventional spirituality in American history by examining closely three "moments" in its career: the Spiritualism of the 1840s and 50s, Theosophy's "journey to the East" in the 1870s and 80s, and the Zen of the 1950s "Beat Generation." Ellwood offers exciting new historical insights into each of these movements.

Finally, Ellwood places spiritual unconventionality in the context of America's religious heritage and American life as a whole, from New England Transcendentalism to the great variety of contemporary religions now present across the United States.

ROBERT S. ELLWOOD, JR., is Bishop James W. Bashford Professor of Oriental Studies in the school of religion at the University of Southern California and is director of USC's East Asian Studies Center. He is the author of numerous scholarly books and articles.

Alternative Altars

Chicago History of
American Religion

A Series Edited by
Martin E. Marty

Alternative Altars
*Unconventional
and Eastern
Spirituality
in America*

Robert S. Ellwood, Jr.

The University of Chicago Press Chicago and London

ROBERT S. ELLWOOD, JR., is Bishop James W.
Bashford Professor of Oriental Studies in the
School of Religion and director of the East Asian
Studies Center at the University of Southern
California. He is the author of numerous schol-
arly books and articles.

The University of Chicago Press, Chicago 60637
The University of Chicago Press, Ltd., London
© 1979 by The University of Chicago
All rights reserved. Published 1979
Printed in the United States of America
83 82 81 80 79   5 4 3 2 1

Library of Congress Cataloging in Publication Data

Ellwood, Robert S.   1933–
    Alternative Altars

(Chicago history of American religion)
Includes bibliographical references and index.
    1. United States—Religion—1945-   2. Cults—
United States.   1. Title.
BL2530.U6E44   200'.973   78-15089
ISBN 0-226-20618-1

Contents

Foreword

At the far edges of my bookshelves on American religious history are a number of titles that put the subject of this book in its place: *Strange Sects and Curious Cults, Strange Sects and Cults, Those Curious New Cults, New Gods in America, The New Religions, Faiths for the Few.* Some scholars estimate the number of people attracted to these groups as anywhere from two to twenty million, and millions more—especially if we include devotees of astrology and the occult—see something in what they represent, even if these interested people do not join cults to express their faith.

What makes sects and cults "strange," and "curious," and why are they "new" for the "few"?

First, the story of these groups violates a kind of canon that for over a century American religious historians have used to define the boundaries of respectability for their readers. No one chartered them to put narrow boundaries around their story or their subjects; these authors simply reflected the viewpoints of their sponsors and clienteles, and thus unofficially established certain faiths as non-strange or non-curious because they seemed old and belonged to the many. A review of this canonical sense will help prepare readers for the current book.

Because New England was the cultural center of the nineteenth-century churches and because the early New Englanders were careful to speak clearly and to leave plenty of documents, New England was at the heart of the story of mainstream religion. The generous early authors gave some weight to the contributions of Virginians, while they treated Rhode Islanders and Pennsylvanians as "strange" and "curious." Eventually these dissenters and mavericks from those colonies won their way and historians charitably enlarged the canon to include with favor all "evangelical" Protestants. The first major book in the canon, *Religion in America* by Robert Baird, used such a line of discrimination. The "unevangelicals" were "Atheists, Deists, Socialists, Fourrierists [sic], Rappists, Shakers, Mormons, Swedenborgians, Tunkers," and, less strange and curious, Catholics, Unitarians, Christ-ians, Universalists, and Jews.

Decades later the historians included all Protestantism in their informal canon until, after a century of Catholic growth, William Warren Sweet began to include Catholics in *The Story of Religion in America,* though as late as 1950 he was still paying at best grudging attention in his best-seller and norm-setter to all non-Protestants. In the decades since, most historians have come to include Catholics and Jews, thus setting up "biblical religion" as *the* American religion. Meanwhile, they have also paid some attention to the equally respectable tradition of the religion of Enlightenment, called variously the "religion of the republic," civil religion, or, in Benjamin Franklin's useful phrase, "publick religion." The most expansive histories—the best is Sydney E. Ahlstrom's *A Religious History of the American People*—included segregated chapters on the subjects Ellwood treats. Ahlstrom, for example, has as his sixty-first chapter: "Piety for the Age of Aquarius: Theosophy, Occultism, and Non-Western Religion." No one else pushed the edges of the canon as far as he, but Ahlstrom remained clear about one theme: Puritanism provided the thread for the story until the 1960s, and when it unraveled, the story became less clear.

The second reason why the groups here scrutinized are considered strange and curious has to do with the fact that the American majority tends to establish a world view and to gain plausibility for it even among those who do not accept the faith. To a complete outsider the traditional faiths may look as arcane and idiosyncratic as the "marginal" ones do. I have heard middle-class Americans chuckle when told of Melanesian Cargo Cults, groups of people who in colonial times and even after World War II developed an elaborate mythology to explain why the whites of the world seemed prosperous and they were not—yet. As American or Japanese troops

landed with abundant supplies on their islands, the tribespeople
explained that their own ancestors would come back at an end of an
age to redeem them, bringing along endless bounty for the once-
deprived people.

What of the laughers? Some of them adhered to the outlook of
the most notable evangelist of our age. He was an intimate of five
presidents, the most admired man of his decades, according to
the polls. Yet he propagated the idea that some time suddenly and
soon a man who lived two thousand years ago would literally return
to earth and reign for a thousand years, and that accompanying his
return would be a great world-ending battle in the Middle East.
Few thought this "curious." Others of the amused were Roman
Catholics, Lutherans, or Episcopalians, who gathered weekly to
receive a little flattened piece of white bread and a taste of wine,
believing that therewith they were eating the flesh and drinking the
blood of their God, communing with him "until he comes again."
Few others thought *them* unrespectable, as indeed they were not,
because their faith had established itself, while those faiths considered strange and curious had not. Yet their beliefs functioned
for these evangelicals and catholics the way cargo cults worked for
the Melanesians—or the way the "new" faiths work for millions of
the "few."

Robert S. Ellwood, Jr., is not out to violate the sensibilities of
those of us who believe in the classic biblical faiths of the Western
world; indeed, he shares one of those faiths himself. Instead, his
purpose is to enlarge the concept and contents of the canon, to
extend the boundaries that define the plausible and the acceptable,
if not the respectable, and to give an honest accounting—always
the first task of the historian—of movements or people who leave
their mark on a populace.

Many of us have come to speak of the spiritual phenomena that
come into Ellwood's scope as "new." But some of them quite
possibly antedate biblical religion and certainly are older than
Christianity. They are believed by most people to be new to American shores. Of course, they had a history in America before the
boom in the seventies. In the conventional telling—and I am
among the conventional tellers—the religions of the East or the
occult first showed up in Salem witchcraft and then, more re-

spectably, as the "Yankee Hindoo" emphasis of Ralph Waldo
Emerson and Henry David Thoreau. After this a few strange people
turned to spiritualism and others followed a mysterious woman into
Theosophy, but not until the World's Parliament of Religions in
1893, when representatives of Hinduism and Zen Buddhism
showed up at Chicago, did citizens have any close contact with
Eastern faiths. While there was always an occult underground, in
the 1930s a number of English authors, Aldous Huxley chief among
them, began to import "the perennial philosophy." Finally in the
1950s came the Zen and "beat" poets, and in the late 1960s the
flowering of spiritualities that have left their imprint on the whole
nation.

Ellwood retraces that history, but shows that it was never quite as
marginal as this telling suggests. Rather than taking readers through
a kind of curiosity shop, he wisely chooses to concentrate on three
narratives or case studies and, by his sustained focus on them, to
raise most of the issues that have to do with "emergent" and
"excursus" spirituality. It is likely that readers will be more aware
than before of its emergence and less likely than ever to think of it
as a *mere* excursus from the mainstream of American religiosity.
Here, instead, is a book that raises questions for a society that is
progressively losing its canon, its norm, its traditional religions by
which others are measured. Professor Ellwood is less concerned with
answering those questions than with providing readers with the
data base and perspective on which to do their own thinking and
resolving.

MARTIN E. MARTY
THE UNIVERSITY OF CHICAGO

Preface

This essay began as a study of "non-normative religion" in America. I have changed the terms to ones more positive and, I hope, more illuminating in connotation. But the original definition of the task remains: to investigate religious life in this country outside the Judeo-Christian mainstream and its significance for American spiritual culture.

Readers aware of the marshy terrain such a quest is likely to enter may first ask what definition of religion undergirds it. The one at the back of my mind is relatively elaborate and restrictive. I am not thinking of religion simply in light of an existential definition, such as Paul Tillich's "ultimate concern," but also as a cultural system, in Clifford Geertz's sense, and as an expression of a social construction of reality in the meaning of Berger and Luckmann.

We will be concerned with socially reified religion which, through an orchestration of concepts, rites, and groups that involve but transcend the individual, formally offers models of meaning-giving ultimate reality and ways of access to it. A good "handle" for dealing with religion in this way is to analyze it in terms of the three forms of religious expression of the phenomenological sociologist of religion Joachim Wach. While accepting that at its core religion involves a numinous, transcendent, or existential reality, Wach indicated that its visible phenomena appear through three forms: the theoretical, the concepts and paradigmatic narratives; the practical, the praxis of rites, prayer, meditation, pilgrimage, services, gestures; the sociological, or its articulation in groups, leadership, and interpersonal relations. My preference is to restrict the use of the word "religion" to that highly visible and discrete class of human phenomena which has an ultimate reference *and* has interlocking expressions in all three of these forms. Thus, we will not be especially concerned with ideas without sociological structures and some kind of praxis to go with them, nor with groups without transcendent ideas.

I am well aware that some of the movements to be discussed do not think that the word religion appropriately applies to them and do not use it of themselves. This is a point of view which I respect and which at some periods, or from some perspectives, I would agree is valid. In connection with them I have often used a term other than religion, such as spirituality. Nonetheless, I think that as a formal definition the foregoing concept of religion allows us to separate out sociologically reified spirituality from purely intellectual movements.

In approaching this task, I early decided not to attempt a full-blown historical survey of non-normative religion. Rather, I have chosen here to focus major attention on theoretical models for understanding American non-normative spirituality, and, by way of illustration, to examine in depth three movements—or, rather, three moments in the lives of three movements. They are, however, movements of immense significance, and ones which well encapsulate three eras in its history: Spiritualism, Theosophy, and American Zen. I trust that this method, far from being disappointingly restrictive, will cast some fresh light on the whole spiritual scene outside the mainstream.

Finally, I would like to add a personal note. Often disquisitions on social movements manage to seem inhumanly dispassionate, if not condescending. They may also seem to communicate less respect for the ideas which have inspired them than concern for the human foibles and frailties, and the historical vicissitudes, which have beset them as they have all human institutions and endeavors. Yet there is a place for both the social commentator and the philosopher; as Swedenborg and the Zen sages have taught, compassion and wisdom are ultimately two sides of the same reality and need each other for completion . . . let the human perspective lead to the first, and philosophy to wisdom. I myself have a high regard for what has been brought to America by much of the non-normative spiritual tradition. I have benefited immensely from reading Shaker, Swedenborgian, and Spiritualist literature; I am a member of the Theosophical Society in America, as well as an Episcopal clergyman; I have studied and practiced Zen meditation, art, and life fairly extensively. But the expounding of all of that would make a different book than this one.

Finally, I would like to express deep gratitude to those who have assisted with this project. The Pulitzer Prize-winning poet Gary Snyder read the chapter on American Zen, in which he is a major figure, and made several very useful comments and corrections. The full manuscript was read by Professor James T. Richardson, of the Department of Sociology of the University of Nevada; by Professor Bruce Campbell, visiting scholar at the Institute of Religious Studies, University of California, Santa Barbara, and an authority on Theosophical history; by Professor William LaFleur, of the Department of Religious Studies, Princeton University; by Professor Catherine Albanese, Department of Religion, Wright State University, Dayton, Ohio; and by Professor Martin E. Marty, of the University of Chicago Divinity School, editor of the series in which this book appears. Their advice and help, often given with a generosity that went far beyond the call of duty, has made this book considerably better than it would otherwise have been. For those failings that remain, the author takes full responsibility.

1   Perspectives

1

Temple and Cave
in America

Two American Churches

Not far from where I live, a quiet, shady street runs through a small suburban town. On one side of that street, as on hundreds of shady streets in as many American small towns, a large Methodist church complex rises. Over the landscaped grounds sprawl sanctuary, offices, auditoria, parking lots, and countless classrooms. The solidity and evident prosperity of this edifice proclaim that it is a local manifestation of the proper, legitimate, respectable religion of the land, akin in that sense to Canterbury Cathedral in England, or the Altar of Heaven of the old Chinese emperors in Peking.

Looking at this substantial place of worship, a keen observer might notice, out of the corners of his eyes, something else across the street. There a modest house has been converted into another sort of shrine. If the visitor were to examine it, he would see that its living room has been lovingly but amateurishly redecorated to make the sanctuary. Its single meeting room was formerly the garage. Much of the lawn has become a miniscule parking lot. In front, a crude sign proudly carries the legend, "First United Spiritualist Church." Behind this simple title and shabby facade lay realms of sacred mystery and marvel undreamed by those whose God is content to remain on the other side of the street.

A former minister of this Spiritualist church, an American shaman if ever there was one—other than Native American medicine men with memories of authentic vision quests—relates a call that was no Wesleyan warm-hearted experience. He says that long ago, on a freezing midwinter night in an Illinois farm-

house, a kindly Indian spirit guide brought him the tangible
spirit of a little neighbor girl whom he had not even known had
died that same night. She wanted to communicate that all was well
with her on the Other Side.

Now, in the former garage converted into a seance room, twice a
week this old habitue of two worlds goes into trance and, assisted by
four familiar guides, delivers messages from Spirit.

I have attended a fair number of seances in that place, and can
attest to their unfailing fascination. On one occasion when my wife
was with me, one of the guides—a garrulous American Indian
spirit—professed to go into our home (which the medium had
never visited) and describe what he saw. There were some misses,
but a few items, including a broken lamp, were striking hits. We
later calculated about 75 percent accuracy.

More intriguing was the audience of some twenty persons, all of
whom received personal messages. The majority seemed not to be
members of the church; a few may even have had their official
connection across the street. One or two were somewhat familiar
with occultism and talked knowingly of chakras and planes and the
like. The majority were clearly from blue-collar families and had
many hard years behind them. They clung eagerly to words from
Spirit regarding deceased loved ones, and advice about travel,
sickness, or errant sons and spouses.

Once I attended a "materialization seance" at the same site. A
visiting Spiritualist minister from another state was the officiant.
He first entered the "cabinet," a closetlike affair with curtains in
the corner of the room, and allegedly went into a trance which
enabled something of his vital substance—"ectoplasm"—to leave
the body and provide material out of which spirits could take
ethereal but visible shape.

Then, the room almost totally darkened, there emerged from the
cabinet a series of apparitions in willowy spectral garb, from little
girls to ancient kings, all bearing messages to various members of the
bemused circle. One of the first to appear was the shade of Nelson
Eddy, who sang a vibrant rendition of "In the Sweet Bye-and-Bye."
The revenant of my mentor on the inner planes, a one-time officer of
Caesar, appeared and presented me with an alleged old Roman coin
as a token of his authenticity; I still keep it in my desk.

But the magical mood of communication between worlds and centuries was broken toward the end of the evening when a young man of proletarian accent, a skeptic in limbo, arose to proclaim he had "seen enough phoney spooks." He flashed on a cigarette lighter and two trousered legs were suddenly clearly visible beneath the current specter floating about the chamber. That figure beat a hasty retreat into the cabinet.

Shortly thereafter the medium stumbled out of the same place, rubbing his eyes and asking what had happened. When he was informed, he asserted that he could have been killed by such a shock to his vital substance when it was out of his body in the form of ectoplasm. He then and there departed whence he had come. The regular minister of the church—whom I respect as a devout Spiritualist divine—entered the tense, muttering room to refund apologetically to each of us the five-dollar "donation" we had made to attend this performance and to request us to leave immediately. He said something about the sort of mediums who give Spiritualism a bad name. But because I considered the evening well worthwhile as entertainment and edification, I was reluctant to accept the refund.

Peter Berger has written that "religion is man's audacious attempt to see the whole universe as humanly significant."[1] There were, to be sure, several audacious elements evident in the little Spiritualist church on that gaudy night. (For that matter, an omniscient eye might have detected audacious features in the quieter church across the street as well.) But I also felt there a desperate attempt to wrench from the infinitely dumb but numinous universe around us, by whatever forcing and contrivance, a human significance. However the living lie, the dead do not die: that heavy certitude I have felt thick as sour cream in the air of every Spiritualist meeting I have attended.

Of course, a comparable affirmation of eternal life could probably also be found in the sprawling, shiny "mainline" church. But its intimations of immortality are presented in a different atmosphere. If it is at all typical of the Middle American Protestantism the building suggests, the Sunday morning rite in the church across the street is not difficult to evoke. A moment's stillness, and one's mind echoes with hymns like "This Is My Father's World," with the sonorous words of scripture, the compassionate pastoral prayer, the announcements of youth group hayrack rides and basketball games, of committee meetings and pancake suppers. The sermon would be warm with the affirmation of honesty, love, and under-standing. Then, the coffee hour, the gathering-up of children from the far-flung reaches of the Sunday school, the ranchwagons and sedans loaded again, long Sunday dinners in a hundred homes, and finally TVs turned to pro football.

The Temple Paradigm

If there is a paradigm for the "mainline" church style of religion, surely it is the temple which Solomon built in Jerusalem when all was at peace, in that city whose ideal form has always suggested men dwelling together like brothers in happy and holy harmony, full of gratitude to God for fruitful families and bounteous fields. Individual and state, heaven and earth, visibly become seamless unities, all people accepting the "natural orders" and the stan-dard, official dispensations of grace as the way things are. No dark, quizzical places linger in a man's soul where he wonders if all this is only pretending, and if the apparent promises of God are not always what they seem.

Instead, the people all joined with the sage king in saying at the temple's dedication, "Blessed be the Lord who has given his people Israel rest, as he promised; not one of the promises he made through his servant Moses has failed." One reads on: "So Solomon and all Israel with him, a great assembly from Lebohamath to the Torrent of Egypt, celebrated the pilgrim-feast at that time before the Lord our God for seven days. On the eighth day he dismissed the people; and they blessed the king and went home happy and glad at heart for all the prosperity granted by the Lord to his servant David and his people Israel." (1 Kings 8:56, 65–66)

The Cave Paradigm

Another paradigm has also haunted the West through the millen-nia, and that is Plato's famous image of the Cave. In it mankind is portrayed, not as a happy community rejoicing in God's peace and bounty, but as prisoners fettered in a cavern. The entry to the cave is open to the light, but the prisoners are shackled so they can only face the other way. All they know of reality is a shadowplay created by a bonfire behind them, before which bearers carry trees and human forms to cast shadows before the deprived eyes of the captives, who, thinking these poor penumbras are the real things, give them names and talk about them.

And, the philosopher continues, suppose one of the denizens of the cave were by some mortal or immortal force to be dragged from his place and taken out into full sunlight. Suppose he were thrust into light even greater that that which threw the pitiful shadows— how would he react?

At first the solar brilliance would hurt his eyes, and he would want nothing more than to retreat back to the comforting darkness of the cave. Yet when he did return, he would be as one blessed by a wisdom the others had never known or had forgotten—though he would also be so bedazzled and befuddled by the ultimate light that he would *seem* even more stupid and benighted than they.

Cave and Temple

The parable of the cave may serve as a paradigm for an opposite style of religious life from that of the temple. The cave image was itself inspired by those initiatory mysteries—Eleusis, Orphism— which stood apart from the sunny parthenons of Greek civic religion to which the leading men of the community led bullocks on festive days.

The temple and the cave remind us that all through the world's religions the communal temple and the initiatory mystery, in one guise or another, stand facing each other. We shall refer to the "temple" style as "established religion" and the "cave" style as "emergent religion." The latter, in an individual, will be called "excursus religion." Every society has its great official and popular fanes which demarcate the official recognition of deity: the huge mosques of Cairo or Teheran, the Grand Shrine of Ise in Japan, the cathedrals of Europe. In these houses of established religion worship is vast, sweeping, impersonal, aesthetically pleasing. The clergy are polished and well-educated, the sermons smoothly

phrased and intellectually sophisticated. Here mayors and heads of
state are pleased to be seen, and here wholesome families gather to
honor births and deaths and to celebrate the public ceremonies of
their people.

This is the temple, like Solomon's. It is the "church" of Ernst
Troeltsch's sociology of religion. Hierarchical and professional in
leadership, but inclusive in membership, established religion em-
braces all within a society who have not made a deliberate, self-
conscious choice to be something else or do not happen to be
hereditary members of a small deviant group. Established religion
ordinarily upholds the normative values of the society—even mod-
erately "worldly" values—either explicitly, or implicitly through
the example of the lifestyle of its leadership and prominent members. It may have a formal creedal orthodoxy and rigorous moral
ideals, but it does not make stringent moral or belief demands in
practice, preferring prudence to scourges, since it must relate in
some way to the spiritual state of nearly everyone in its community.
Indeed, one can usually not uncomfortably hold skeptical thoughts
within the temple, so long as one holds them privately. Many may
have such an ambivalent relation to the belief of the established
religion even as they participate in its rites and value the cultural
and communal benefits of its tradition. At the same time, the
temple will also have its devout. But from either perspective, the
temple looks established in every sense, and beside it small deviant
groups cannot but appear bizarre and uncouth.

Established religion is the Catholicism of Italy, the Islam of
Arabia, the Buddhism of Thailand, the American Christianity of
the "mainline," family-oriented Catholic and Protestant churches.
On one hand, established religion merges imperceptibly into "civil
religion"—on the other, into the faith of those happy ones for
whom what is a deep and serious commitment happens to be no
different from the faith of their fathers and what is respectable in
their environment. For them the temple is all the truth they need.

The Different Ones

Others, even in the midst of temple rites, know deep down they are
prisoners in the cave. In the bosom of kin and community, they feel

not at home but inexpressibly different, out of harmony. Their inner sails are set to a crosswind, they are fledgling swans amid ducklings.

This sense of being spiritually "different" often starts with subjective turbulence together with acute self-consciousness; the "different" one is always, in his or her own view, more complex and aware than the rest. He or she looks out to see the same cracks in the gleaming facade of the temple as in his own soul and wonders at those still smilingly entering its portals. Perhaps, like the young Carl Jung,[2] he dreams of God defecating on a cathedral, and muses about better churches not made with hands and known only to him.

The different and more complex one may come by his difference in diverse ways—or its real source may be unknown. He may be a Greek slave in the days of the Roman Empire transported from familiar grove and shrine into one of the teeming Mediterranean cities; a Chinese of old who nodded during the stiff Confucian rites; an Englishman for whom the stately Anglican worship had only the exterior beauty of a vessel of old chased silver.

To such as these speak attractive voices, inner or outer, saying, "Come out from among them. You are ready for things they are not, and you need to show at least in a part of your life that you are not the same as they." It is a call to some other wisdom, some other initiation, which makes plain and immediate what is only dimly recognized in the official temple. It is the call of the Magus, the esoteric Taoist, the Tantrist, the Sufi, the occultist, the sectary.

The summoner's role will be that of Plato's shambler back from the light. In the West, at least, his or her allegiance is more likely than not to be to the undying Platonic and Neoplatonic spiritual tradition in some form, whether called Gnosticism, Kabbalah, Hermeticism, Theosophy, or Spiritualism.

But, also like Plato's stumbling initiate, he will doubtless appear incoherent and confused. He or she will be called an idiot or a madman or, most likely, a charlatan by the folk of the temple. Indeed, he or she may well be a combination of all these, like the shaman of yore.

Yet also like the shaman, and the light-scarred initiate, the summoner has somewhere known he or she was marked out as different from most, and can see things opaque to the multitudes. The charlatan contemptuously expresses this sense of being different in an endeavor to befuddle the others with deep words and sleight-of-hand. The mystagogue expresses the same sense in humble or proud proclamation of an alternative truth even in the face of ridicule and stones. Perhaps they are not as different as they seem. The two, in fact, often abide together in the complex personality of the spiritually different one, the right hand not knowing what the left is doing—or the right using the left to make a few technical adjustments which will help confirm the faith of others in what the wonder-worker himself deeply believes. More than most men of the temple, the returner to the cave and those drawn by his words show extremes of spiritual courage and depravity, or complex intermingling of the two.

To be sure, the American temple has known its share of people with seemingly contradictory characters. The Hawthornesque puritan whose strange inner stirrings belie his election to grace and the ambivalent Elmer Gantry evangelist are stock figures in the American imagination. Not a few successful priests and ministers combine deep commitment with passion for the power and prestige their calling can afford.

But the ambiguities of the temple are different from those of the cave in important ways. The temple is, as the religion of the community, the custodian of normative moral values, and any sacerdotal manipulation must be tacitly understood by the community to be following an acceptable style and as ultimately supportive of community values. Every community must have rights of exclusion and inclusion, of forgiveness and rejection, and of drawing the lines between them. Anyone operating within a temple structure will have a good idea what sort of behavior supports its self-image, and what does not. For every community has an idealized image, supported more by symbols and styles than concepts, of what an ideal personality is, and knows quite well what "fits" and what does not. It may be no real sin for a cleric to be ambitious, rich, or gluttonous, though he must shun drink and adultery. Or, as was almost the case in some Tantric and Taoist circles, it could be the other way around. There are kinds of crime or immorality which "fit" better in a social context than others, and so are far more easily forgiven, if the overall style of the perpetrator supports the self-image of the society. Often the wily schemer, like Jacob, Odysseus, or the trickster Coyote of Amerindian folklore, may be a beloved hero of legend whose emulators are half-admired. Or again, a cleric like Friar Tuck, self-indulgent yet lovable and warmly human, may be liked better than the moralist by many.

But the initiate from the cave seems not to fit with either the temple's virtues or its accepted vices. His ambition, unlike that of the aspirant bishop in a "mainline" church, is considered a sign of little grace; his wealth (if he has any) is held to be the gains of charlatanism, though it will probably not equal that of many established ecclesiastics in this land who live on tithes and royalties without similar imputation; his gluttony singles him out as a hypocrite, though other men of the cloth have been beloved for their girth. At the same time, he will have his devoted coterie, who do not so much defend his faults as simply not see them.

Models of Occult Conversion

The process of the individual excursus of "different ones" into a congenial group has been spelled out in more detail in Lofland and Stark's model of conversion to a non-normative religion.[3] According to them, the background factors are:

1. Perception of considerable ongoing tension, strain, deprivation, or frustration. This fits our reflections on the dissonance between the "different ones" and the establishment religion environment.

2. Possession of a "religious" rhetoric and problem-solving perspective. This implies that somewhere along the line the literature or presence of the mystagogic tradition must have reached the prospective adherent of emergent religion, who found in its teaching a way of rationalizing the tensions cited in (1).

3. Self-definition as "religious seeker." This stage involves both rejection of traditional, establishment religion, and of "secular" processes (such as psychoanalysis) as solutions to the problem.

The individual at this point would be more than ready to find his or her spiritual identity at least in part (for we must always bear in mind that many seekers are willing to carry what amounts to dual

membership in both conventional established religion and emergent religion) in those options which present themselves to "seekers" rather than in what is conventional. Lofland and Stark go on to
suggest further stages which result from "situational factors" in the
process rather than "predisposing characteristics."

4. A turning point is reached in which old lines of action are no
longer operable and contact with a "cult" member begins.

5. Development of bonds between the "pre-convert" and members of the new group begins.

6. This relationship and weakened ties with people outside the
group results in "verbal conversion."

7. Finally, "total conversion" comes when interaction with the
group becomes intensive and often communal, so that the new
member becomes "deployable."

It should be emphasized that probably only a small percentage of
seekers reach the stage of "total commitment" and availability as
"deployable" agents of the new movement. Later we shall speak of
the distinction between the intensive and diffuse expression of
non-normative movements; the last stage of the Lofland and Stark
model would clearly pertain to those who are drawn to the former.

Salient characteristics of this model, and of our own categoriza-
tion of "the different ones," have been confirmed by other studies.
Balch and Taylor, in their study of members of the UFO cult started
in 1975 by two individuals who called themselves Bo and Peep,
noted that most members were "not converts in the true sense of
the word." There was not a "radical reorganization of identity."
Rather, most were people who had had a consistent record as
"different ones." It was the last stage in the process of people who
had been for a long time protean in life-style, alienated, and
involved in cults, communes, self-actualization techniques, and
esoteric world views. This group was not, then, a radically new
identity—but the decision to join it was a *"reaffirmation* of their
seekership." Most had been in such groups before, and most were
able to rationalize in advance the possibility of disillusionment by
saying that "the Two" were not important in themselves, but the
whole episode would just be another opportunity to "grow," even
if it turned out to be a hoax. This attitude maintains a confirmed
population of "different ones" and enables them to live with the

charlatanism that sometimes seeks them out, and even to "grow" according to their own esoteric lights despite, or through, the shadow side of their esoteric world.[4] Other studies have shown that people who value the eclectic inner quest are likely to be better educated and more intellectually sophisticated than the average, and perhaps they are able in their own way to sort these things out.

The paradigm suggested by these writers has been reinforced by Frederick R. Lynch's study of adherents of a group he calls the Church of the Sun.[5] He has divided the process of conversion and commitment into four phases. The first consists of intellectual curiosity and individual reading in occult and mystical literature; we can presuppose behind this interest some long-standing degree of alienation and sense of being "different" that the seeker is attempting to interpret. The second stage is more subjective; its elements may be emotional conviction, personal psychic and mystical experiences, together with tension and stress. In the third stage, the preconvert meets a charismatic occultist and/or visits a congenial occult group. Finally he adheres to it to receive social support, even as he senses individual growth and development.

Metaphors for Established and Emergent Religion

Our issue is not to assess the relative virtues and vices of establishment and emergent religionists, but to understand why it is that they are perceived, and perceive themselves, in different ways, even when they do or say fundamentally the same things. It is clearly a matter of differing roles within the society, which amounts to a matter of perception. The initiate is perceived, by both his detractors and supporters, as a novelty and the bearer of novelty. To his foes he is a dangerous disturber of a stable and tranquil social order; to his enthusiasts a light-bringer of a new age. L. Ron Hubbard has been attacked as the founder of the "dangerous new cult of Scientology" and labeled as he who "wears the boots of responsibility for this universe" by himself and his followers.

But claims comparable to this have been made in America for a long time. One thinks of Jemima Wilkinson, the "Publick Universal Friend" of early nineteenth-century upstate New York, Mother Ann Lee of the Shakers, John Noyes of the Oneida Community, or

Thomas Lake Harris of Fountain Grove. These people and their movements were considered, like Scientology or the "Hare Krishnas" of today, "new and different," as though these terms were synonymous.

Yet the very existence of the nineteenth-century predecessors, and even before, suggests that the different is not always new in form or social role. Instead it may be a part of an ongoing pattern of alternative spirituality. Just as we have not always recognized what the study of Balch and Taylor showed—that most converts to new, non-normative groups are likely to have been in several similar groups before, and are not really converts in the sense of making a radical change in self-identity and life-style—so we have not always recognized that the whole non-normative religious world is not as new or alien as it seems. What underlies these conceptions, or misconceptions, is the operative basic conceptual metaphor for religion, that which plays the role of what Stephen C. Pepper has called a "root metaphor."[6]

We often think of the sociological expression of religion as taking two forms. In the Troeltschian tradition, these are commonly called "church" and "sect," or "church" and "withdrawal groups," the latter broken down into "sects" and "cults." As indicated, I prefer the terms "established" and "emergent" religion. Established religion is that which is, like the "temple," culturally and institutionally pervasive in the society, and which is also assimilated by folk culture and embodied in many of its motifs.

The dictionary meanings of the word "emergent" are several, all of which suggest characteristics of a contrasting manifestation of religion: emerging out of a fluid that covers or conceals; arising suddenly and unexpectedly; arising as a natural or logical consequence of a prior event; appearing as or involving the appearance of something novel or in a process of evolution; and, as a noun, a plant visible above others, as a tree much higher than the level of the forest. A quality of emergence suggested by several of these definitions is that the absolute novelty of its appearance is deceptive; it is something that was there all the time or is fully understandable in terms of known logic or processes. But the emergent form was concealed; it did not or does not become visible until certain changes in the total environment occur, or a certain angle of perception is achieved. When this happens it is likely to strike one as a novelty, as something vastly different and amazing.

An emergent religion, then, is one which appears suddenly and unexpectedly, and which stands out from the sea of established religion like a new volcanic island or a rock revealed by an unusually low tide. Though it may be a result of an understandable process and even something which in a sense was there all along, it gives an appearance of both novelty and striking contrast to the established faiths that surround it.

Let us return to the matter of root metaphors and see in what way they contribute to this perception. What conceptual metaphors do we commonly and half-consciously use to understand the role of established religion? I would like to suggest they are geological. We think of the established religion, or what we conceive to be the established religion, of a society as coterminous with entities like "culture" and "society," which we then imagine as static, underlying substrata out of which individual lives, and more ephemeral social movements, arise and decline like grass or summer flowers. Under the influence of ideas like Comte's distinction between "social statics" and "social dynamics," we think of established religion and what goes with it as unchanging ground—like the See of Peter, a rock. We may even think of it, like "culture," as comprised of several geological layers: the bedrock of "folk religion," the loam of institutionalism, the topsoil of the intellectual "great tradition." But short of earthquakes, all are as unmoving in relation to the span of ordinary lives as the earth upon which our cities and temples are built; they slide only inches per century.

In the late twentieth century, it should hardly be necessary to spell out the inadequacies of this metaphor. While the distinction between established and emergent religion has not been erased, we have seen that the conceptualization of the former as static and coextensive with "ground" entities like "culture" and "society" does not fit the facts. Institutions as paradigmatic of established religion as the Roman Catholic Church, the Confucian tradition in China, or traditional religions in Africa have undergone rapid change or been toppled from primacy within their spheres of influence. Whatever the contrast between established and emergent religion, it is not between that which changes and that which

changes not, or at a slower rate—the former can change at a rate
which parallels the rise and fall of new spiritual movements when
conditions are right. Moreover, established religion is not necessarily coextensive with "culture" or "society"—a dominant church
certainly will affect different people or groups to very different
extents, and may touch important segments of the population very
little, yet still be the most important religion of the society in the
sense of holding the "established" heritage.

More important, the past was not as different in these respects as
the static view of established religion and culture indicates. To be
sure, there are those who will hold that the twentieth century is a
time of unprecedentedly rapid and drastic change, when cultures
which *were* geologically static for millennia have been bulldozed
into the harsh light of modernity. Undoubtedly modern change has
important special characteristics and can be seen in significant
respects as a unique global transition. But its uniqueness can be,
and often is, misleadingly wedded to another conceptual paradigm,
one which has been common coin of prophets and social commentators from ancient Greece and Israel to the present: the past as
a kind of timeless mythic *illud tempus* when people lived more
quietly and were more religious than now, against which a present
of change and, usually, fall from grace, can be showcased. This
reading of the history of religion is hardly valid. As Paul Radin has
shown, primitive societies have their share of skeptics and of the
irreligious just as modern societies do.[9] The Middle Ages were
hardly a static "Age of Faith" on either the inner or outer planes,
except, for different reasons, in the eyes of Whig and Catholic
romantic historians. Few significant societies have long endured
without political and spiritual turmoil engendered by intercultural
confrontation.

In contrast to the geological metaphor of established religion,
under what metaphorical umbrella do we commonly contemplate
emergent religion? It is, I think, biological. Victor Turner, referring
to the work of Robert A. Nisbet, has underscored the significance in
the social sciences of metaphors of "growth" and "development,"
and, conversely, of the "sickness," "decay," and even "death" of
societies.[10] It should be obvious that this metaphorical language
makes the observer aware of certain phenomena, but may well

obscure his perception of others. As in grand Hegelian and Marxian schemas, or dispensationalism, the significance of the small but, arguably, only real historical units, microevents and individual lives, is likely to be collapsed into the significance of where they fall in the process.

The grand conceptualizations of history rooted in the biological and evolutionary metaphors of Hegel, Marx, Spengler, or Toynbee, are (except for the second) not in high favor at the moment. But in the study of emergent religion they are still with us. We tend to think of a "new religious movement" in terms of a beginning, a process of development or unfolding, moments of crisis and transition, periods of maturity, and finally perhaps decay and death. This metaphor has been assisted by the popular use of Weberian categories for understanding new movements: the Weberian prophet or mystagogue is the "founder"—the "seed," one might say—of the movement; the "routinization of charisma" process in the movement's second generation seems clearly to legitimize thinking in developmental terms.

Of course, all of these categories are valid; they all have reference to real observations which have been confirmed time and again. But let us reflect on what might be hidden, as well as what is revealed, by a fundamental set of "root metaphors" for religion which picture established religion as layers of "geological" substrata virtually coextensive with culture or society, and new, nonnormative religious movements as "biological" growths which rise out of them and finally collapse back into them as they decay.

Metaphors of Coexistence

Suppose we were to think instead of metaphors like the ones suggested by our discussion of emergence: the sea, and the rock always beneath it but only occasionally revealed; the forest in which from certain perspectives a tree stands out against the skyline. What we are getting at, of course, is a dualistic rather than a process metaphor. We are thinking of what we have called the temple and the cave, the Methodist and the Spiritualist churches, "mainline" religion and what is commonly (though, if our metaphor were to be adopted, misleadingly) associated with "cult" or "new" religions.

Suppose we were to think of these pairs of categories as representing two modes of religious experience and behavior that conformed equally to aspects of human subjectivity, were equally long-lasting, and were also equally susceptible to change. The chief difference would be that the "temple" sort tends to take expression in the established manner, and the "cave" sort in the emergent. The latter, particularly in the context of American culture, fulfills an attribute of its intrinsic nature by rising and falling, coming and going, from the line of sight of the temple porch. As a true opposite, it is the reverse of those values by which the temple is comprehended. It lacks conspicuous institutional continuity, is represented more by a series of charismatic than routinized leaders, and exalts the unstable-seeming initiate from the cave rather than one who is able to handle the affairs of a society's normative values.

But the "two sides" metaphor—no more "true" than the biological one—brings in some important points about this elusive and reverse tradition. First, it gives conceptual priority to the tradition itself, rather than to the rise and fall of individual personalities and movements within it. Second, it reminds us that the tradition has a history of its own and does not begin anew with every new outcropping of it. Third, it shows us that the two sides are in continual interface and interaction, not least within individuals themselves. Fourth, it keeps in mind that the alternative tradition is an opposite, and that much of what is true about its structure, meaning, and work can only be rightly understood by turning upside down the criteria that we apply to the temple.

We think, for example, of temple institutions as being huge and solid, and those of the other side—like the Spiritualist church—as being ephemeral and almost microscopic. In a sense, they are. Spiritualist churches come and go with the popularity of various mediums, who even buy and sell them. The Spiritualist church described earlier in this chapter was founded under its present name only in 1969 or thereabouts, and the minister who endeavored to make it the flagship of a new Spiritualist denomination has already left for another state. Yet the point is that new Spiritualist churches, and other even more important manifestations of the emergent wing of American religion, keep appearing even as others decline. Comparing them to the mighty "church" of Troeltschean sociology, is like comparing the amoeba to the whale—they are tiny, short-lived, continuously dividing, yet in one sense far more immortal.

The Significance of the Metaphor

Certainly a metaphor like this sets up two "ideal types," and such images very easily lead to serious misconceptions, not least in appreciation of interaction. As I shall argue more fully later on, the metaphor's significance is not chiefly in the realm of social expressions of religion. If one were to label all churches in America as temple or cave, the result would be misleading both statistically, for the two have differing relations to that kind of expression, and inferentially, for the relationship between them is such that many groups would have characteristics of both. In fact, as we shall see, the real divide is not in the history of sociology, but within the individual and social psyches of Americans—and here (not in sociology) the dualism of the model has some ineluctable significance, since it is related to the basic binary patterns of human thought.

But it might be well to explore further the sociological values of the dualistic metaphor. A good example of the other approach might be found in J. Milton Yinger's monumental work in the Troeltschean tradition of sociology of religion, *Religion, Society, and the Individual*.[11] The sort of religion we are concerned with is what here finds its structural expression in the "cult," an entity at the opposite end of the scale from the Universal Church, the Ecclesia, or even the Denomination. It is characterized as being of small size and short life, centered around the charismatic leader, having beliefs at great variance with those of the community, basically concerned with mystical experience and personal problems. They are, and significantly a biological term is used, religious "mutants." Spiritualism is cited as illustrative of cult religion.

G. K. Nelson, in his admirable study of Spiritualism, argues that Yinger's characterization does not do justice to it. Far from being short-lived, some Spiritualist institutions have survived over a century, while admittedly perpetuating a religion at great variance with community beliefs, and centered on "mystical" experience and personal problems. More important, even though the great

majority of Spiritualist institutions come and go, the movement
seems able to replenish itself without benefit of the kind of educational facilities and institutional solidity which undergirds "mainline" churches.[12] It seems, in other words, to play by different
rules.

Our model, on the other hand, would emphasize and give a
conceptual framework for the continuities of Spiritualism—as well
as (to name only the three traditions discussed at length in this
book) the relationship of Theosophy with Spiritualism and of
American Zen to Theosophy. It would underscore a metaphorical
reading of each individual movement, or personal experience, of
the "cave" sort as only an epiphenomenon of a vaster presence
which is, in its way, as puissant and lasting as the temple. But it is
different, and works by different laws. Its strengths and weaknesses
are, in fact, the opposing complement to those of the temple: it has
protean flexibility where the latter has visible continuing structure;
it has appeal to subjectivity as established religion evokes one's
sense of family and community and place, as it continually changes,
divides, regroups.

As James T. Richardson has pointed out, a cult—and one could
add the emergent spiritual tradition as a whole—has as its major
criterion its "oppositional" character.[13] Its beliefs and practices
both are counter to those of the dominant culture, or when that
culture is in a state of dissolution, to those of other subcultural
groups. In fact, this opposition is not only in belief and practice,
but in the entire "style" of being religious informed by a very
different sociological experience which nonetheless has its own
continuities. We thus affirm the main thrust of the "structuralist"
argument of Roy Wallis, that "cults" are distinguished by certain
structural features much at variance with normative churches. Wallis mentions individualism, eclecticism, and a "fragile" character
which is often focussed on a charismatic leader; "cults," in his view
are not distinguished by any particular doctrine, but by symbols of
opposition to social norms.[14]

But one can also agree with Richardson that ideological content is
an important symbol of this opposition. I would further argue,
without minimizing the structuralist aspect of a definition of
"cult," that ideology and structure in any social movement are

usually profoundly if subtly intertwined on the "deep structure" level, so that certain types of ideology tend to bring forth certain structures, and vice versa.

In European and American culture, at least, there is an ongoing "cultic milieu" or "emergent religion" tradition to which new "cult" or "excursus" movements almost inevitably relate themselves, and from which they draw, to reify their oppositional stance, style and substance. However different on the surface in content, and however new a revelation they claim, this tradition often provides implicit models for the structure and ideology of a new-formed excursus oppositional group, and usually an implicit validation of its existence.

Our model far better fits the self-conception of alternative groups than does the biological, for if anything unites the subjective experiences of these groups, it is conviction that what they are participating in is not rightly understood by emphasizing the small-ness, recentness, and marginality of the group. They may have explanations both metaphysical and sociological for that, and in-dividuals may understand the relation between their own sense of "differentness" and the appeal of a minority group. But they will also insist that their group is older and deeper than the more visible churches. Thus Spiritualism, not unaware of its parallels with pa-leolithic shamanism, calls itself "the oldest religion in the world." Theosophy speaks of its lore as "the Ancient Wisdom." Zen claims to be the essential but unspoken message of the Buddha, if not something even older than the Enlightened One. However one chooses to evaluate these claims, a hermeneutical method which does not obstruct phenomenological empathy with the self-under-standing of the religion under study is desirable. More than de-velopmentalism, this method may, in fact, offer a crucial clue to understanding not only their inner life, but their place in American society.

2   *Excursus Religion*

Visits to the Other Shore

If emergent religion is the alternative to which those who turn away from established religion of the temple have recourse, their journeys are individual excursions. If the emergent religious tradition has certain unifying themes, and a hidden history which shows continuities among its many manifestations past and present, for each voyager the journey is unique and solitary because it enacts a personal subjective quest. However much both goal and pilgrim path may pre-exist or conform to well-trodden patterns, the experience ordinarily comes to a person conditioned by normative cultural religion as an excursus away from the familiar and toward that which draws just because it is strange, yet in its very strangeness seems to offer a promise of new kinds of self-discovery.

In 1809, speaking at Nurnberg on educational theory, G. W. F. Hegel made these remarks:

> Inherent in the strange and remote is a powerful interest, . . . the attractiveness of which is in inverse proportion to its familiarity . . .
> Initially it is in this remoteness that depth must be sought; this is a necessary seeking for illusion. But the depth and strength which we attain can be measured only by the distance to which we have fled from the familiar center in which we first found ourselves embedded, and to which we strive to return. From this centrifugal impetus of the soul derives its compulsion to achieve for itself the desired separation from its natural essence and condition. . . . But that which separates us from ourselves contains at the same time all the starting-points and threads of the return to ourselves, of its inner affinity, and of the rediscovery of ourselves, but now finally of ourselves according to the true and general essence of the spirit.[1]

W. R. Irwin has spoken of this individual Hegelian process—when for the subject even the owl of Minerva nods to dream, or, becoming distracted, tarries in her flight down the centuries—as "the excursion and return of the soul."[2] Minerva's human servitors then turn aside from the idea whose time has come, whether nineteenth-century Western triumphalism or the alleged secularity of the twentieth century, to savor something else.

The religious quest that leads away from the ordinary and established religion could be called an excursus—and, collectively, excursus religion. Its opposite might be termed familiar religion, with a certain emphasis on the origin of the word in *familia*, for it is intertwined with the ethnic and community structures communicated to one through family. Excursus religion, then, is individual or group participation in what on a large scale is emergent religion.

For the excursus of any individual or small group is likely to lead soon or late to the enchanted forest of the enduring, if often hidden, pattern of emergent religion. That is because the singularity of the quest seeks completion in identification with a tradition, however arcane; both the vast but invisible cloud of witnesses and the loneliness of the initiate in this world help define his experience. A society, therefore, will have not only its stock symbols of identity with the social structures, but also its stock symbols of alienation. As we shall see, in America such symbols as meditation, monism, feminine spiritual leadership, and orientation toward a distant and exotic culture have been among those signaling an excursus toward the emergent shore. Often the humor of a culture reveals better than more formal statements its stock symbols of alienation and excursus; in American wit about religion, the long tradition of jokes featuring wild-eyed sandaled men preaching imminent doom and bemused middle-aged matrons gushing over soulful-eyed swamis bears them ungrateful testimony.

Excursus religion is a spiritual movement away from ordinary social and psychic structures alike, for a quest will steadily reassemble both as they impinge upon consciousness to mirror each other. Excursus religion can be discussed from both social scientific and psychological perspectives, and nothing about it is more instructive than its revelations concerning the profound interaction of these two spheres of human operation. But let us first, in this chapter, emphasize the social scientific approach in American historical perspective.

Grid and Group in America

I would like to start by attempting a brief application of certain categories of the anthropologist Mary Douglas to the American religious situation. There is a place in this model for non-normative cultic religion which reveals, I believe, some fundamental facts about it and its role in American spirituality. Douglas's fundamental hypothesis is that cosmological theories have their roots in social experience.[3] While this is by no means a new idea, it provides a novel and very stimulating model for the correlation of cosmologies and societies. The model rests on the assumption that humans desire consonance at all levels of experience; the same style and texture is sought in subjective, intrahuman, and transcendent relationships.

Douglas's model consists of two basic variables, "grid" and "group." Grid refers to the systems, classifications, and symbols by which one brings order to experience, and so to society and to the cosmos. A social example of grid in practice is caste in India. Group refers to social pressure and indicates the degree to which the group establishes its boundaries and constrains its members' identities. It indicates the extent to which one's place in the caste system inescapably shapes the contours of life. Every society has both grid and group forces, but their relative strengths vary considerably, producing not only very different types of human social life, but very different types of religious symbols to articulate it and views of divinity and transcendence to validate it. Particularly significant clues lie in the society's attitudes toward the meaning of sin and the cause of suffering; toward the roles of trance, magic, and ritual; toward purity and pollution; and toward the meaning of personal identity. Let us examine attitudes relevant to religion which pertain to each of the four kinds of social organization the model yields.

Here are the categories and relevant attitudes as summarized by Sheldon R. Isenberg and Dennis E. Owen.[4] It is important to note that each set begins with the attitude toward purity. Then, working through the attitude toward the closely related ritual and magic categories, and through attitudes toward identity and the two aspects of self-hood (body and the powers of mind—trance or meditation), finally reaches the interface of self and the transcendent in the category of sin. It projects the whole system in a cosmology and a cosmic view of suffering and misfortune.

Strong Group and Grid

Purity: strong concern for purity; well-defined purification rituals; purity rules define and maintain social structure

Ritual: a ritualistic society; ritual expresses the internal classification system

Magic: belief in the efficacy of symbolic behavior

Personal Identity: a matter of internalizing clearly articulated social roles; individual subservient to but not in conflict with society

Body: tightly controlled but a symbol of life

Trance: dangerous; either not allowed or tightly controlled and limited to a group of experts

Sin: the violation of formal rules; focus on behavior instead of internal state of being; ritual (magic) efficacious in counteracting sin

Cosmology: anthropomorphic, nondualistic, the universe is just and noncapricious

Suffering and Misfortune: the result of automatic punishment for the violation of formal rules; part of the divine economy

Strong Group, Weak Grid

Purity: strong concern for purity but the inside of the social and physical bodies are under attack; pollution present and purification ritual ineffective

Ritual: ritualistic; ritual focused upon group boundaries, concerned with expelling pollutants (witches) from social body

Magic: ineffective in protecting individual and social bodies; a source of danger and pollution

Personal Identity: located in group membership, not in the internalization of roles, which are confused; distinction between appearance and internal state

Body: social and physical bodies tightly controlled but under attack; invaders have broken through bodily boundaries; not a symbol of life

Trance: dangerous; a matter of demonic possession; evil

Sin: a matter of pollution; evil lodged within person and society; sin much like a disease; internal state of being more important than adherence to formal rules, but the latter still valued

Cosmology: anthropomorphic; dualistic; warring forces of good and evil; universe is not just and may be whimsical

Suffering and Misfortune: unjust; not automatic punishment; attributed to malevolent forces

Weak Group, Strong Grid

Purity: pragmatic attitude; pollution not automatic; bodily waste not threatening, may be recycled

Ritual: will be used for private ends if present; ego remains superior; condensed symbols do not delimit reality

Magic: private; may be a strategy for success

Personal Identity: pragmatic and adaptable

Body: instrumental; self-controlled; pragmatic attitude

Trance: not dangerous

Sin: failure; loss of face; stupidity

Cosmology: geared to individual success and initiative; cosmos is benignly amoral; God as junior partner

Suffering and Misfortune: an intelligent person ought to be able to avoid them

Weak Group, Weak Grid

Purity: rejected; anti-purity

Ritual: rejected; anti-ritual; effervescent; spontaneity valued

Magic: none; magic rejected

Personal Identity: no antagonism between society and self but old society may be seen as oppressive; roles rejected, self-control and social control low

Body: irrelevant; life is spiritual; purity concerns absent but body may be rejected; may be used freely or asceticism may prevail

Trance: approved, even welcomed; no fear of loss of self-control
Sin: a matter of ethics and interiority
Cosmology: likely to be impersonal; individual access, usually direct; no mediation; benign
Suffering and Misfortune: love conquers all

I would like to propose that American society in the young Republic was, as a whole, one of weak group and grid. This was especially true on the frontier and more a matter of expansive American self-perception and Jeffersonian-Jacksonian idealism than of fact. Very strong grid and group patterns remained in some subcultures, particularly with regard to slavery and social class. But self-perceptions are important, and certainly the general ethos of the new nation reflected a combination of enlightenment rationalist rejection of ritual and magic, a deistic impersonalizing and democratizing of the cosmos, and the frontier's freedom from oppressive social roles and social control.

Against the almost oppressive vacuity of weak group and grid, however, arose certain reactions. Clearly, the fundamentalist-evangelical religion of past and present grounded in the great revivals exemplifies strong group, weak grid characteristics. The crucial importance this tradition places on establishing a boundary between the circle of purity and pollution (that is, between the "saved" and the "world") but through group membership and internal state rather than through ritual or formal roles, and its corresponding insistence on distinction between appearance and internal state, bears that out. So does the tradition's well-known and sometimes almost obsessive mistrust of anything that smacks of ritual, magic, trance, meditation, or "the occult," and the vociferousness with which polluting persons, things, or ideas are often shunned or cast out. Finally, one sees the cosmological consequence of fundamentalism and evangelicalism in its anthropomorphic and dualistic theology, and not least in its sometimes lively sense of demonic intervention in the affairs of humankind. In the revival situation, of course, both the group pressure, which is its dynamic, and the construction of the alternative world of its cosmology and perception of personal identity are intensified to the utmost.

Another American spiritual tradition which has probably equaled evangelicalism's influence is the cult of optimism and success based on belief in the power of mind and attitude to transcend problems. This is the tradition which, rooted in transcendentalism, appears in "New Thought," Christian Science, and, more recently, "positive thinking" and many comparable quasi-religious, quasi-psychological teachings about the "science" of constructive thought. This tradition (excluding the strong group aspect of Christian Science) has many characteristics in common with the weak group, strong grid pattern. Perhaps that is because of its sociological background in the primordial American weak group ambience joined with the implicit status-consciousness of the later successful capitalists who have been its most typical adherents. One finds in the literature of this tradition a basically pragmatic attitude in which failure is the real sin, in which all sorts of semi-rituals and semi-magic may be used as a means of strengthening the positive thoughts which are the forces through which the ego attains success. The cosmology generally amounts to a benign monism in which meditative trance is not inappropriate (for there is a mystical and "metaphysical" cast to the theology), and in which many wells of power may be tapped by the one who has both initiative and adaptability.

Now we come to the kind of religion which is the topic of this study, the "non-normative" religion more strikingly discontinuous with the cultural background than the above and attained by excursus. My hypothesis is that its basic characteristics are those of strong group and grid. However, some of these characteristics need to be translated to understand their application to a tiny dissident group, instead of a vast society like traditional China or India. Moreover, it needs to be understood—and this is a point to which we shall return later—that strong grid and group represent an ideal which compels, in the spirit of Hegel's attractiveness of the strange and opposite, just because it *is* the most direct antipode of the basic American weak grid and group. It is an ideal, however, which can only be completed symbolically, and in the relating of present excursus religious life to paradigmatic histories and cosmologies overflowing with tokens of invisible but very real strong grids and groups to which the initiate belongs. Excursus is the spirituality of fascination with symbols of strong grid and group.

Thus, even when the group is small and ephemeral, its leader-

ship is likely to have fairly unusual and imposing titles, suggesting
continuity with ancient mystery schools, churches of the apostolic
succession, or lineages of Eastern gurus or masters, and to stress that
authentication. The cosmology is likely to feature a nondualist
Absolute rather than a personal God, and sin is a violation of rules
which is punished automatically by karma, thus fulfilling the rule
of order on the metaphysical plane. But between the Absolute and
the more chaotic world here below there is likely to range a vast but
ordered hierarchy of intermediate masters, spirits, polytheistic
gods, or kabbalistic spheres. This pleroma suggests at once the
order and compulsion of a vast strong grid and group assembly to
which one is privy, and the reality of numinous but anthropomorphic beings with whom one can have a warmer relation than to
the impersonal Absolute. It is one's place as a novice in this
hierarchy that one internalizes, as well as whatever place one may
have in the sociological order, even though that role might bring
one into conflict with empirical society.

The group's putative history serves a comparable function. At
the end of the last chapter, we alluded to the tendency of religions
in the emergent tradition to see themselves as older than more
normative churches, whatever the appearances. Continuity with
shamanism or the ancient mysteries provides a strong grid and
group dimension in time, as does rapport with invisible hierarchies
in space—or perhaps one should say hyperspace.

As we observed in connection with the cave metaphor, initiation
has a definite place in a strong grid and group spiritual world. Its
characteristic concern for purity is evidenced in concern for initiation (for initiation is purification), although it may also be
expressed in such practices as vegetarianism and the formation of
communes where strong grid and group can be reified.

Although excursus religion may be as ritualistic and magical as a
ceremonial magic order, or as unritualistic as a theosophical lodge
which offers little more than lectures, a sense of the importance of
symbol and symbolic behavior pervades nearly all of it. There may
be, however, some inconsistency in the matter of trance, for according to our model it is considered "dangerous" and "either not
allowed or tightly controlled and limited to a group of experts" in
strong grid and group social organization. The great importance of

meditation, mediumistic trance, and the like in American excursus religion seems at odds with this criterion. Perhaps so. Yet the need for skill and authenticity in the practice of meditation is, in fact, the chief reason for existence of a number of important groups. Organizations like Zen centers, the Maharishi Mahesh Yogi's Transcendental Meditation movement, yoga centers, the Divine Light Mission, and many others certainly wish to promote widespread use of meditation. Yet the fact that they offer legitimated teachers of it who are often members of a long lineage of such teachers indicates it should be taught only by experts, and implies it is useless or dangerous when it is not. Such control has also been one rationale for the formation of Spiritualist denominations, as weak as they have been. Thus, although the widespread use of meditation has been an important symbol of differentiation from other segments of American religion, and although the enhancement of subjectivity it allows is very important to the psychology of excursus religion, it has not escaped equally energetic constraints.

Cosmic and metahistorical strong grid and group, then, constructs a heavenly city of purity, order, and identity in which the man or woman of excursus devoutly wishes to dwell. We must now consider further the way to it and the signs of its appearing.

Liminality and Communitas

As Isenberg and Owen suggest, the work of Victor Turner offers models which complement and extend the insights of Mary Douglas very nicely.[5] What we are concerned with is the appeal of one grid and group arrangement in the context of another, and this means understanding alienation, initiation, and the appeal of an alternative reality. An important area of Turner's work has been the analysis of initiatory passage and the enactment of social ideals.

In *The Ritual Process*,[6] Turner explores the three steps of initiation defined in Gerardus van Gennep's classic study of initiation, *The Rites of Passage*. These are (1) the separation of the candidate out from his group, (2) margin or limen, and (3) reaggregation or reincorporation of the initiate as a member of a new group, or of the old group with a new status.

Of these the middle stage, liminality, is doubtless the most

mysterious. It is the status of the novice during his time in the
initiatory lodge, tomorrow's knight at his nocturnal vigil before the
altar, the future king being jousted and jeered by his prospective
subjects. It is a time of the reversal of all customary structures and
restraints. The subject is ritually naked and downcast, betwixt and
between. But since at the same time this state negates all the
restrictions of structure, in a paradoxical way it is an opening of the
doors of infinity, akin to that mystical experience which also requires a stripping away of all worldly garb. These two sides, degradation and the plenitude of a *coincidentia oppositorum,* are well
expressed in the language which compares liminal states to death,
the womb, invisibility, bisexuality, and journeys in the wilderness.

Liminality is originally a process state, a state of transition. But
for some—especially when the quest seems endless—it can become
a permanent state, a continual calling. This is the meaning of
monks and holy wanderers of all sorts, who manifest it to themselves and to the world through special garb and a reversal of
ordinary usage in the matters of sex, family, money, authority, and
habitation. They symbolize to the community that an opposite of
the "natural" is a possible human ideal, that structure can be
transcended, or, rather, replaced with an antipodal structure. Liminality, perhaps inspired by the ideal of the monk, is also a quad-
rant on the inner compass of many who do not wear it as a robe;
they are like the people of the cave paradigm.

Understanding liminality is clearly very important to understanding excursus religion, for it is into the sea of liminality that the
latter ventures. Yet it is not a journey without charts, for in
emergent religion ways of negotiating liminality can be made traditional, as they are in numerous ordinary religious settings. Certain
people and social organizations embody and institutionalize liminality: they are able to do so because liminality usually both breaks
structure and is provided for by the social structure in approved
contexts. Nothing is more basic to Hindu society than recognition
that to become a sadhu is the acknowledged and honorable way to
move out of the structure of caste obligations. In America, excursus
religion is what might be called "established means" of touching
the liminality borne by such avatars of otherness as spirit mediums
and Zen masters.

But even if such groups and people provide institutionalized and legitimatized glimpses into another world beyond that of the primary structures, as do all groups which participate in Frederick Streng's definition of religion as "means of ultimate transformation."[7] they do point to something beyond, of which persons, groups, and symbols are only images. That, according to Victor Turner, is the ideal of a social or perhaps eschatological state which transcends structure. In this state individuals are related in the "I-thou" manner rather than through roles. Reactions are spontaneous. It is the goal, we are told, of utopias and countercultures, and it is adumbrated in festivals and pilgrimages. Turner calls this state communitas.

Can the desire for unstructured communitas correlate with the excursus quest for plenitude of grid and group? I believe that it can, and, indeed, that in this quest strong grid and group are intended as symbols of communitas. In a traditionally strong grid and group society, the search for communitas might take other forms. But in America, strong grid and group is intended to articulate a sense of infinite but unimpeded relationships extended to every corner of space and time—in the words of the title of one famous Spiritualist book, an "unobstructed universe." It is actually structure, a plenitude of group and grid structure, which makes this possible, for the lines of its sinews are lines of communication, whereas for the excursus mind, lack of structure implies a chaos in which no real transcendent (or interhuman) communication or relationship is possible. The sense of meaningful roles in the context of ultimate reality and infinite dimensions arises from seeing oneself as a part of the unending hierarchy of heaven and earth—whether of spirits, masters, or buddhas—and is protected by strong grid and group symbols.

Mary Douglas herself seems to miss this point when she says, "No one would deliberately choose the elaborated code and the personal control system who is aware of the seeds of alienation it contains."[8] There are those for whom the lack of code and control seems far more alienating, and their presence—especially when chiefly reified as an internal symbol system related one to cosmic transcendence—is far more a preservative of place and so of "standing" before the universe. As Isenberg and Owens posit, when we

seek relationships unmediated by roles—Turner's pure communitas
—we find that the very intimacy we sought is foreclosed, for
intimacy requires communication, and communication requires
structure.[9] Language itself is structure and is symbiotic with the
general structures of thought and society. These last—insofar as the
self is a social construct, exemplified by acquisition of language and
internalization of family and social place—are requisite to there
being anyone capable of sharing intimacy or seeking communitas.

Indeed, those occasions which best embody communitas—the
festival (and even orgy), pilgrimage, utopian societies—are in practice bound to have a structure, often a very strong structure, precisely to facilitate the new social and cosmic intimacy they incarnate.
As we have suggested in the case of the monk, the outsider's
liminal state is represented far more by symbols of reversal of the
ordinary structures than by any absolute transcendence of the realm
of symbol.

The same is suggested by the lives of those who, like the UFO
cultists mentioned in the last chapter, progress by endeavoring to
"grow" from one facet to another of the "cultic milieu." Each
"experience" is itself a symbol, as is the life-pattern as a whole—
with its "oppositional" or reversal relationship to the dominant
culture a major message. But the particular experiences, at their
fullest, may indeed be experiences of liminality. Liminality is that
breaking of structure which, through its own symbols and experiences, adumbrates communitas. It is about as far as we actually get
in this sublunar world, for communitas like Streng's "ultimate
transformation" cannot be completed among humans as we are
without paradox, and like the Buddhist nirvana cannot be concep-
tualized as attained, but is only as an awakening symbol in the
mind.

We shall find, then, that the processes of excursus religion
actually follow models like the initiation model analyzed by van
Gennep and Turner. Individuals drawn to excursus religion first
undergo a detachment from ordinary society. Frederick Evans,
Madame Blavatsky, and Jack Kerouac first left home for a period of
extensive wandering, and societies like the Shakers and Theosophists were groups of people with little sense of direction but a
definite sense of separation before they coalesced into counter-

societies. Then there is the liminal state, a state of deep initiatory
separation when the transcendent and communitas reality seems
close and the ordinary social realities seem unreal. This is exemplified by the early days of the Shakers under Mother Ann Lee, the
Theosophists on the journey to India to be later described, the Zen
year described in *The Dharma Bums*. Thirdly, the period of reaggregation comes. This is not, however, a simple reabsorption into
the prior social order, any more than the initiate becomes just what
he was before. Rather, it is a rationalization of the life of the group,
or of the incorporated member, into its own symbol-of-reversal
structures that allow it to continue both distinctive from surrounding society and yet placed within it. Here it is that symbols of the
ongoing emergent religion tradition are likely to become prominent (the Spiritualism of the Shakers), and also that strong grid and
group symbols move firmly into place. (The nascent excursus religion is likely to show some characteristics of strong group and
weak grid.)

Excursus religion, then, is likely to manifest strong grid and
group internal symbols and structures, which demarcate it from
the basal weak grid and group of American society, and the strong
group or grid only of evangelicalism and positive thinking. These
symbols and structures are partly drawn from the treasures of the
long-standing emergent religion tradition and are partly internal or
putative. There are, however, definite forms which the visible tip of
its expression are likely to take.

Excursus Religion and the Forms of Religious Expression

Let us examine excursus religion in terms of the three forms of
religious expression proposed by the sociologist of religion Joachim
Wach.[10] These are: the *theoretical*, the religion's conceptual and
verbal expression in philosophy, doctrine, and myth; the *practical*,
the religion's praxis in worship, rite, prayer, pilgrimage, and so
forth; and the *sociological*, the styles of group, leadership, and
interpersonal relations the religion indicates. In all these areas, we
shall find the excursus experience generates its own symbols.

A common characteristic of excursus religion in all forms of
expression is this: despite its overall oppositional stance, it seeks to

find some niche in which it is not directly competitive with normative religion. It does not set up altar against altar, or doctrine
against doctrine, in opposition to the Judeo-Christian establishment, so much as present itself as dealing with aspects of life other
than established religion, and with teachings which, rightly understood, only complement the received confessions. These movements are ostensibly noncompetitive with the great denominations,
even as they survive on religious interests and needs aroused—but
perhaps not met—by them.

This characteristic is most apparent in the sociology of excursus
religion, and it is this form of expression we shall consider first.
Sociologically, emergent and excursus religion avoids being directly
competitive with established religion by taking either more diffuse
or more intensive forms than the normative. Instead of the network
of institutionalized churches of the standard denomination, it will
have intensive centers which approach being total institutions, as
well as other forms of private participation or interest in the spiritual path which are not seen as competitive with normative religion. Thus, as we shall see, excursus religion is capable of the
intense community and full-time practice of a Shaker community, a
Zen center, or the life of a Blavatsky and an Olcott during and after
their journey to India.

This manner of life approaches that of what Erving Goffman
would call a "total institution": comparable to existence in a
prison, insane asylum, royal court, boarding school, or monastery,
it determines nearly all of one's behavior, all one's expression of
identity.[11] The horarium from dawn to dusk, the manner of eating
and sleeping, the dress and speech and, presumably, one's thoughts
and prayers—all are controlled. At its epicenters excursus religion is
dotted with such "asylums." They are not necessarily permanent
residences, for many come and many go. As Hegel realized, the
"Other" has a strong attraction, but there is also a strong undertow
to return, for once the initial enthusiasm wears off, any life-style
which does not have the support of the nonenthusiastic sociological
factors undergirding normative religion is hard to sustain. But those
who have been in and out may still retain a degree of interest or
even nostalgia, and the intermingling of these people with the
"world" helps to diffuse the religion's influence.

The other side of excursus religion's noncompetitiveness is a kind of diffuse influence which is very different in kind from that of normative denominations. Very few "standard" denominations—Methodist, Baptist, Roman Catholic—can be said to have had the widespread, noninstitutionalized yet highly identifiable influence on the art, literature, and intellectual life of non-members that Western Zen or even the Shakers have had. Very few "mainline" churches have the high percentage of occasional participation by non-members of Spiritualism, theosophical lectures, or yoga centers. This style of occasional, nonaffiliative participation is different from what would be practiced with regard to a "rival" denomination because of excursus's noncompetitive image. Innumerable non-Hindu Americans meditate in the Maharishi's manner or do yoga—but very few non–Roman Catholics say the rosary, and very few synagogues have a regular plurality of non-Jewish visitors. There is a good deal of dual or multiple membership, and even more of participation, in non-normative religious circles.

This diffuse influence is no less important when it is only extended through reading and involves no group participation at all. Many clergymen have known parishioners who, in terms of attendance, contributions, and donations of time to countless committees and activities were surely pillars of the church, to confess—often with a certain trepidation in the presence of the cloth—to a private love of Zen or Theosophical literature. Writings in the New Thought or positive thinking tradition, as well as certain evangelical authors, of course, have a comparable cross-sectarian appeal, but one does not easily imagine a staunch Lutheran nourishing a secret passion for Baptist books. Rather, reading interests represent an American religious map with contours ill-defined but doubtless widely differing from those of official denominationalism, and one in which the true strength of emergent religion would be better plotted than in church statistics.

It should be noted that these two facets of emergent and non-normative religion, the intensive and the diffuse, correspond well with the two forms Ernst Troeltsch gave to what he called mysticism, the immediate spiritual experience which in his sociological analysis of religion formed a "third type" of expression beside church and sect. Mysticism, he said, may be spoken of in a "narrow, technical, concentrated sense," a form which undercuts structures and forms new groups; and there is a "wider form" of mysticism that is diffuse and supports existing groups as well as deepening experience.[12] If groups in the emergent tradition represent reifications of Troeltschean mysticism, within its specific forms, such as yoga or Zen, can be found a "narrow" and a "wider" or diffuse expression.

A second important area of sociological interest is leadership. In excursus religion, the founding and, to a great extent, the continuing leadership is charismatic; even if, as in many Spiritualist churches, there is a great show of routinization in the elaborate constitutions and hierarchies, the real focus is the charisma of the mediumistic minister. The charismatic personality in emergent religion is one who has personally and paradigmatically undergone excursus. Like the shaman of old, and the magus who might be called a "shaman in civilization," he or she has made a passage through liminality, even perhaps initiatory psychopathology, and returned with remarkable spiritual credentials. So it was with Ann Lee, Madame Blavatsky, and many Spiritualists and Zen masters.

The crisis of the second generation—of continuing a movement after the passing of the charismatic founder and the original enthusiasts sparked by his or her fire—is especially acute in causes where there is little social reinforcement. It has been handled in various ways, but generally by means which enable the religion to continue as an excursus—that is, as a faith which draws people seeking an initiatory experience rather than taking up the family and community identity roles of religion—though inevitably, in the course of the transition, the excursus has become standardized and the leadership has become professional. Yet they may or may not differ significantly in their style from that of the first generation. Spiritualism has managed to retain something of its original character in each generation through the appearance of new mediums little different from those who have gone before. Zen also has a self-replenishing charismatic leadership in principle, though the training process is quite stylized. Theosophy has become quite definitely changed in the direction of routinization in its second and especially third generations of leadership, no longer claiming the sort of charisma and transcendent communication of its founders, but content simply to propagate its teachings.

It may also be noted that excursus religious groups have most of the general characteristics of withdrawal groups: a tendency to reach isolated people or a single status class (young people, older women, and so on), rather than the families and demographic cross-sections one would expect ethnic or community religions to reach; easy but definite entry procedures; provision for meaningful participation by nearly all members (or at least serious members) in responsible as well as receiving roles.

How is this sociology enacted in the praxis of the excursus religious group? The noncompetitive stance is typically maintained by advancing (particularly in the diffuse promotion) a single, simple practice which can produce fairly immediate and perceptible subjective change and can be practiced alone or in a small, ad hoc group quite independent of the kind of elaborate activities and structural ramifications of the parish church. Meditation, yoga, mediumship, chanting, and exciting concepts like those of Theosophy (as much as anything, this last is a spiritual way in which the transformative power comes from simply thinking over mind-expanding ideas) would be examples. These techniques are not for the sake of social identity even when done privately, like the Muslim prayer, but for their intrinsic effect on the doer.

Also, the excursus religion will have some practices which simply reify the excursus experience. That experience is one of separation, liminality, and reincorporation as a body in another context; its rituals, especially those of initiation, may mimic it. One thinks of those Neo-Pagan and Witchcraft groups which mount impressive "classic" initiations, even to blindfoldings and mild scourgings. More likely, the ceremonies are simply rites of identity, giving one status in the group and demarcating the group from outside society. They will define the set-apart order, as does Zen with its robes; or establish a group and place identity, as does pilgrimage to India or Japan; or create an assembly with a special state of consciousness, as does the long, rapid group chanting of Nichiren Shoshu of America. These practices, in contrast to those discussed in the preceding paragraph which are related to diffuse distribution, tend to form an intensive group or express the existence of one.

Finally, a few reflections on the theoretical expression of excursus religion. Almost by definition, it is a gnosis—a wisdom which has of itself, when truly known and acted upon, a saving power, which was always true but known only to an elect and now is again revealed to those with ears to hear. The gnosis concept correlates, of course, with the sociology of a small withdrawal group.

Beyond this, the teachings are diverse, yet certain themes are widespread. Generally we have an ultimate monism, but between it and this world of toil and shadows is spread what might be called an intermediate polytheism: an assemblage of masters, spirits, buddhas, gods, or archetypes who give texture and color to the One, and who can reach down to guide pilgrims along the way. This cosmology is, of course, characteristic of strong grid and group societies such as India, China, or medieval Europe; it offers a model both of cohesion into oneness and of hierarchy. It also offers an excellent paradigm of the excursus experience. It suggests an ultimate unity and many possible avenues of excursus toward it; its intermediate figures are generally lords once human who have advanced much further down the infinite way—but who can turn back with a word of hope and a helping hand.

The emphasis on creation is slight; the excursionist has instead in view an eternal, though perhaps evolving, world. Indeed, in our age of historical consciousness, he will probably see the internal transformation he has wrought through intellectual realization and the effect of the technique as the first fruits of a new age. From the Shakers onward, most excursus religion in America has had an eschatological thrust, linked to the current secular dream as well as to the tradition's ruminations about mystical evolution.

Yet another interesting form of expression, as much praxis as theoretical, has been a renewal of cosmic religion. From the "Holy Hills" and seasonal "cleansings" of the Shakers, to the sensitivity to nature of Zen and the explicit cosmicism of modern Neo-Paganism, the excursus journey has been not only toward the infinite but also toward a return to a sacred earth it feels the Judeo-Christian tradition has too much slighted. There is an uneven yet meaningful trend toward demarcating sacred space and time with seasonal rites, and even sacred centers. To be sure, American Christianity has managed to recover the Samhain, Yule, and Beltane of the Puritan's pagan forebears in the festive celebrations of Thanksgiving, Christmas, and Easter. But various excursus groups have gone on to schedule meditations or rites by the waxing and waning of the moon, not to mention the arcane dictates of astrology.

Moreover, whether in UFO cults or Buddhism, there seems to be a desire to recover the powerful religious meaning that holy places, places charged with power and worthy of pilgrimage, can have. American Christianity (unlike that of the Old World) has lost all sense of sacred places, but that has not deterred others. The UFO-related Aetherius Society has "charged" a number of sacred mountains in this land. As I was writing this chapter, I received a mailing from Feraferia, a colorful Neo-Pagan movement, indicating that it has established a "Ley Line" like those so much beloved of British esotericists.[13] But this one, extending for some 450 miles in California, is marked at regular intervals by Reichian orgone accumulators.

Symbols of Excursus

Peter Berger and Thomas Luckmann, in *The Social Construction of Reality,* have described the socioreligious process of projection, reification, and internalization. Feelings, anxieties, dualisms, and ecstasies within are projected and given body as the images, rites, structure, and common ideologies of a social order. These, on the wings of the language that names them, are then internalized as symbols through which one thinks and names oneself. Within and without, symbols are the religious coin of the realm.[14]

This model is viable so long as one realizes that the chain is unending, that religion no more "begins" in the subjectivity that is projected than it does in the outer reifications which are then internalized to create a modified subjectivity to be projected again. It should not be viewed as a reductionistic explanation, but rather as a description which simply acknowledges the ceaseless interaction of human inwardness, society, and cosmos to which religion gives voice. In this light, then, let us elicit some further symbols of excursus religion which accent its particular kind of human experience.

A very basic symbol is the group. In all social religion, of course, the sociological expression is highly symbolic. But in the case of excursus religion, beginning as it does with individual sense of alienation and call, the very existence of a group is in itself a powerfully important symbol. The immense significance of forming a group, however tiny or ephemeral, is evident all through the tradition, with its plethora of titles, charters, and post office boxes. Any entitled group, however small, is very different from an individual religious quest. Even the spiritual relation of only two people, master and disciple or two fellow seekers, is quite distinct from the subjectivity of a solitary soul, however expansive. The existence of any sort of group gives the experience a putative legitimation and a standing within the fabric of society as a whole which individual religion does not have in the same way; it may even be seen as the distinction between legitimate religion and madness.

In America, the group not only gives the religion a legal footing, but authenticates it as a part of our pluralism and a vindication of constitutional freedom in a public way. The group satisfies an implicit feeling that all real religion *ought* to have something in all three forms of religious expression, and it gives the religion a safety valve against spiritual inflation; it does not only exist in liminality, but must also be able to handle the things of this world regarding its corporate life. The leader must be able to control, like a shaman, his ventures to the other side, in such a way that he can also manage budgets, by-laws, and cantankerous individuals. All of this, our attitudes proclaim, indicate he is not a schizophrenic visionary, but one who has passed through the initiatory psychopathology to become a legitimate exerciser of religious freedom—and this social attitude is internalized by the religionists to make them want to reify and legitimate their vision in a group and in its accoutrements—buildings, offices, covenants, and stationery.

Within the religion, other symbols of excursus are evident. We have mentioned the recovery of cosmic religion, with all its rich symbols of sacred space and time, which sometimes occurs. We have also mentioned the rebirth of functional polytheism on the "intermediate" level. We could also cite a corresponding plurality of paradises or paradisal visions which emerge in the lore and art of excursus religion—a perception of "many mansions" on the other side, or of paradisal possibilities in terrestial nature. Almost imperceptibly, the last merges into social utopianism, the ideal of the "peaceable kingdom."

Especially in America, a significant symbol of excursus religion is feminine leadership and even feminine identity in the divine. In "mainline" American churches feminine clerical or professional leadership has never been more than nominal, and in the day when the Shakers, Spiritualists, Theosophists, and Christian Scientists were emerging with substantial feminine leadership, was virtually nonexistent. More important still, the characteristics of these movements clearly include signs of a quest for an authentic feminine spiritual identity—a quest reflected in the concepts of divinity itself, as in the bipolar masculine and feminine deity of the Shakers and the Christian Scientists; and in the typically "maieutic" rather than forensic concept of spiritual process. Even Zen has had, in America, a greater degree of feminine leadership than established churches.

A symbol of a somewhat different sort is wandering. Excursus religionists, especially the founders, leaders, and intensive practitioners, tend to be peripatetic. But "not all who wander are lost," and the seeming vagrancy has meaning. It is, as we have seen, first a symbol of liminal experience and status. Second, it may be in the nature of pilgrimage, like the journey of Blavatsky and Olcott to India, and so express not only liminality but also another symbol, an exotic place or remote holy land which encapsulates the otherness the excursus seeks. Third, as in the case of Johnny Appleseed and a Zen master in America like Soyen Shaku, it may disseminate the religion throughout the land by making the wandering a part of the message, inasmuch as the personality of the communicator is a part of it.

Still another symbol is the controlled use of trance or meditation. We have discussed ambiguities regarding trance in connection with grid and group. While the casual welcoming of trance in the original post-independence weak group and grid spiritual situation made possible its employment by early Spiritualists and their mesmerist antecedents, in excursus religion trance is controlled in ways which legitimate its charismatic lineages. But in that context it is most important, for it then symbolizes the possibility of intrapsychic reflection of the strong grid and group cosmos and of subjective communication with it. In a word, it speaks of the possibility of unmediated and tangible ultimate transformation.

This brings us to the next topic, one which is linked to sociology by the social symbolic meaning of meditation: the psychology of excursus religion. To that we shall now turn.

3   Inner Worlds   The Psychology of
                      Excursus Religion

From Mount Shasta to Other Planets

The "I Am" Movement, famous in the thirties and early forties, and still active through several groups, was started by Guy Ballard and his wife. In 1930 Ballard, a mining engineer, was hiking on the slopes of Mount Shasta in northern California when he had an experience which, he said, changed his life "so completely that I could almost believe I were on another planet, but for my return to the usual routine in which I had been engaged for months."[1] Shasta, a gorgeous and isolated snow-crowned volcano in the midst of dark forests, a natural "holy site," has long had a special fascination for American esotericists; around its base are now centers of at least a dozen groups who believe special "lines of spiritual force" are operative in the mighty peak's vicinity.

It was a very warm, lazy day, and Ballard often stopped to rest. At lunchtime he found a clear, cool mountain spring. Stooping to fill his cup, the engineer felt an "electrical current" pass over his body. Then, turning around, he saw a remarkable man who gave him a vitalizing drink superior to spring water and discoursed on philosophical matters.

This experience may be compared with that of Paul Twitchell, founder of Eckankar, a now-substantial spiritual movement which centers on soul-travel, effecting inward journeys to higher worlds. Twitchell reports that he was initiated in the practice while in India on a journey of spiritual seeking. He writes:

One evening I lay down in a hotel room in Srinagar with the hope that the following morning would find me making contact with a *rishi*, who

42

lived almost inaccessible to those like myself, who were seeking some
experience with God.

Almost as quickly as my eyes were closed, I awoke in the *Atma Sarup*,
the soul body, to find myself walking along a sandy beach where the
wild surf lashed the shore and a wind whipped the pines along the edge
of the strand.

Something about the landscape was ethereal and my pulse was quick-
ened by the thought that this was an out-of-the-body projection via the
dream technique. The colors, the invigorating air, and the beauty of
the pale, white clouds against an azure sky were beyond words. It
seemed as if there was God in everything.[2]

In these auspicious surroundings, as one might have expected,
Twitchell did meet his spiritual guide, clothed in light.

One more of many such accounts is that of Orfeo Angelucci, a
UFO contactee whose case was given considerable attention by
Carl Jung.[3] Angelucci tells us that Friday, May 23, 1952, started out
as an ordinary day.[4] But after he went to his swing-shift job at an
aircraft plant, he began to feel ill and peculiar. He reports that an
odd prickling sensation ran through his arms and up his back; he
had a slight heart palpitation and his nerves were on edge. He says
that he always felt that way just before an electrical storm, but that
night was clear and the stars were bright.

Shortly after midnight Angelucci drove home, exhausted. The
nervous tension increased. His eyesight became blurred and the
noise of traffic around him was oddly muffled. Then, continuing
along a deserted stretch of road by a river, he saw a brilliant light
descend. Almost in a state of shock, Angelucci stopped, left his car,
and approached it. He was greeted by friendly voices from another
world, and began a period of conversing and travel between
paradisal spheres in outer space with these extraterrestial guides.
Though unlike Ballard and Twitchell, he has founded no group of
his own, Angellucci has written books and been a regular speaker at
religiously-oriented UFO meetings; to this extent his experience has
led to institutional acceptance and a certain fame. When I heard
him at the Giant Rock Space Convention, he commented that upon
meeting the marvelous visitors, he felt an exaltation "as though
momentarily I had transcended mortality and was somehow related
to these superior beings," and that he then "felt another world, or
something akin to a whole other universe." Clearly, Angelucci

experienced an initiatory shock which enabled a jump from one paradigm or "reality" to another.

These three twentieth-century American examples suggest a basic psychological feature of those who are deeply involved in excursus religion, especially as founders or transmitters: they sense the existance of two worlds, an ordinary world and an alternative one of wonder and meaning, and they enjoy the rare privilege of moving between the two as visitors and envoys.

All serious religion, of course, has something of this dual reality. Ordinarily, however, the reality of the alternative is strongly sustained by powerful symbolic and institutional reinforcement. I myself was at one time close to an intensely, poignantly romantic Anglo-Catholicism. I often dwelt, as in an alternative world, in a fairyland Middle Ages of pilgrimage and piety somewhere between the Seven General councils and Lyonnesse. This alternative was supported by the whole panoply of gothic imagination. Ecclesiastical architecture, church ceremonials, vestments, incense, and music were such as to make walking into the churches of this persuasion a sensuous as well as a subjective entry into the portals of another world.

Institutionalized excursus religion, especially in its intensive centers, may have symbolic and social reinforcement comparable to this. But in the initial phases of a new wave of its transmission—that is, in experiences like those of Ballard, Twitchell, and Angelucci—and for most of those reached by its diffuse influence, the external institutional support will not be present. Instead, the major phenomenon will simply be people who sense they are "different," or discover it through experiences like these. They experience a subjective turbulence and acute self-consciousness which seems to make them more complex than others. To put it another way, they have not only a social identity like everyone else, but also a dissonant non-social identity in some way not placed by the ordinary structures of society, which needs to be reified.

This awareness of two identities dwells in rich interaction with excursus and the perception of other worlds. It is related to the Hegelian excursion and return of the spirit—for that is a journey which, like the excursus of excursus religion, is essentially intrapsychic. Journeys to India, like that of Twitchell and, before him,

Olcott and Blatvatsky, are only symbolic reifications of what is at
base a journey in the mind to another world also in the mind. It is a
journey from one's social identity—the self comprised of family,
status, work, and so forth—to one's non-social identity, to another
"self" which seems to have nothing to do with these things. Social
identity correlates with establishment religion; non-social with
emergent.

Of course, a journey to the non-social identity can ultimately end
in a new social identity. As in the case of Guy Ballard, the new
social identity can be one as leader of an institutionalized movement which reifies and legitimates the non-social identity through
giving meaning to the experiences that created it. It can be within
the ongoing "cultic milieu" described by Balch and Taylor. The
sense of two identities, or, rather, the overcoming of the problem of
two identities, is projected in two ways: outwardly, in the search for
reification in symbol and social group; and inwardly, where voices,
visions, and states of consciousness seem to validate the world of the
alternative identity. It is with this second projection that we shall
now be concerned, though we cannot forget that the two sides
unceasingly interact.

Transits from World to World

Let us examine more closely the meaning of two identities and their
expression in excursus religion. What seems to be involved is, first,
a sense of an inner reality, or an inner reality in rapport with some
cosmic reality, which does not wholly correspond to the structures
of the world. The latter are imperfectly internalized, in that something is leftover inside—and perhaps outside as well—that does not
mesh with the internalized structures. Since humans are dissatisfied
with a lack of equilibrium between inner and outer, this is a
situation which cannot be endured. The solution is to project
inward or outward the "leftover" surface to make out of it a
structure which can then be reified and internalized.

This does not mean, though, that the nonintegrated inner reality
has no content. It will, in fact, be a constellation of memories,
associative feelings, and concepts that somehow have a life of their
own; This particular grouping balks at merging into "establish-

ment'' social and conceptual patterns that would link it to an ''official'' ultimate reality. But it may not be until these attitudes and ideas find an appropriate excursus which somehow does this for them that they are themselves able to emerge into consciousness by the aid of its power. (For the term ''emergent religion'' suggests something emergent as out of a sea, and this is suggestive as an intrapsychic metaphor.) Often, the associative pattern will be one reaching far back into early childhood.

These are people for whom the establishment church may convey one set of childhood memories: the awesomeness of liturgy, coloring pictures of angels and saints in Sunday school, other children or young people in various sorts of activity groups. That church was always something structured, social, and connected with acquired concepts or beliefs, however much internalized. But reading, say, Theosophical literature, for some reason brings to the surface memories perhaps even earlier and probably very different in setting. In them one may be alone, dreamy or reflective, and close to nature and its powers.

Several years ago I talked with an adept in ceremonial magic. He said that he viewed the evocational rite as the induction of a temporary, therapeutic schizophrenia, when real but intrapsychic entities could be called forth, given face and form, and commanded. He said also that the magical arts brought back the sense of wonder one had as a child.

Again, these unassimilated corners of the psyche which take religious expresssion may burst out as the sheer emotional ventilation of some Satanist rites, or create the kingdom of the gods in the fantastic rituals of Neo-Paganism. The point is they are manifestations of something long-standing in the individual's psyche not synchronized to the ordinary structures; something related to the ultimates with which religion deals and so calling for religious symbols; and something which makes a person feel sufficiently ''different'' that non-normative religion best bespeaks not only the psychic content but also the relation, or rather lack of relation, to society's norms that the realization entails.

Yet alternative reality is not always there. In this respect it is identical with Turner's liminality. Many enter it occasionally; some are at least symbolically in it as a lifelong vocation. But generally the experience of other worlds means that one must make transitions, and, indeed, it is necessary to do so. As we noted in the preceding chapter, the legitimation of a religious experience by society requires that ability, for the adept must prove his sanity by being able to move from his other world to the practical world of social relations and business affairs, and back again.

Alfred Schutz, as a phenomenological sociologist, has developed William James's notion of "sub-universes," and given the process of moving in and out of them definitions of use to us.[5] Schutz presents the "world of everyday life" or "working" world as a subuniverse or "finite province of meaning" among countless others, but insists that it is the paramount one, the mode of experiencing oneself and the universe which is the point of reference for all others. Whether or not this means it has an ontological priority is a question outside the phenomenology of experience. But Schutz tells us there are other worlds—"the world of dreams, of imageries and phantasms, the world of scientific contemplation, the play world of the child, and the world of the insane." Each of these has a cognitive style distinctive to itself, and so creates realms of experience with inner consistency, although these are not compatible with the cognitive style of "working" or "everyday life."

What of the transition from the ordinary to one of these other realities? Schutz says the transition is accompanied by a sort of "shock." It is, he says, like falling asleep to enter the world of dreams, and awakening to leave it; it is marked by the signs which betoken suspension of ordinary belief—like those evident when a story is being told, or a game is being played, or a ritual begins with procession or drum.

In the case of the three men with whom we opened this chapter, the transition is evident. Two of them reported a strange electrical feeling, a sudden uncanny perception, and a definite sense of encountering something of another order. The third apparently assimilated his transition to the "shock" of falling asleep and entering the dreamworld. The convulsions of some shamans entering and leaving trance, and the "jerks" of trance mediums as they enter the world of spirit, are comparable.

These cases were allegedly spontaneous and unexpected. They

may, however, fit the research-supported argument of Ralph W. Hood that mystical experiences in nature occur when something suddenly appears which points to the "limits" of everyday reality, especially when the occurence is stressful but was not stressfully anticipated.[6] But what of those like the shaman's or medium's, or the ritualist's and meditator's, which are highly intentional? Are they of the same order?

Not exactly, of course. But it must be remembered that religion strives to obliterate this distinction as much as possible. The contrived transition of the faith's epigone must convincingly be an entry into the same alternative world whither its founder went in his paradigmatic transition, or else the point is lost.

For this reason religions use techniques and images which amount to "condensed symbols" of its paradigmatic experience or person, and also extensive repetition of ritual or rhetoric. These, almost like post-hypnotic suggestion, can trigger a response in a believer similar to that of the original experience, or his own first faith, even though the sign may be so condensed as to seem superficially different. Examples are chanting, liturgical drama, lectures employing suggestive images or calling up emotively powerful concepts used over and over, or even comparable words on the printed page. The seance atmosphere and the "jerks" of the medium, and the sharp clapper in the Zen meditation hall which calls one to mindfulness are also examples.

The difference between the original experience and its induced recapitulation is not that the former is genuine and the latter derivative. To think of it in original-spontaneous versus imitative-contrived language grossly oversimplifies. Our three cases would appear to bear that out, for it is clear that in content these experiences were simply reversions to ancient beliefs in masters, soul travel, or UFOs and superhuman visitants from the sky. On the other hand, one does not doubt that many of the many who have, in "I Am" and Eckankar, sought to repeat Ballard's contact of ascended masters or Twitchell's out-of-the-body travel have had experiences which, to their own satisfaction, validated the goal and seemed to them as fresh and real as the paradigm. The fact that it was later in chronological time did not mean that it had all the connotations of "derivative." Subjective experience has only a nodding acquaintance with clocks and calendars at best, and what is real to it is neither more nor less real because of its relation to another experience, or to the means by which it was triggered. Whether one understands its induction to have been by a deliberately learned technique like those taught by "I Am" or Eckankar, or by an unconscious trigger and projection of some sort, or, for that matter, by supernatural intervention, may not, after all, say much about the quality of the actual experience once it is released.

The nature of the triggering, then, may not determine the essence of the experience as transition to another "world" where one realizes a non-social identity. What it does determine, of course, is the relation of that identity to one's social identity. One will be drawn to triggering methods—or to unconscious "triggerings"—which promise a realization of a non-social identity quite similar to one's own, so much so one hopes for no dissonance between the two. If one adapts a learned triggering, then one has a certain set of social identity options available: as private practitioner, or as member of a group which reinforces the transition in its own ways, possibly tending to over-routinize it. If one has a "spontaneous" experience, one may either keep it to oneself, or take up the prestigious but lonely burden of the prophet.

Divine Madness

At several points we have alluded to comparisons between contact with other worlds in the excursus religionist's subjectivity, and "temporary schizophrenia," in the words of the magician. The comparison with madness is highly suggestive, and certainly worth exploring, in light of controversial contemporary views of insanity which recognize in it therapeutic as well as destructive possibilities, and recall the "divine madness" of Plato.

R. D. Laing is the best-known exponent of the new view of madness.[7] His thesis is that what we call ordinary reality—the "working" reality of Schutz—is in itself schizophrenic. Its structures create distortions of human personality which "work" because they are reinforced by society, but only at great cost in inhibition and pain to individuals. To become mad is the only way many sensitive persons can deal with the greater madness around them, and often the private madness produces a world which is not only better suited to them than the outer insanity, but also gives them a self-knowledge and inner strength that finally enables them to live better in an insane world.

According to Laing and his school, then, the real task of the psychotherapist is not to coerce the patient to accept his or society's or the psychiatric profession's opinion of what "reality" is, but accompany him or her on the trip through madness. Like Normon O. Brown's Dionysiac personality, his id and ego unite to create a personality dynamic enough to defy "reality," rather than developing a Freudian ego which accepts the reality-principle.

In reading Laing's work, one is impresssed by how often his patients seem to undergo religious and occult experiences. It is not only that, as Carl Jung recognized some time ago, the symbols in the minds of the mentally disturbed, like those in dreams, often show convergence with the archetypes of religious myth and rite. The passage of some of Laing's people through their psychoses, including contact with supernormal entities along the way, also parallel in structure traditional ritual and spontaneous initiations.

Laing describes one woman at his Kingsley Hall in London who regressed through childhood to infancy and even to the fetal state. She said she wanted to go all the way back to find herself, and live in a way that was not false. She reached a point where she was no more than a bundle of bones, had to be helped to take food and to defecate, and was often near physical death. Then she returned to adulthood gradually over a period of several weeks as a new person with a new personality.[8] The parallel to what is symbolized by religious rituals of death and rebirth, such as baptism, and to the more spontaneous initiatory ordeals of shamans and magi, is striking.

Even more striking in the present context is Laing's account of a former seaman who had a complete mental breakdown and had to be hospitalized for ten days. During this time he seemed helpless and dissociated. But although he could not communicate it to anyone, his experience during the breakdown was dramatic. At the depth of his outward decline, he felt he touched a source of power within himself, and had a sense of being on an immense journey through eons. Moreover, the patient felt that above reigned

not only God, but also intermediate beings like gods "far above us
capable of dealing with the situation that I was incapable of dealing
with, that were in charge and were running things, and at the end
of it, everybody had to take on the job at the top."[9]

This decription and the pilgrimage through the eons in countless
reincarnations, culminating in the right and duty of being a lord of
cosmic destiny, seems an apparently spontaneous re-creation in
mental crisis of the Theosophical world view. In it the Masters, like
the Bodhisattvas and Rishis and Sufi "Pivot Saints" of classic
Eastern lore, are human beings developed tremendously beyond
the norm and are the benign administrators of the invisible government of the world.

If one were to examine the initiatory experiences of many in
excursus religion, especially those in it intensively, he would probably find nonclinical and better controlled parallels to these; even
experiences of those reached by excursus religion's diffuse influence
perhaps represent "miniaturizations" of these breaks and rebirths
through manipulation of subjective "condensed symbols." Again,
whether the process is spontaneous-seeming, as in the case of the
founders of "I Am" and Eckankar, or learned and induced, as for
the ceremonial magician, is not of critical importance from the
psychological perspective. In both cases it may be a working
through "madness" and learning from it. It is developing and
stabilizing and giving substance to one's non-social identity as a foil
against the opposing "madness" of the society which informs one's
social identity. The excursus religionist is aware in his own way of
the drab, one-dimensional quality, even the schizophrenia, of mass
society and its prevailing world views.

While this is not the place to discuss the theoretical validity of
Laing's hypotheses, which have certainly not gone unchallenged, I
think it is fair to say that they offer an unusual and illuminating
insight into the inner experience of excursus religion and the subjective face of its tension with society. In Laingian terms, perhaps the
ideal would be, as we have suggested, to find the point of precise
equilibrium, a Buddhistic middle way, between the outer madness
of society and the inner madness of unbridled subjective excursus,
so that one could draw the strength and perspective of each as a
corrective to the other, without being trapped in the black hole of

each alone. This is the way of the magus who, like Castaneda's Don Juan, has a shamanistic "lightness" which enables him to move between worlds, manage practical as well as transcendent affairs, and keep his balance on the thin edge of interfacing realities.

The Modern Magus

A person who maintains this equilibrium between sub-universes possesses a peculiar fascination. He shimmers with a certain glamor, as though his life was itself a mystic spell. Like all magic, it may be partly illusion, but one is drawn back to the thaumaturge time and again because one is never quite sure what is sleight-of-hand and what is really a glimpse into some alternative universe—or whether even the sleight-of-hand may not have some significance beyond trickery. Like the shaman of old, the adept is mainly concerned with creating a universe of meaning in which the spiritual reality that he believes in is perceived as the absolute and fundamental truth. This means that it must be reified as evident truth on all levels of perception so that no crack is left for cognitive dissonance. If that end requires certain technical adjustments to maintain consonance in the world of such gross senses as outward sight and hearing, those adjustments are not very different from the belief-fomenting glamor of any rhetoric or symbol-manipulation.

As in the case of the shaman, neither words nor ecstatic scenario nor trickery nor wake of myth and wonder are in themselves the shamanistic mastery of equilibrium. The shaman-in-civilization, whom I have previously referred to as the "magus," and who is the mainstay of the emergent and excursus religious traditions, actually comes into being in and through relationships.[10] The transformative catalyst he becomes for the circle around him is more important than what he says or does, in itself. The most significant feature of the charismatic figure, the magus, is that he becomes a symbol in the minds of others—a symbol that is powerful enough to effect a reordering of the disciple's mindset, to raise or lower the threshold of the unconscious, or to "cleanse the doors of perception" so that modalities or patterns of reality are seen which were not before. The words of the magus are important, but important because of their associative power rather than on what a strict and

detached intellectual analysis might prove about them; the wonders
he is alleged to have accomplished are significant, yet the question
of whether they would be verifiable under laboratory conditions is
not really to the point—the important thing is that in the context
of the relationship they become symbols and bearers of the transcendence incarnate in the magus. Remarkable spiritual figures from
Jesus to Madame Blavatsky have worked extraordinary phenomena
as signs in the context of interaction with followers, but have not
commanded stones to become bread to meet their own private
needs outside that context, despite much provocation.

This sort of relationship, whether with a wonder-worker or a Zen
master who simply shows uncanny insight into one's psyche, marks
the difference between the magus of the excursus path and the
philosopher or clergyman. It is not so much different ideas that set
them apart as it is different relationship styles marked by different
symbols of the meaning of the relationship. There is a distinction
between the philosophies of Alfred North Whitehead and the
Russian mystagogue Georges Gurdjieff, even though both expounded a process philosophy which drew from the wells of
platonism and both were interested in mathematical symbolism.
There is probably some difference in their respective competence
with the tools of the philosopher's trade. But a major difference
between the two is that while, to the best of my knowledge, there
are no groups devoted to Whitehead's thought outside academic
circles, Gurdjieff has scores of groups devoted to discussing his
philosophy and practicing the "work" that accompanies it. Both
philosophers have had influence, but it has differed in kind, owing
to the very different nature of the relationship between the mentor
and the followers and that relationship's symbolic meaning for the
latter.

It would be instructive to compare those men of ideas whose
influence has taken the form of shaping intensive groups and a
sense of master-disciple relationships—like the Buddha, Gurdjieff,
and even Teilhard de Chardin—and those, like Aristotle and Whitehead, in which it has not. For the former, the master becomes
internalized as a transcendent symbol around which aspects of the
psyche governing several levels of activity—social, motor, even
memory and ego-formative—become arranged. For the latter, the

philosopher is a person with important ideas. In that cleavage lies the distinction between philosophy and religion.

The difference surfaces basically in two factors: a different personality on the part of the mystagogue and a different technique. We have cited the glamor and mystery, the sense of being on the border of realities, borne by the magus. We have also mentioned his capacity to be internalized as a subjective symbol in the minds of his followers. What this really means is that his personality, his image, becomes a condensed symbol of more than himself— whether of the experienced history of him in relation to the disciples, that is, of the relation itself; or of a particular kind of transcendence; even, like Teilhard, of a spiritual generation.

The second difference is in technique. While the academic philosopher will use and teach only intellectual techniques, the religionist will work in all three of the forms of religious expression. He will use non-intellectual techniques of communication and reinforcement, and will probably teach sensual and motor means of self-incorporation into the transcendence he mediates.

What makes a person a mystagogue? Whether a Ballard, Twitchell, or Angelucci, a Gurdjieff or Blavatsky, he is a person marked by experiences of liminality and even initiatory madness, probably symbolized by wandering and visions or voices; he is a person whose non-social self has a life of its own and the power to form its own society.

Consider Helena Blavatsky, the dominant figure in nineteenth-century Theosophy. Though she was brought up in aristocratic circles in Orthodox Russia, and though she occasionally had wistful yearnings toward conventional faith and life, the major features of her inner life were occult initiations, communication with transcendent masters, and the paranormal powers they worked through her—all of which created in her a non-social self that could only be socialized through new sets of relationships centering on its own phenomena.

This personality was intertwined with a long-standing sense of alienation from society and tension from it. This quality as it expresses itself in the life of the magus of excursus religion has rarely been better or more forcefully expressed than in a letter Blavatsky wrote in 1884 to the Russian writer Vselovôd S. Solovyoff,

at a time when charges of fraud had been published against her
under the auspices of the British Society for Psychical Research and
many had turned away from her. Solovyoff, brother of the mystical
philosopher Vladmir S. Solovyoff, had been in Blavatsky's confidence for a period in 1884. Despite their friendship, he published
this letter, albeit with her permission, together with other correspondence and memoirs in a book, *A Modern Priestess of Isis*,
intended as an exposé of the mysterious madame. Combined as it is
with Solovyoff's rather priggish moralizing about his enigmatic
countrywoman, this publishing venture has its distasteful aspect.
Nevertheless, much of the material, as Solovyoff recognized, is of
great psychological interest.

In the letter, Madame Blavatsky first asks the reader to picture in
the mind this scene. "There is living in the forest a wild boar—an
ugly creature, but doing no harm to any one so long as they leave
him in peace in the forest, with his wild beast friends who love
him." But this comrade of the wild things is suddenly turned upon
by a pack of fierce hounds, and has no choice but to turn and
"show himself wholly as he is, from top to bottom," as he attacks
back at the horde until he falls.

She goes on to say that she will write a full confession of her life,
and gives a few hints of what that document will contain, com-
bining allusions to great turpitude with claims about the immense
good her Theosophy has done. Then she says "I will even take to
lies, to the greatest of lies, which for that reason is the most likely of
all to be believed. I will say and publish it in the *Times* and in all
the papers, that the 'master' and 'Mahatma K. H.' are only the
product of my own imagination: that I *invented* them, that the
phenomena were all more or less *spiritualistic* apparitions . . . I will
say that in certain instances I *fooled* people; I will expose dozens of
fools . . ."[11]

Here we see an attempt at self-understanding by a complex
personality whose non-social self is powerful yet needs expression
through the medium of some sort of relationship. Solovyoff later
says, "She imagined that everything in the world was founded on
personal relations, and that to this there was no exception." She sees
herself as set against the world, friend only of the strange and wild,
with powers capable of great depravity and great good. She has an

immoderate capacity for self-dramatization, and the temptation to lie and deceive is always there and doubtless sometimes indulged, yet always in the context of something else which is not a lie but is almost impossible to communicate about, so much is it a part of the non-social self. Yet communicate it she must, for the something else paradoxically must grow in relationships, even if it has roots in experiences closer to the private heavens and hells of those bruised and blessed by initiatory madness.

In personalities like those of Blavatksy, Gurdjieff, and many another luminary of counterspirituality, one observes qualities not only of the paradigmatic shaman and magus, but also of the trickster and "ritual clown." The trickster is that figure in many mythologies who cleverly outwits both gods and men and manages to establish a precarious immortality for himself on the tenuous boundary between heaven and human society. From that outsider's vantage point he laughs at the pomposity and gullibility of both realms.

In many human communities something of the same role is taken by the trickster's emulators, the ritual clowns who may follow an up-lifting performance by priest or shaman with a comic burlesque of it, or even interrupt sacred solemnities with rough humor and obsceni-ties. Those holidays which, like Purim or Carnival or the Hindu Holi, treat religion in a light vein have much the same role, and their traditions, like the clowns, have been thought ultimately important to cosmic (and human) equilibrium.

The strange ways, defiance of conventional morality, and mock-ery of normative faith for which many colorful figures outside normative spirituality are notorious can be put in trickster perspec-tive, among others. Those with this quality are not likely to be long idolized by many. At the same time, the sport they make of the solemn assemblies of established religion—sometimes with the rau-cous derision of a Blavatsky, sometimes without scornful words but only by showing an alternative way—is often salutary. Even the dangerous disregard of ordinary virtue may, especially when that virtue is overlaid with sanctimoniousness, have its point. Heinrich Zimmer, in *Myths and Symbols in Indian Art and Civilization*, writes of "that touch of 'amorality' which must form at least part of

one's intellectual and intuitive pattern, if one is not to fall prey to
predetermined bias and be cut off from certain vital, highly iron-
ical, and disturbing insights."[12]

Meditation and Expansive Consciousness

In the psychology of excursus religion, special attention must be
given to meditation, since in the American scene it has played such
an important role. Varying definitions have been given for meditation, but generally the crucial point is that in meditation the
consciousness is directed away from outward things and reflected
back upon itself—upon particular sacred images or thoughts which
are conjured up in the mind, or upon the formless essence of
consciousness, or even upon a simple observing of the ordinary
processes of thought. This act properly becomes "one-pointed," to
use the Eastern term, in that it gives rapt attention in the present to
its focus, excluding all else. The process may be aided by posture, or
even dance, and by sensory stabilization through attention to a
single sight or sound. The meditation act should induce a tranquil
or ecstatic state of consciousness. It may deepen into the trance of
mediums and others, or broaden to include work or play done with
a rapt but calm state of attention, especially when these are interpreted as religious states.

Meditation is not, of course, unknown to the Judeo-Christian
religious tradition, and has a part in the traditional spirituality of
the Roman Catholic and Eastern Orthodox churches particularly.
Undoubtedly much Judeo-Christian prayer is psychologically not
very different from meditation. But it must be conceded that
meditation is attention to consciousness itself, whereas prayer is
psychologically and symbolically structured as an "I-thou" relation
to a personal God conceived of as essentially outside the psyche.
This is a problematic but not insuperable matter, as Christian
mystical theology and kabbalistic Jewish thought concerning meditation shows. However, it has meant that in religion in which
meditation is central—in Judaism and Christianity it has always
been at best a sort of "option" for a minority of mystical bent, and
has not seldom been regarded dubiously—the tendency is inevi-

tably toward an immanentialist and monistic ontology oblique to
much Western religious experience, especially as represented in the
"establishment" churches.

This has meant that for Western non-normative religion, meditation has often been very important, a prime tacit symbol of that
religion's oppositional character. The reasons are threefold.

First, meditation offers an excursus for those to whom the whole
meditation experience is alien. Whatever its ontological validity, in
a culture structured around interpersonal meanings on both the
terrestrial and cosmic planes, meditation focusing on one's own
inwardness presents a new and wonderful world. That is all the
more the case when intersubjective meanings appear to relate only
to the expression of one's social self, and the non-social self is left
with no appropriate venue—unless meditation inflates it until it
momentarily attains the dignity of being virtually the whole.

Second, meditation, whether in Eckankar, TM, or Spiritualism,
serves as an important symbol of an alternative spirituality. In itself,
the practice of meditation symbolizes that one is engaged not in a
religion that mainly cements family or community bonds, or places
one in a cosmic interpersonal relationship, but in a religion that
involves deep internal exploration and the modification of states of
consciousness to actualize that true self which, presumably, one will
find at the end of the quest. Because the presuppositions and
language of meditation are different, its practice symbolizes—
above all to oneself—that one's adventure is different. Sociologically, a serious interest in meditation will inevitably align one, in
America, with different kinds of people than will a major interest in
"establishment" religion.

Third, meditation or something like it is essential to excursus
religion because it can give that sense of immediacy and cosmic
participation necessary to counter the sociological pressure to conform to the establishment religion of one's culture. A bare ideology, or even rite, is not sufficient to stand against those forces; they
must be met with an equal subjective impetus that is to a great
extent self-validating.

All these reasons for meditation's importance in American excursus religion can be summed up in the concept of meditation as
expansive consciousness—expansive as a movement toward the

Other Side, and as a foil against pressures to conform to established
religion.

Polymorphous Sensuality

Still another interesting set of psychological correlates can be found
for excursus religion—a set that concerns the senses employed. Ernest
G. Schachtel, a psychoanalyst, has distinguished the "proximity
senses"—touch, taste, smell—from the "distance senses" of hearing and sight, and explained that in early childhood we make a
partial transition from concentration on the former to concentration
on the latter.[13] This creates a new and more extended environment,
but one in which the person is less immediately involved as a
psycho-physical organism.

If a religious map of America, or of the world, were drawn along
the lines of whether distance or proximity senses were dominant, it
would be different from the maps drawn to demarcate formal
beliefs, and would be quite instructive. Magical rites and tantrism,
for example, often include sexual rites and generally involve, as
does sex, evocative use of the proximity senses. Catholic sacramental worship employs a rather genteel token acknowledgment of
all the senses in its use of incense, kissing of holy objects, and
bread, as well as icon and song and sermon. But classical Protestant
worship suggests a vehement denial that meaningful religious communication can come through the proximity senses; it reflects
"maturation" in its view that hearing and seeing (of the word, and
of the unmediated reality of the creation) are alone reliable or
sanctified.

Excursus religion, ranging as it does from magic and Neo-
Paganism to highly ethereal "metaphysics," represents the whole
sensory gamut. But it is worth noting that a tendency toward
recovering the sacred possibilities present in the whole sensory
spectrum often emerges. Even in a movement like Pentecostalism,
as in Spiritualism, Theosophy, and Zen, a barely veiled sensuality
lurks just beneath the spiritual surface, expressing itself in "phenomena," in unusual styles of marriage and community, in an
ecstatic relation to nature.

Kenneth Grant, in his valuable and sympathetic study of modern ceremonial magic, and particularly in his work on Aleister Crowley, the notorious mage of the twenties and thirties, emphasizes the physical and physiological basis of magical phenomena and the extent to which its rites and symbols are shot through with tantralike sexual images. The power of magic, he indicates, really resides in the profound union of the person with his or her physical energies that it can effect; magic is a union of metaphysical concepts with psychodynamics, sexology, and endocrinology, all aligned to will. It is far from being only a "spiritual" matter. Indeed, Grant tells us, contrary to what some seem to believe, in initiatory mystery traditions like magic, it is the spiritual or philosophical explanations that are exoteric, concealing what are actually physiological experiences of great power, and not the other way around.[14] Magic and ritual seem to evoke a primal stage of human development when psyche and physiology were much more intimately integrated than after the distance senses, and the ego, began to create worlds of consciousness separate from the "world" of the physical body, its wordless energies, needs, and knowledges.

Not all excursus religions, of course, are as frank and full-blooded a return to primary sensuality as sexual magic. Some, rejecting even the tepid sacramentalism of conventional Christianity, appear only overspiritualizations of religion reinforcing body-spirit dualism. They are in the lineage of the ancient orphic and platonic allegorizing of physical aspects of initiatory and shamanistic ecstasy.

Yet it is interesting to note ways in which excursus religion, both in what it recovers and in what it too obviously represses, is sometimes an excursus toward an unconventional relationship with the senses and the sexuality so potently linked to them. The reader may wish to reflect on the proximity sense meaning of the virulent Shaker dance and spiritualism in the context of Shaker celibacy, the transparent sexual mysticism of Thomas Lake Harris, the recovery of tangible evidence in the "phenomena" of Spiritualism and of Madame Blavatsky, the association of the highly ceremonial Liberal Catholic Church with Theosophy, and the decorous exaltation of all five senses by conventional Zen, together with the paradoxical libertinism of some its American "beat" devotees.

Let us end this chapter, though, with the observation that the real excursus of excursus religion is inward. The sociology, praxis, and doctrine, even the relation to the body and the senses, all finally serve only to symbolize excursus and to create a psychic space in which it can take place. In conventional religion these features often are the religion, in the sense that a major function of it is to provide social placing. This is also the case in excursus religion, in that the excursus may represent a liminal social position; but for this reason it has no power unless it provides a compensatory inner journey. The bulwarks of a different social group, actions, and beliefs free one to make this journey, which can be understood in terms of the platonic "divine madness."

2   Histories

4

Shakers and Spiritualists

An Ancient Sybil

According to the old sagas, at the Norse settlement of Herjolfsness in Greenland, an interesting event happened about the year 1000, shortly before Leif Eriksson's voyage to Vinland or America. A prophetess named Thorbjorg attended the winter feast of Thorkel, a farmer. She wore a blue mantel adorned with stones down to the hem. On her head was a black lambskin hood lined with white cat's fur, and she wore catskin gloves. Her staff was capped with a brass knob studded with stones, and from her belt of touchwood hung a large pouch full of the charms required for her craft. On her feet she wore hairy calfskin shoes with thick laces that had tin buttons on the ends. The evening of her arrival she ate a meal consisting largely of a gruel of goat's milk and a main dish made of the hearts of various animals; this she ate with a brass spoon, and a knife with a walrus-tusk handle.

Late the next day the sybil prepared to do her witchcraft. She needed the assistance of women familiar with the spells, known as warlock-songs, that would summon up spirits. None of the women present did, save a maiden of good family called Gudrid. But those were the days when Christianity was spreading among the folk of the North, and Gudrid, though she acknowledged that she had learned the warlock-songs from her foster mother Halldis in Iceland, declined at first to sing them, saying, "This is the sort of knowledge and ceremony that I want nothing to do with, for I am a Christian."

Other guests argued convincingly that singing the songs could not really hurt her, and might be of help to others. Finally, under pressure from Thorkel, the host, Gudrid acquiesced. Thorbjorg seated herself on a ritual platform, the other women forming a circle around that awesome feminine figure, and Gudrid chanted the mystic stanzas. It was said that none before had heard lovelier singing.

The prophetess thanked her, saying, "Many spirits are now present which were charmed to hear the singing, and which previously had tried to shun us and would grant us no obedience. And now many things stand revealed to me which before were hidden both from me and from others."

Thorbjorg, presumably in a state of mediumistic trance, then foretold the future. Looking into the days and years ahead, she perceived the imminent end of the famine and epidemic that had lately afflicted the pioneer community and saw a bright destiny for Gudrid. Then she gave individual readings for all present, said mostly to be accurate, and departed. A messenger was sent to summon back Thorbjorn, Gudrid's father, for he had refused to be present while such paganism was going on.[1]

As for Gudrid, she later married a certain Karlsefni and accompanied him to Vinland. There, the Graenlendinga Saga tells us, she dwelt in the tiny Norse settlement for a year and gave birth to a son, Snorri. She, and the other settlers, had difficult encounters with the Skraelings, as the natives were called. Though she remained resolutely Christian, once in Vinland she had a puzzling apparition of a short, pale woman with unforgettably large, luminous eyes who entered the house and, after asking Gudrid's name, introduced herself as Gudrid also. Was it a *döppelganger* or a projection of some alternative personality? Gudrid never learned, for just then she was interrupted by a loud noise from outside as Karlsefni's men killed a Skraeling who was trying to steal some weapons. The vision vanished and was not seen again. The party returned to Iceland.

Later, after the death of her husband and her son's marriage, the redoubtable Gudrid made a pilgrimage to Rome, and ended her days as an anchoress in Iceland. Two of her great-grandsons were bishops.[2]

Three points from this narrative of Norse spiritualism are striking

in connection with our endeavor to understand the alternative altars
of America. First, we may note the concentration of feminine
spiritual force which empowered the sybil's seance. The medium
was a woman; she was surrounded with a supporting ring of fe-
males; and only the song of a woman could soften the will of her
spirits. Men might be (as some still argue today) the only acceptable
ministrants at the altars of Christ, the new power; but in Thorbjorg's world the menfolk, however strong in battle, were only
humble suppliants before the powers controlled by the other sex.

Second, we note the dimensions of the conflict between the
religion of the spirits and that of Christ. The Norsemen were
relatively tolerant for their day, but, even so, those like Thorbjorn
who had forsaken the hammer of Thor for the cross were not at ease
with such doings—though one senses in Gudrid, a woman and a
Christian, an unconscious ambivalence, reflected in her ability to
sing the shamaness's songs with unexpected force once her scruples
were overcome. The conflict certainly did not die easily; memories
of Thorbjorg's breed were undoubtedly brought much later to
Massachusetts by the Norsemen's Anglo-Saxon cousins, and had an
influence on certain events at Salem. And, as we shall see, this
heritage—influenced also by the comparable shamanism of the
Skraelings or Amerindians, and by many other lineages—was in a
sense reborn in more liberal times in such American phenomena as
Shakerism and Spiritualism, not to mention the tiny Witchcraft
and Neo-Pagan movements of today.

Third, we note that Thorbjorg's message was one of a spiritual
world immediately accessible, comprised of finite but pluralistic
powers, and promising a future brighter than the present. We have
already observed that these views of the spiritual world are characteristics of excursus religion generally, at least where the familiar
religion is historical and monotheistic Christianity. They are particularly characteristic of Spiritualism.

Ecstatic Religion

Let us reflect a little more on the theme of sexual antagonism in
religion. We should not overemphasize its importance in understanding excursus religion in America, for there are several other

symbols of reversal of the ordinary that are of equal importance. But it should not be underemphasized either, particularly as a psychological dynamic. Consider how many new movements originated in America were founded by women—Shakerism, Spiritualism, Seventh-Day Adventism, Christian Science, Theosophy, Divine Science. Or consider those that, while founded by men, established unconventional relations between the sexes—the Latter-Day Saints (in its early polygamy), the Oneida Community. Or those, like the New Thought churches and Pentecostalism, that have had an unusually high proportion of women preachers and members. Virtually all the movements just named have a rich history of new revelation suggestive of spiritual immediacy triumphing over history, a spiritual cosmos more monistic or pluralistic (or both) than that of the Lord of Sinai, and a view of a new spiritual start in the New World and of a brighter future that often reaches apocalyptic proportions—even as did the oracles of Thorbjorg.

Whether, as Jungian analysts would argue, characteristics like these—drawn from the unity of the womb, the pluralism of the family under the maternal arms, and the apocalyptic process of giving birth—represent an inalienable feminine pattern of spirituality too long repressed is a matter beyond the scope of this book. Others would argue that it represents only the ecstatic and apocalyptic religion typical of oppressed groups who have little to hope from the reason, law, and hierarchical authority that cater to those dominant. Since the latter are invariably men, as well as of the proper race and class, we have no empirical grounds for saying what the religion of women would be like in other circumstances.

There is little doubt, though, that we are dealing with a recognizable phenomenon and set of associations. The predominance of women in ecstatic, possession, mystical, and healing cults is a worldwide fact. It is as evident in Haitian voodoo, the ancient Greek Dionysiacs, and the Japanese new religions, as in the somewhat more decorous Shakers, Spiritualists, Theosophists, and Pentecostalists of America.

I. M. Lewis, in *Ecstatic Religion*, gives a vivid account of the *zar* cults of Islamic East Africa. Women in this ostensibly highly masculine society will from time to time be possessed by vigorously assertive spirits which, through the mouths of the entranced wife or kinswoman, make demands on men. Although ordinarily the women obey rather than give orders, these importunities for gifts or favors are generally met, for the power of the spirits to bring misfortune to those who defy their wishes is well known.

Lewis argues that such cults are "thinly disguised protest movements directed against the dominant sex."[3] Excursus religion has certainly had such overtones for many. Madame Blavatsky of Theosophy once put it forcefully enough: "Woman finds her happiness in the acquisition of supernatural powers. Love is but a vile dream, a nightmare."[4]

Lewis also makes the significant point that the spirits involved in this type of feminine possession cult are not so much concerned with upholding the moral order of the established society—which, in any case, is probably a rationalized ethic supporting male hegemony—as they are with simply giving joy, ecstasy, excitement, healing, and an inchoate sense of countervailing power. They are, in other words, spirits embodying the flavor of an opposing, feminine liminal world. While the invisible communicators of American Spiritualism and related movements have, indeed, delivered reams of moral discourse, often replete with fulsome Victorian platitudes, on notable occasions their values have also seemed highly oblique, and the general sense one gets of the movement is that much of its real appeal lay less in what its otherworldly guides and teachers said than in the atmosphere of wonder and power that commerce with them exuded—though, of course, much the same can be said of any experience of the numinous.

Two Women: I

The shaman, as we have seen, is one who has passed through an initiatory madness, death, and rebirth, emerging in control of spirit helpers, able to transcend the boundaries between worlds, so that he can travel to or communicate with gods and departed souls and give boons to healing and divination to humankind. The shamanic paradigm leaps to mind as one reads about many important figures in the excursus religious tradition, but none recall it more effectively than two women who began their work on these shores when the nation was young.

It was in 1776 that the eighteen-year-old Jemima Wilkinson of Cumberland, Rhode Island, appeared to die from the plague. Her body grew cold and stiff. But then it became warm again, rose up, and began to speak. And the voice that spoke through it confirmed that, indeed, Jemima Wilkinson had "left the world of time," but that her body was now to serve as the vehicle of the Spirit of Life from God, and should be known as The Publick Universal Friend.

For forty-three years thereafter The Friend worked from within that body. During the first fourteen of them she traveled about the northeastern states calling upon the citizens to lead Christian lives and winning converts. Her doctrine was generally orthodox enough, save for a lack of respect for lawful marriage, for she often persuaded followers to leave spouses who were not equally dedicated to The Friend, and came more and more to counsel complete chastity. Hers was a dramatic presence well able to lure the hearts of impressionable followers from earthly bonds. Strikingly tall, with ample dark hair, passionate eyes, and lovely coloring, she wore a low white beaverskin hat and a full white robe. She was accompanied by two associates: Sarah Richardson, who was alleged to be "the prophet Daniel operating in these latter days in the female line," and James Parker, who, dressed in prophet's robes, gave voice to the spirit of Elijah. At The Friend's open meetings, these persons would declaim, fall to the ground in rapture, or describe visions of heaven as the Spirit gave them utterance, and The Universal Friend would stand between them to plead the love of God with graceful gestures and winning voice.

It can easily be believed that, though she had her share of enemies and was even once tried (and acquitted) for blasphemy, The Friend also won wealthy and prominent admirers and converts and did not lack for this world's goods. Indeed, toward the end of her traveling ministry, she had built for herself an open coach, shaped like an upturned half-moon, with seats of gold tapestry, and both on the front panels and over her head were engraved the letters U.F. Many regarded The Spirit of Life from God as none other than the returned Christ, an opinion she neither affirmed nor denied.

In the early 1790s The Friend ceased traveling and settled with 260 followers pledged to obedience and celibacy in the Finger Lake district of New York State. Here a community was built, centering

about a large, beautiful house for The Friend overlooking Lake
Keuka. Here the mystic queen lived in state, waited on by seven
maids of youth and beauty, and gave divine counsel to suppliants
from near and far. She and her people reported frequent visions,
wonders, and exchanges with the Other World out of time.

As years passed, though, dissensions and apostasy, especially in
the matters of communal property and celibacy, racked the community. It was also weakened by the loss of the many who "left
time," as the prophetess called dying, and were not replaced. The
decades also left their mark on The Friend, whose fleshly vehicle
came to know age and illness, much to her distaste. She once
commissioned a portrait, then refused to allow it to be shown when
the artist captured too honestly the ravages of the years on what was
once a divine beauty.

Some stayed faithful until the end of her earthly course in 1819.
Then certain adherents who had expected her to be immortal were
distraught, and others were disappointed when she did not return
after three days, as they had anticipated. But still others of the
Jemimakins, as her devotees were called, continued by occult means
to consult the spirit of The Publick Universal Friend for advice until
at least the end of the century, and she is still a local legend, if not
cult, around Yates County, New York.[5]

Two Women: II

In 1774, just two years before the transformation of Jemima Wilkinson, a tiny band under the leadership of another changed and
chaste woman of prophetic gifts arrived in the New World. She was
called Mother Ann Lee, and she was foundress of the United Society
of Believers in Christ's Second Appearing, commonly called
Shakers.

Ann Lee had been born in Toad Lane, Manchester, in 1736,
amid the squalor of an eighteenth-century British industrial town.
Her father, a blacksmith, was not prosperous; the child grew up
without education and worked in a cotton factory from an early age.
(Most of her first followers were of similar background; the idyllic
rural communal life which became the Shaker ideal was not so
much a product of the frontier, as a reaction to the notorious evils
of the first industrial cities.)

Even as a child, Ann found the matter of sexual relationships extremely distasteful. We are told she often admonished her mother against the "impure" act, so that her father was driven to take up the whip. Nonetheless, she married a man named Abraham Stanley and had four children by him, all of whom died in infancy—she read those sad losses as a sign she was not called to cohabitation. After her children's deaths, she went through nine years of deep mental distress. The condition was, judging from the accounts, something more than simple depression. She would weep and moan through long sleepless nights, and wasted away to a virtual skeleton, weak as an infant. This stage can be compared to the archetypal shaman's initiatory pathology; the period was also "filled with visions and revelations of God."

Her process out of this divinely disturbed state was greatly aided by her becoming affiliated with the "Shaking Quakers," a small group of ecstatics on the fringes of Quakerism influenced by French Camisard refugees in England. Finding a sympathetic group in which one's own mental disturbances have sacred meaning can often transform those disturbances from weakness to sources of extraordinary strength. It can release new powers of leadership and creativity, while granting social legitimacy to what had been a private vision in conflict with the world's construction of reality. Thus in 1770, after uniting with the Shaking Quakers and, indeed, while in prison for her testimony on their behalf, she received after deep distress a "full revelation of the root and foundation of human depravity, and of the very transgression of the first man and woman in the garden of Eden."[6] (One is reminded of Sun Myung Moon, the visionary founder of the Unification Church, who perceived that the secret basic sin of Eden was that Satan had sexual relations with Eve.)

After her revelation, Mother Ann grew in strength and in the power of her testimony; before long she was effectual leader of the Manchester Shaking Quakers. Though she suffered much persecution from the officials, her course was set. Hers was to be a religion that combined that group's singing, dancing, "shaking," and ongoing ecstatic revelations, with sexual abstinence as the way of the kingdom of heaven. Her followers believed she was none other than the second appearance of Christ.

In 1774, following special revelations and promises from God,

Ann left for America with her husband, brother, and several other "Shakers." They settled at first in New York City, and quietly found work. Ann was employed as a laundress, but after a time had to stop work to care for her husband, who had become very ill. She was reduced to the depths of poverty, at one point having nothing but a cold room and, for nourishment, a cruet of vinegar. After his recovery her husband demanded cohabitation with his wife, and when she vehemently refused left her and the movement for good.

In 1776 the little flock settled at Niskayuna (now Watervliet) near Albany, New York. The territory was then frontier country, and there it was that the Shaker communal life had its beginnings. Their early history is one of hardships. Hunger weakened them before the agricultural projects got under way. Mother Ann and others went about on preaching tours, and, both at home and abroad, the pacifist Shakers were accused in those revolutionary years of being British spies, as well as blasphemers, and were set upon by angry mobs and irate officials.

Yet the community grew. The tours won some souls, even if at the price of stonings and beatings which undoubtedly shortened the lives of both Mother Ann and her brother. The Shakers reaped a harvest from an upstate revival in 1779, as they did from the Kentucky revivals a couple of decades later. The Shakers followed in the path of revivals, often preaching at camp meetings. Most revival preaching itself, of course, was not oriented toward Shaker beliefs, yet always there were some spirits awakened by evangelism who found thereafter that they could not rest until they had embraced the level of communal and continent perfection that the Believers exemplified. Until her death in 1784, Ann Lee was truly a mother to her struggling yet growing fellowship of heaven, a strong presence among them, full of rich and edifying counsel.

It was not until three years after the passing of Mother Ann that the movement was formally "gathered in society order" and the quiet empire of Shaker communal houses commenced its remarkable cycle of expansion and decline. At its peak, around 1830, Shakerism had some nineteen communities between Maine and Kentucky, each with several hundred members. They were noted for their diligence and legendary cleanliness, their hearty (and often vegetarian) fare, and their practical inventions—for the Shakers can be credited with a number of innovations from the needle with the eye in the middle (now adapted to sewing machines) to the circular saw. Under Mother Ann's motto, "Hands to work and heart to God," these societies outwardly lived lives of labor and peace. Within, however, the Spirit was leading these called-apart "families" in different directions.[7]

The Shakers

The Shaker community can be considered virtually a paradigm of the non-normative religious expression in America, for it represents most of the prevailing characteristics of excursus religion (except that it did not have much diffuse following, though it did have a widespread general cultural influence). We will examine the characteristics of Shakerism relevant to our purpose in terms of Joachim Wach's three forms of religious expression: the theoretical (myth and doctrine), the practical (worship and practices), and the sociological. These characteristics encapsulate basic features of excursus religion generally.

The basic teachings of Shakerism centered on belief in the dual nature of God, incorporating equally both male and female principles. As the former was incarnate in Jesus, so the latter was in Ann Lee. This second incarnation inaugurated a new age of the church in which men and women were absolutely equal (as they were in the communities), and in which humankind was raised much closer to the kingdom of heaven. Shaker elder Frederick Evans wrote:

> The old heavens and earth—united church and state—are fast passing away, dissolving with the fire of spiritual truth. Out of the material of the old, earthly, civil governments, a civil government will arise—is even now arising—in which right, not might, will predominate. It will be purely secular, a genuine republic. Men and women will be citizens. All citizens will be free-holders. They will inherit and possess the land by right of birth. War will cease with the end of the old monarchical, theological earth.... In the new earth sexuality will be used only for reproduction; eating for strength, not gluttony; drinking for thirst, not drunkenness. And property, being the product of honest toil—as those who will not work will not be allowed to eat—will be for the good of all, the young and the old.[8]

That may sound more like nineteenth-century radical socialism than the evangelical piety, but the Shakers, despite the ecstatic

pietism of their beginnings, were not fundamentalist sectaries, even
as their belief in the second feminine coming of Christ was scarcely
orthodox. Shaker thought was far more closely allied to the radical
movements of the day, both spiritual and political, than to ordinary
pietism.

We are told by one interpreter that the Shakers "do not generally
believe in the miraculous birth or divinity of Jesus, but consider
that he was divine in the sense of having power to rise above the
lower propensities," and it was the "Christ-Spirit" that was manifested in him and Ann Lee. We are told also "they accept the
Christian Bible allegorically and literally [sic], and include among
Bibles the Koran, Talmud, Zendavesta, and other books sacred to
various nations."[9] The progressivist idea of successive spiritual
waves spiraling ever upward, manifesting higher and higher levels
in early Christianity, Quakerism, and finally Shakerism in the New
World, itself so superior to the old, was popular: another Shaker
writer says, "Each spiritual wave, in accordance with the laws of
accelerated motion, rose above the preceding bearing the masses
higher up the altitudes of wisdom"[10]—this and much else in the
same vein suggests chiefly the mood of progressive optimism,
tinged with scientistic metaphor, widespread in the age of Emerson
and Whitman. Add to this the lively and sympathetic interest of
many Shakers in such social idealism as that of Robert Owen and in
such high-spirited radical movements as the Locofoco Party.

This liberal quality in a religion that had its origins in the
Manchester slum's Shaking Quakers is not surprising if we note that
ecstatic religion rooted in oppressed groups, like the more recent
Pentecostalism, is really very different from the dogmatic style of
fundamentalism with which it is often grouped. Pentecostalism is a
unique way of experiencing Christianity, whose experiential freshness has often led to doctrinal innovation. In 1916, for example,
the Assemblies of God church was split between trinitarians and
those who believed in the "oneness" doctrine, which held that
baptism should be in the name of Jesus only, who in himself
embraced the fullness of God, and who is the only God. But the
radicalism of such unusual beliefs, like Jesus' being the only God,
and like the Shakers' belief in the dual nature of divinity, may be
overlooked, since they do not follow the patterns of ordinary
liberalism.

Such beliefs are not obtained in ordinary ways either. While they may be founded on "searching the Scriptures," the ecstatic or pentecostalist divine does not read the Bible deductively or analytically. His Spirit-filled eclecticism may free-associate the most unlikely verses, moods, and current situations into strikingly unusual intuitive patterns of meaning. He moves with agility from luminous verse to subjective feeling or expression of repressed powers to contemporary application, unbounded by dogma.

An ecstatic like Mother Ann may, in one breath, say something which sounds like the simplest biblical literalism, and, in the next breath, something in the nature of a private revelation never before heard on land or sea. The Bible, in such cases, clearly functions as a symbol of that "otherness" for which the speaker is yearning, as well as a vehicle for words by which to internalize the luminous other. The operative factor in the "direct" revelations is not biblicism but inspiration, and inspiration of a sort consonant with the excursus religious experience.

Shaker doctrine was subjectively expansive, setting an inner construction of reality based on a perception of "otherness" derived from visionary experience against the social construction of reality of the "world's people." In this doctrine were symbols of the exaltation of the structurally weak—women, and also weak classes in society. The doctrine, like the practice, made transcendence immediately available through continuing revelation, coming in the successive waves it postulated. In this sense, even though it can be seen as an idealized Progressivism, historically conditioned by the Industrial revolution, there is an important anti-historicist theme in Shakerism, as in all utopianism and millennarianism. Its eschatology serves to take the communities of Believers out of ordinary time into participation only in the ideal time of transcendence and divine purpose, where Shakers observe as though from elsewhere the follies of the "world." This is characteristic of excursus religion, for it represents a way of moving out of the structure of society, history, and consciousness, through "cave" initiatory experience, to the erection of inner and symbolic bulwarks against outward structures.

As for Shaker worship, it was regarded as a bizarre yet unforgettable and strangely moving experience by all who saw or participated

in it. Nearly all day Sunday and several weekday evenings were given
over to worship, and parts were rehearsed previously. Worship included precision marches a drillmaster would admire. There were
rapid dances to music with odd and shifting African or Indian
rhythms, which sounded peculiar yet gripping to nineteenth-
century ears and anticipated something of the music of the twentieth century. Song after song was sung with the same effect of
mysterious, almost dangerous, beauty. Finally, long periods were
reserved for simple emotional outbursts of praise and "gifts" offered spontaneously, as in the more staid, conventional Quaker
meeting. Gifts of singing and movement were most common, but
there were also gifts of tongues—songs or speeches, sometimes transcribed, in an unknown tongue. Now and again personages, in the
1830s and after, from the spirit world gave messages, and sometimes Shakers received imaginary baskets of fruit and flowers from
the Other Side.

Belief in spirit visitations seemed to grow naturally out of the
primordial Shaker experience of visions and special revelations,
often very graphic in their depiction of paradise. This belief was
certainly enhanced by familiarity with the works of Swedenborg on
the part of informed Shakers like Frederick Evans. It reflects a sense
of the pluralism and complexity of the alternative spiritual world
which is an important feature of excursus religion, and which was to
influence directly its course in America.

The spirits who visited Shakers were mostly biblical characters or
departed Believers. We read such intriguing notes in Shaker memoirs as, "This evening Jacob of old and his twelve sons attended our
meeting," or it might have been Noah or one of the prophets or
Mother Ann or another of the founders. Most remarkable of all, a
record from North Union, Ohio, says, "In the year 1843, when the
Millerites were looking for Christ to come ... he was among the
Shakers spiritually ... He took up his abode at North Union for
the space of three months."[11]

It was in 1837 that a major Spiritualist movement swept through
the Shaker communities. It led to tremendous enthusiasm, uncon-
trolled emotionalism, and highly charged worship services. It is
surprising to realize that it was Spiritualism which led to renewal of
Shaker art and ritual; apparently legitimation by an enraptured

medium was required for the aesthetic side of the Shaker personality to show itself. With Spiritualism came the use of mediums for the testing and proving of members, but also a richer symbolic and aesthetic life. Early Shaker furniture and crafts (which now bring exorbitant prices in antique shops) had the austere beauty of that which is purely functional and honestly made, and whose lines are clean and true. Shaker creations bore no trace of ornament or fanciful twist.

Yet these same masters of plain workmanship, after the spiritual influx of the "Era of the Manifestations," produced a remarkable series of "inspirational drawings," swirling pen or pencil traceries or watercolors showing symbolic maps of heaven or opulent trees of life, all suggesting paradisal vision and the quintessence of aesthetic play. It is noteworthy that these pictures, considered to have sacred meaning within the community and rarely shown to outsiders, originated during the few years of greatest Spiritualist activity but reached their greatest florescence in the decades just after it. There was also, in this other world being opened to mortal eyes and ears, new songs such as that brought by "Mother Ann's little White Dove, November 5, 1843," or by "a little bird which was taken from a spiritual tree that was planted in our meeting room, March 9, 1844."[12]

The new wave also brought rites oddly reminiscent of "cosmic religion." Spring and autumn rituals that included processional singing through the fields and buildings for the blessing of the crops or "cleansing" were initiated. Even more intriguing was the establishment of "Holy Hills of Zion" on Shaker farms. Under inspiration, a hexagonal tract of land would be cleared and fenced, and a "Lord's Stone" bearing a secret inscription set in its center. Here with rapturous singing and dancing and frenzy, twice-yearly "love feasts" were held in the 1840s. They were wholly closed to outsiders, but were times not only of spiritual celebration and offering, but also of meeting with American Indian spirits and the spirit of Mother Ann, whose mysterious "second appearing" was believed to be taking place in the "Era of the Manifestations." Shaker Spiritualism led to many problems and, in the opinion of some, contributed heavily to the decline of the movement. Other nineteenth-century utopian ventures, such as the Rappite and

Owenite communities at New Harmony, Indiana, and the Oneida
community, were swept by Spiritualism in their final periods. But it
must be emphasized that mid-century Spiritualism, far from being
a "decadent" occultism, entwined itself with the optimistic rhetoric of democracy, progress, and the advent of new age. Thus,
Frederick Evans, as radical as his fellow-Spiritualist Robert Owen,
was quite capable of praising men like Voltaire and Thomas Paine
as precursors of the coming just society in which the tyrannies of
church and state would be abolished, yet in the same passage
contending that Spiritualism was a new influx designed to further
that work by converting, through its rappings, moving tables, and
so forth, the "scientific Materialists."[13] This last task, the Shakers
believed, must be accomplished before the perfect church and
social order, foreshadowed by the Shaker communities, can be
established here below.

Two fundamental characteristics of excursus religion are evident
in Shakerism. One is the reversion to sensorimotor expression. The
dances and raptures indicate that when the repressions of structural
society—the "world order"—are reversed, a great desire to feel and
express oneself physically can be released. This is all the more the
case when other symbols of reversal, such as the denial of sexuality,
are also operating.

The second characteristic is the influx of symbolic pluralism, in
the form of the spirits. This feature is open to debate, for it can also
be cogently argued that new religious movements are more monotheistic and more centered on single symbols—a single founder,
revelation, rite, place, time—than are established religions. Popular, folk, or even establishment religion inevitably has a certain
polycentric quality, symbolized by a diversity of spiritual powers of
whatever name: gods, spirits, angels, saints. Mother Lee's movement represents the kind of reaction against this multiverse that
often leads to intensive monotheistic or salvation religion focused
on single symbols. But the implicit pluralism of the ecstatic style
militated against this, as did the open liberalism of many Shakers.

But a more fundamental example of symbolic pluralism is connected with the third of the forms of religious expression, the
sociological. After Ann Lee, the basic symbol upon which Shakerism focused, the symbol upon which rested its separateness from

the diffuse environment, was the community itself. With the community in the unifying role, then, other facets of religion were free to exfoliate. Indeed, exfoliation was necessary. Once the doorway of community formation had been passed through, Shakerism was a separate world, loosening more and more ties with the old world, especially in its subjectivity and in that half of Shaker life of which outsiders saw but little, the worship. Here, on the other side of the door, a new world had to be constructed. This new world would have to be an expression of the ideal, the communitas (in Victor Turner's term), which the community symbolized. As a symbol of total communitas, of I-Thou relationships in which all structural barriers, whether of sex or of life and death, are broken down, it includes the spirits of the departed and all the powers of the Other Side. Finally, in the seasonal rites and the consecration of the Holy Hills, it completes the communitas symbolism to make a new, sacred cosmos opposite the world's order.

The sacredness of the community is demonstrated by its reversal of worldly patterns of relation between the sexes and by its members' distinctive dress and speech. As always, though, religious community is the total of a number of individual processes of transformation. To each individual in it the community will be the end of two transitions, first to a certain independence and ego enhancement when he or she makes the decision to join the community, perhaps at the cost of stormy parting from kindred, and then of an ego loss, possibly welcome after the great act of self-affirmation, as identity and personality sink into that of the new fellowship—which, in the case of a "total institution" like the Shakers', will construct virtually all of life.

Frederick Evans and Shakerism

Let us look at this passage in the light of the life of one distinguished Shaker, Frederick Evans. He was an agnostic as a young man, and a radical for most of his life, but lived more than sixty years in Shakerdom—"on the back side of this world," as he put it. Evans was born in England in 1808 to middle-class parents. He was resentful of school and church, and his happiest memories were of wandering the English fields observing the crops and animals and

talking with the common people. At the age of twelve he was
brought to America by his father and brother. The brother,
George, better educated than Frederick, became a publisher of
radical papers and tracts with titles like *The Workingman's Advocate* and *The Bible of Reason,* in which he urged land reform,
equality of men and women in all respects, and abolition of "chat-
tel slavery and wage slavery." George Evans was among the founders
of the Locofoco Party in 1835. Reading widely in philosophy and
the world religions, but favoring Thomas Paine and Voltaire, Frederick Evans was firmly antagonistic toward "all the wrongs perpe-
trated by Church and State," and believed in materialism and
"Socialistic-Communism." He determined with some friends to
form a community based on these principles.

But in 1830, while gathering information on utopian community
life, he visited the Shaker house in Mount Lebanon, New York.
Expecting a group of fanatics, he was much impressed by "the air
of candor and openness"—indeed, after a week, he called them a
society of infidels, the highest compliment, he says, of which he
was then capable. And his rationalistic antipathy toward past evils
wrought in the name of religion only endeared the Shakers to him
more, for they had suffered greatly under false and evil religion,
and saw in themselves the promise of a better day.

The Shakers prayed for him, and Frederick Evans experienced a
spiritual change. It was something so subtle, so strange, that he
could hardly put it into words. Only a few seemingly minor signs
were enough to suggest to this young confirmed materialist that
there was something more than what he had known.

"In one of the first meetings that I attended, I saw a brother
exercised in a slight way outwardly; and it gave me the first *evidence* that began to produce in me faith in the *spiritual.*" "One
night, soon after retiring, I heard a rustling sound, as of the wind of
a flock of doves flying through the window (which was closed)
towards my bed; and ... I believed it to be supernatural...."
After these tokens, he found he had within him powers, including
powers of reason, he had known not of. Visitations of angels came
to him at night for about three weeks, and with them a power that
moved through his body, starting at the feet. At the end of this,
he could not but believe, through his rationality itself, in the

existence of a spiritual world, in immortality, in the reality of communication between souls out of the body.

At the same time, he had a strange dream: there was a great fire, and a nude man of perfect physique standing by it. The man stepped into the fire, which encircled his whole body. Next the dreamer observed that, though of perfect beauty, the man was, as Evans delicately put it, "so organically changed that no fig-leaf covering was required."[14]

With such signs on both inner and outer planes, how could he resist the call to join this community at once radical, spiritual, and celibate? He easily convinced himself that the Shakers were the truest of all rationalists, able to defend their beliefs, for they were based on their own experience, and that better than anyone else they put the principles of socialism and reform into practice. So he went from the politics of alienated idealism to an order exemplifying the same ideals almost outside of this world, but in communion with the better realities of the spiritual world.

All of this indicates general characteristics of the sociological expression of excursus religion. The community, because it must bear the burden of being the salient symbol of the oneness and communitas the movement seeks, may be exceptionally close-knit at its core—even a total institution. At the same time, of course, it will have, as did the Shakers, circles of admirers (perhaps in other religions) outside its institution or in peripheral contact with it. It will also have, as did the Shakers, large numbers of "in and out" adherents, for it cannot offer structural inducements to compensate for loss of fervor or weariness with intensely spiritual life. Finally, it will be a community of "core" people who have, ideally, passed through an initiatory transformation of sufficient strength to make them secure in their membership.

The Shakers were far from the only expression of excursus religion and search for communitas to appear in the spiritually restless America of the first half of the nineteenth century. Without speaking of transcendentalist New England or the camp meetings of the frontiers, the spiritual children of Mother Ann Lee had many interesting colleagues in upstate New York, where they first settled. They provide an instructive pattern of variations of the excursus type.

Carl Carmer has pointed out that there stretches a belt scarcely twenty-five miles wide across New York state from east of Albany to Buffalo which invites the wonder of the religious world. He calls it, for the phenomena that took place in it in the first half of the last century, Spirit Way; it is also the "Burned Over District" where sparks lingering from revival fires lit the oil of stranger lamps.[15]

Here was the 1779 revival, an afterglow of the Great Awakening, and here was the Shakers' original Watervliet settlement which increased its numbers as a result of fall-out from that 1779 work of grace. In Spirit Way was also the last settlement of the Jemimakins and the last resting place of the Publick Universal Friend. Here, in 1824, the great evangelist Charles Finney began his ministry of hell-fire preaching and social concern; and here not long after, in 1827, Joseph Smith found the golden plates with their tales of fabulous spiritual adventure in early America. And here it was that, beginning about 1833, William Miller commenced preaching the end of the world and the second coming of Christ on October 22, 1843, and his followers gathered in white robes on hilltops and housetops to await the consummation of the ages and meet the Lord in the air. Out of this movement came indirectly the Seventh-Day Adventist Church.

Here it was also that the Oneida Community, founded by John Humphrey Noyes, flourished from about 1835 to 1885. It offers an interesting contrast to Shakerism. Noyes believed, as the Shakers did, in the present possibility of Christian perfection, and that perfection required that all beings must love each other equally well. But at Oneida this admirable goal did not eventuate in celibacy, but in a system known as Complex Marriage. Through it every member of the community was entitled to have sexual intercourse with any member of the opposite sex, though only under the supervision of a Central Committee. The committee generally approved requests when contraception through retention of the semen was to be observed, but exercised stricter control over the procreation of future members of the society, in an endeavor to practice scientific eugenics. The one great sin Oneidists were to avoid was "special love"—a particularized sexual or other attachment between two members at the expense of equal love for all. Oneida, then, reversed the ordinary "structural" pattern of social and family life and relations between the sexes as much as did the Shakers, but in the opposite direction.

Finally, it was within the purlieu of the Spirit Way that, in 1848, the Fox sisters heard the mysterious rappings which they and many others took to be messages from departed spirits. That event, whatever else may be said of it, was exaltation of the structurally weak, for Margaretta and Catherine Fox were female, aged 15 and 12 respectively, and of a poor rural family. From the Fox sisters stems the Spiritualist movement. But much else besides this episode must have gone into the explosive Spiritualist enthusiasm of the 1850s, for the match from Hydesville, New York, struck dry grass indeed.

Within a year or two of the "Rochester rappings," and the attendant newspaper stories, there were spirit circles in most major American cities. In some places, like the Western Reserve section of Ohio, it was said the regular churches were half deserted for the conventicles of the new craze. Tales of the Shaker experience account for part of this, and tales of Amerindian shamanism account for part. But a major factor was an intellectual tradition providing a structure all fit and ready to be filled by the influx of actual experience, such as the Fox sisters provided. To that tradition we must now turn. Rarely has the way been better prepared for an excursus experience than in this case.

Swedenborg

To understand non-normative spirituality in American history, one could do much worse than begin in eighteenth-century Sweden with the remarkable scientist and mystic Emanuel Swedenborg. Spiritualism, Theosophy, and "New Thought" have all been deeply influenced in their intellectual constructions by his ideas, or, rather, by his highly creative reworking and popularization of that platonic idealism tinged with theurgic mysticism which has ever been a fountainhead of emergent religions in the West. Both as source of ideology and as paradigmatic model of the modern man of initiatory experience, Swedenborg has influenced counterspirituality as has no one since Plato himself.

Born in 1688, Emanuel Swedenborg was the son of a Lutheran

court chaplain and bishop. His father was an outstanding man in his day; strictly pious, he was nonetheless a cleric of broad sympathies, an advocate of church union, and an enthusiastic reformer. Like his more famous son, the bishop had a lively awareness of invisible spiritual realities; he believed firmly in the ministrations of angels among men and declared that from time to time he conversed with his guardian angel.

Emanuel Swedenborg, however, turned to science before he turned to religion. He was appointed to the Swedish Board of Mines, and did significant work in metallurgy and mining engineering. In the manner of his time, though, Swedenborg was by no means a narrow specialist. He proposed a version of the nebular hypothesis of the origin of the solar system many years before Kant, Herschel, or Laplace; his work in anatomy, crystallography, and other fields was comparably in advance of its time, and had less effect on the development of European science than it deserved partly because Sweden was then a land well outside the mainstream of intellectual life.

His searching intellectual interests, though, did not exhaust themselves in such inquiries. He became interested in the problem of the nature of life, and the result was his book *The Economy of the Animal Kingdom* (1740–41; revised as *The Animal Kingdom*, 1744–45—the "animal" of the title is from the Latin *anima*, "soul," so refers to the realm of all things animated by life). In the book, Swedenborg posits that the soul, the principle which sets living matter apart from inert, cannot be located anatomically. The closest one can come to it is in life's energy, in the "tremulations" which characterize organic matter; but the real source of life seems to lie elsewhere. At this stage we may note the use of scientific information and method (at least as a start) in what is really a spiritual quest. But here, and in a book *On the Worship and Love of God*, which he wrote at about the same time, Swedenborg moved from science to reason, then to the use of analogy, and finally to careful intuition, saying the mind can *see* truth, as well as learn it by observation and reason.

All this is typical of the alternative tradition. It represents that side of mysticism which is really closer to science than to historical-revelation religions, or to the community orientation of the temple.

Like science, it views a universe of quiet and eternal truth which must be patiently explored, rather than Sinaitic revelation; and like science it has no high opinion of the verification validity of majority opinions. Indeed, modern science and esotericism have a common background in late medieval and renaissance Rosicrucianism and alchemy.

In 1744–45 Swedenborg passed through an initiation to a new manner of life. Because he kept a remarkable set of diaries of his dreams and visions, the process is not hidden. Late in 1744 the scientist experienced a series of dreams which induced profound humility, for they brought home his sinfulness and his tendency toward intellectual pride. Then, in April of 1745, came a decisive vision in which a man appeared to him while he was eating dinner in an inn; the man later introduced himself to the Swedish seer as none other than the Lord God himself. He told Swedenborg he should write as he was guided about the spiritual meaning of scripture; he was also shown, not for the last time, the realms of spirits, and heaven and hell.

Thereafter Swedenborg was eminently a resident of two worlds. Although he soon retired from his position with the Board of Mines, he traveled widely and was a respected member of the European intellectual community. At the same time, he frequented the other world, where he learned the state of departed spirits, and conversed with the shades of past worthies. Based on these experiences, he wrote heavy tomes of theology and scriptural exposition. So much were these two sides combined in the same man that it was not uncommon, in the midst of some learned conversation, for the Swede to raise eyebrows by commenting, "Yes, I just recently discussed that point with the Apostle Paul," or with Luther or Aristotle.

What were the basic ideas of Swedenborg's mature thought? First, he affirmed that spiritual realities are prior to material; everything visible that exists does so because of a spiritual force. The complexity of the visible world, then, owes to a complexity of the spiritual; things are what they are because of an elaborate system of correspondences between the two realms, an *analogia entis,* to which the key is the scripture understood allegorically. The pivot of the visible realm (as in his earlier nebular hypothesis) is the sun, which reflects God, who is the spiritual sun of the spiritual world. (This is a common motif of ancient and renaissance Neoplatonism.)

We may pause here to note a couple of themes already apparent in Swedenborgianism. First, there is the evident drive to put sacred things in "scientific" form. Swedenborg was looking for a language to express relations between the infinite and the finite which would have mathematical and scientific exactitude; this he found in correspondences. Second, there is evident a kind of rationalism or mentalism which makes thought or spirit, independent of space and time, prior to the visible universe and able ideally to know all places and times in all worlds. Both these themes are evident in his spiritual progeny, from William Blake and Ralph Waldo Emerson (both of whom are indebted to the Swedish sage) to Spiritualism, Theosophy, and "New Thought"—with its belief in healing and controlling through proper thinking, and its love of the word "science," as in "science of mind," "Christian Science," and the like.

As a theologian, Swedenborg denied the traditional Trinity but taught that the entirety of God—Father, Son, and Holy Spirit—was in Jesus Christ. The Father is the inmost principle of divinity within Jesus, the Son its manifestation, the Spirit its outward-working energy. (The doctrine can be compared with that of the "oneness" Pentecostalists.) The Spiritual Sun which is God for us shines wholly through the glorious clouds of the human flesh of Jesus Christ; it is to Jesus that Swedenborgian prayers are addressed.

Another unusual Swedenborgian doctrine concerns the Last Judgment—Swedenborg claimed that it had already taken place in 1757, and that he had been allowed to observe it as a representative of the world of humankind. But just as the coming of God in Jesus Christ was not done in exactly the way the Jews expected, so was the Judgment not exactly what conventional Christians expect—and still fruitlessly await, even as Jews still await the Messiah. Instead, the Judgment took place wholly in the spiritual realm, and cleared away certain evil forces to allow the Second Coming in the form of a powerful new spiritual influx. Evolution in the material world cannot come by natural causes, but can only be the result of a new spiritual arrangement and power input, since by the law of corres-

pondences all below reflects its invisible spiritual causes. Swedenborgians argue that those who reject Swedenborg's account of the
Judgment and spiritual Second Coming must be prepared to offer
some equally far-reaching explanation of the unprecedented
changes in human life and consciousness since around the middle
of the eighteenth century.[16]

Swedenborg's notions may at first sound odd. But it is not for
nothing that William Blake, who was greatly influenced by the
Swede, has joined Nietzsche as a patron saint of recent "radical"
and "death of God" theology. For all its queer kabbalism, Swedenborg's thought can be interpreted not only as a throwback to
Neoplatonism, but also as presenting a new "secular Christ" and a
new dispensation for "mankind come of age." In his vision of the
1757 Judgment, he saw emblazoned in heaven the words *nunc
licet,* "now it is pemitted."

There is a third side to Swedenborg's offering, and that is his
accounts of the worlds of departed spirits, based on his numerous
journeys to them. These realms, which directly reflect the thoughts
of their inmates, have an almost psychedelic splendor, yet are also
places of learning, for the sage tells us spirits advance from joy to
greater joy there as they grow in wisdom and love. Heaven and hell
both exist, but they are states rather than places, and spirits may
move from the latter to the former as they are able to abide it—but
those of certain temperaments tend to wish each other's company.
Higher spirits continually greet and guide novices on the other
shore. Whatever one makes of his visions, Swedenborg's spiritualism can be said to have a modern ring about it, in that it evidences a
"triumph of the therapeutic" over the forensic and punitive concepts of the afterlife that prevailed in his day.

But for all that, Swedenborg was also a man of his time. He may
have seen heavens of glowing luminosity, but he did not perceive
natural beauty in this world. Once, journeying from Florence to
Leghorn, he wrote, "the road was fine, *but* there were mountains
on both sides." His style of excursus religion had nothing to do
with the still-to-come romanticism and romantic concept of beauty;
it was, rather, intellectual theosophy indebted to Descartes and
Boehme, but not to aesthetics. In art Swedenborg favored only the
most direct realism.

All this must have some relationship to the prodigiousness of his

verbal expression, the photographic literalness of his presentation
of his visions, and his elaborate yet wooden dissertations on religious language and symbol, in which every important term in the
Bible is made to have a single, direct, symbolic meaning. The
meanings are often provocative, yet they suggest a certain fixation
on words found also in the writer's rejection of sacramentalism—on
the grounds that only motives, not acts, are saving—and his remarkable affirmation that the Word of God in the Bible *is* God.

Swedenborg was ascetic in many respects. He was virtually vegetarian and rarely drank; he was a lifelong celibate who vowed
not to marry after an unhappy love affair as a very young man. But
the dreams he records as coming just before his decisive vision in
1745 contain explicit sexual elements, and he was the author of a
justly celebrated book on marital love, in which he pointed out
that, in contrast to the spirit worlds, where marriages may be
consummated and completed, in this life so few marriages really
work out on a deep level that we have hardly any idea what
"conjugial love" really is or can be. His austere regimen and
volcanic inner life were apparently salutary for him; his tall, thin
frame crowned by snowy white hair was tough as a willow, and he
wrote his most lucid and important book, *The True Christian
Religion*, at the advanced age of eighty-three. Of him Jorge Luis
Borges wrote:

> Taller than the others, this man
> Walked among them, at a distance,
> Now and then calling the angels
> By their secret names. He would see
> That which earthly eyes do not see:
> The fierce geometry, the crystal
> Labyrinth of God and the sordid
> Milling of infernal delights.
> He knew that Glory and Hell too
> Are in your soul, with all their myths;
> He knew, like the Greek, that the days
> Of time are Eternity's mirrors.
> In dry Latin he went on listing
> The unconditional Last Things.[17]

Johnny Appleseed

John Humphrey Noyes, of the Oneida community, once said that
Spiritualism was Swedenborgianism Americanized. While this may

be an overstatement, it is far from completely false. Swedenborg's books, popular for their sensational material despite the heavy style and bulk, were well known in the new world.

The ideas contained in them had an important intellectual influence on Emerson; on William and Henry James through their Swedenborgian father; and on other transcendentalists, who, in turn, influenced the "New Thought" movement and Christian Science. The fundamental idea that moves through the latter two, that specific spiritual causes aligned to thought affect material events, was certainly transmitted to the founders of these popular American religions via the Swedish sage. Then there was, and is, the Swedenborgian church in America, properly called the Church of the New Jerusalem (called by its followers the "New Church"), which, though small, goes back to colonial times and has been influential. The church, and literature published by it, made millions vaguely aware of Swedenborgian ideas about spirits, the nature of the afterlife, and judgment. This, in turn, set the stage for Spiritualism, although one should hasten to add that the Swedenborgian Church strongly discourages mediumship, feeling in strong group and grid fashion that its founder's gifts were very exceptional and that the efforts of others to imitate his interworld communication are likely to end in trouble. In the turbulent and adventurous America of the last century, though, such warnings seemed hopelessly stodgy.

One link between Swedenborg and Spiritualism was John Chapman (1774–1845), better known as "Johnny Appleseed." An orphan raised in western Massachusetts, Chapman went to the frontier early, but not before he had come into contact with Swedenborgianism and been converted. Never married, vegetarian, friend of pioneer, Indian, and animal, he was something of a native American saint, and there grew up around him the folk legends suitable to a popular holy man. He carried his appleseed business as far west as Ohio, providing an item of greatest economic importance to the pioneers. But in the frontier cabins he left not only apples, but also Swedenborgian literature, especially chapters of Swedenborg's *Heaven and Hell*. "Good news fresh from heaven!" he called it.[18]

The more recondite elements of the Stockholm philosopher's

work may have eluded the frontiersman, but the graphic accounts of what happens to one's soul after death were his meat. His life was hard, brutal, and deprived. His labor was endless, hunger was never far from the door, and half his children might well die of disease. Many of his communities knew no higher entertainment than drunkenness and brawling. Yet at the same time there was in his breast a free-floating idealism—he was building a new land where the shackles of the old order would have no hold—and he yearned to know, with a definiteness that could withstand relentless Yankee skepticism, the state of his loved ones who had passed over before him.

The new dispensationalism, the gutsy heterodoxy, and the concrete spiritualism of the Swedenborgian tracts left by Johnny Appleseed had their appeal for the pioneers. The New Church as an institution did not particularly flourish on the frontier, but many a lonely evening must have been spent around cabin fires talking about whether it was true that souls on the other side gather in communities according to temperament, or whether truly conjugal husbands and wives are reunited for eternity. When the new Spiritualism with its mediumship and churches came along in the 1850s, it is no wonder that the areas Johnny Appleseed had worked most assiduously, such as the Western Reserve region of Ohio, turned eagerly, if temporarily, to the new faith, leaving conventional churches half empty.

Mesmerism

Another European influence joined with Swedenborgianism in fermenting the yeasty American brew that led to Spiritualism. That was the teaching and work of Franz Anton Mesmer (1734–1815), the father of modern "Mesmerism" or hypnotism. Mesmerism was concerned with psychosomatic medicine and psychotherapy, and also with a more speculative philosophy about "animal magnetism," which sought to interpret Mesmer's uncanny-seeming discoveries. Underlying these teachings was Mesmer's doctrine of a subtle, universal substance which gives life and vitality; sickness is due to its loss or imbalance. At first Mesmer sought to regulate its influx by magnets, but later discovered that it could be transmitted by persons even better through a process called "animal magnetism." The techniques varied; there was stroking, suggestion, and the famous seancelike sessions in which several patients sat around a vat of dilute sulfuric acid while holding hands or iron bars in contact with the chemical. In any case, the treatment was easily capable of producing hypnotic trance-states which could measurably aid in a cure if the ailment was psychosomatic or psychiatric.

It was a short step for the next generation of savants to take matters further in two directions: scientists like Braid, Charcot, and Freud developed from Mesmer's work, and from other sources, medical hypnosis and psychoanalytic ideas of the unconscious; those of more occult bent sought out the cosmically cognitive meaning of the mesmeric state and the paranormal potential of the powers involved in Mesmerism.

Mesmer did nothing to discourage the second option. In his *Memoir* of 1799, he presents as scientific fact the power of animal magnetism to awaken latent powers that enable people to penetrate universal mysteries, to experience extrasensory perception and precognition, and to heal. He states that it releases an inner sense and power, available also in somnambulism, to which all time and space is one; with it one may see past, present, and future, and to it the secrets of dreams, diagnosis, and philosophy are unveiled. Mesmer felt that much of the work of sibyls, oracles, alchemists, mystics, and occultists of the past was valid, though for reasons that had previously not been understood. It was on this basis that Madame Blavatsky later praised Mesmer enthusiastically, calling Mesmerism the most important branch of magic, and, indeed, the true base of what is called magical or miraculous.[19]

This is the Mesmerism which, especially as it was a subject of experimentation by all sorts of enthusiasts in the New World with more curiosity than caution, helped turn Swedenborgian doctrine and Transcendental mysticism into Spiritualism and Theosophy.

New England Transcendentalism

Another movement which, in convergence with Swedenborgianism and Mesmerism, had a far-reaching impact on the American emergent spiritual tradition and helped effect the thorough American-

ization of those imports was New England Transcendentalism. This
name is primarily associated with a group of thinkers who lived in
and around Boston in the 1830s and 1840s, including Ralph Waldo
Emerson, Amos Bronson Alcott, Orestes Brownson, James Freeman
Clarke, and Henry Thoreau. They contributed substantially to the
appearance of later movements such as Spiritualism, Theosophy,
and Western Zen in several ways: through their establishment of an
American style of contemplative and mystical thought rooted in
metaphysics of the Platonic, Swedenborgian, and Indic sort; through
their popularization of Eastern religious philosophy; through their
example—in this respect Thoreau at Walden and the Brook Farm
communal experiment were especially significant—of an American idealistic "drop-out" life-style which was intellectually and
socially an important statement.

Catherine L. Albanese has shown in a provocative study that the
basic idea of the Transcendentalists was the ancient concept of
correspondences, derived partly from Neoplatonism through Swedenborg.[20] (The latter's works were very widely read and discussed
in American intellectual circles in the 1830s.) The universe was
structurally identical with the human form, and its meaning was
embedded, had one eyes to see, in every segment of it. All this
meant that the cosmos was harmonious and fundamentally benign.
Transcendentalism has evolved from Calvinism through Unitari-
anism, laying aside the sterner doctrines of the older orthodoxies,
but preserving a sense of intrinsic laws in the universe and the
Puritan's moral earnestness in a far more open and impersonal
cosmos. It was an ideology for the intellectual elect of the era of
Jacksonian democracy, of the rapid expansion of the frontier, of
seemingly unlimited opportunity, and of the worldwide contacts
effected by Yankee traders.

But in a deeper sense Transcendentalism was conservative, even
as was Gnosticism and European occultism before it, and Spiritualism, Theosophy, and Western Zen subsequently. Like them it
sought, in a remoter past than the immediate, intellectual supports
for understanding what was palpably a new day of the Spirit. To
interpret, and find spiritual ways of living with, the new fact which
was democratic and progressive America—an America intoxicated
with the ideas of change, expansion, and a brighter tomorrow—

Transcendentalists looked not to Calvinism, Lockeanism, Deism, the nation's direct intellectual antecedents. It searched out instead subtler and more ancient doctrines which could give even wider meaning to the new experience: the divine in all persons, the universe in all its parts, timeless motifs enacted in the historical dramas of the present, intuition rather than reason the tool for confronting events and key to the universe, contemplative retirement the mainspring of truly significant action.

For example, Albanese speaks of the "kinetic revolution" in Transcendentalist thought. Its glorification of movement and change obviously reflects the current frontier situation, but motion typically becomes for those thinkers a universal absolute. Emerson repeatedly speaks of rest as decay, of motion as a form of perfection, of challenges to leave the shore and plunge into the Unlimited and the Immensities. But this absolutizing of movement itself as a basically spiritual, cosmic thing obviates the concrete historical importance of particular movement, such as the westward expansion of the frontier. As historians the Transcendentalists were, in fact, antihistorians: for them history had a unique meaning for each person, as a project for learning one's own cosmic identity; on the other hand, a person could learn all history of true significance for himself from out of the depths of his own consciousness.

The genuine heirs of the Transcendentalist movement, then, were not the practical-minded pioneers, but those for whom movement itself was a spiritual symbol, a token of liminality and transcendence. Those were travelers in the excursus tradition who literally and significantly acted it out, like Mother Ann and The Publick Universal Friend and "Johnny Appleseed," and, as we shall see, the early Theosophists en route to India, and the later Zen "Beats" going "on the road" or living the life of "Dharma Bums."

New England Transcendentalism was not explicitly religious. Thoreau said he would rather hear cowbells than church bells on Sunday morning. But it has nourished religions and quasi-religions. More than that, one does not hesitate to say that, because of the impeccable intellectual credentials of its principal thinkers, it has done more than any other force to legitimate in America the whole bundle of alternative spiritualities which have come to these shores, and to present paradigms for their domestication.

Andrew Jackson Davis

An important source for Spiritualist thought was Andrew Jackson Davis (1826–1910), the "Poughkeepsie seer," a prolific writer whose work was supposed to have been initiated in part by the shade of Swedenborg. Davis is a classic example of a person of indifferent background who, after a remarkable initiatory experience, found a place for himself in the emergent tradition and became a mouthpiece for radical religion.

Davis's parents were uneducated and poor; his father was a coarse, hard-drinking drifter who continually berated his son for the boy's lack of "manliness." Despite a miserable childhood, Davis did manage to learn some letters at a Lancastrian school. At sixteen, he left home to become apprenticed to the keeper of a shoe shop in Poughkeepsie, New York.

In the 1840's, Mesmerism and Swedenborgianism were both popular in America; they were widely discussed and written about, and the former was widely practiced by amateurs and professionals alike. Davis, while still in his teens, combined the two. In Poughkeepsie he fell in with a circle which practiced Mesmerism, and was reportedly an adept study, quickly developing remarkable powers of clairvoyance, medical diagnosis, and mystic vision while in hypnotic trance. Soon he left the shoe shop to support himself as a trance healer and stage hypnotist.

A few months after he began the Mesmerism experiments, when he was seventeen, came Davis's major mystical experiences. This was also shortly after his mother, to whom he had been closer than to anyone else, had been delivered from her hard lot by death. Davis was awakened one night by his mother's voice, and he went downstairs. Then, apparently in astral travel, he journeyed through icy mountains and over deep valleys. He saw a flock of sheep in great confusion; he helped the shepherd to bring them into order. Then three figures appeared to him with messages.

First an old Quaker presented a scroll bearing the cryptic words:

As they were, so they are
As they are, so they will be!

Then appeared the celebrated physician of antiquity, Galen, who gave Davis a marvelous staff of healing. Next appeared the tall, cerebral figure of Swedenborg, who pronounced Davis "an appropriate vessel for the influx and perception of truth and wisdom." Davis sought to leave and return to Poughkeepsie, and at the last minute Galen withheld the staff, saying that before he took it the novice would have to learn to keep an even mind.

But a few days later, after a long Mesmeric session, Davis retired with an odd feeling he had forgotten or lost something. Suddenly in his dark room he saw glowing the rod of Galen and a translucent sheet with these words emblazoned on it: "BEHOLD! Here is thy Magic Staff. Under all circumstances Keep an Even Mind. Take it, Try it, Walk with it, Talk with it, Lean on it, Believe on it Forever." From then on this mysterious cane made up of diamond segments, visible only to mystic eyes, was the adept's joy and reliance.[22]

Shortly after his mystical experiences, Davis announced that he would begin dictating out of trance a series of revelations on philosophical matters. His amanuensis was a Universalist minister named William Fishbough. (It should be noted in passing that clergymen of this denomination were commonly involved in early Spiritualism.) The seances at which these deliverances were given were usually attended by a small circle, which from time to time included Edgar Allan Poe, the Fourierist Albert Brisbane, and Thomas Lake Harris, of whom more later.

The result of these trance revelations was Davis's great work, *The Principles of Nature, Her Divine Revelation and a Voice to Mankind*, published in 1847. Despite its nearly 800 pages, this book spoken by an author of only twenty years and claiming divine inspiration created a sensation. It covers many subjects, including the creation of the world from "liquid fire," the origin of the solar system, and the geological history of the earth. It presents a summary of ancient history from a deistic perspective, showing no special favor to Christianity. There are favorable discussions of Swedenborg and Charles Fourier. Accounts of the spiritual constitution of humankind and of the seven spiritual worlds around earth show how the soul evolves after death. Finally comes a denunciation of the ills of society, including those of clergymen, and an appeal for the creation of a Fourierist utopia.

The book, widely read between 1847 and 1876, was praised and attacked vociferously. The questions of its authenticity as revela-

tion, and of how so young a man of such unprepossessing background came by such learning, was discussed avidly then as later.
That complicated issue cannot be resolved here. While there is little
that is truly original in the work, and long passages are no more
than paraphrases of Robert Chambers's *Vestiges of Creation,* of
Swedenborg, and of Fourierist writings; and while the scribe Fishbough was (as his articles in various journals indicate), a man of
some learning who could have contributed more than he allowed to
the project, there is a certain quality to the *Divine Revelations*
which is fresh and which sets the tone of early Spiritualism. For
Davis, as his many subsequent books reveal, was a writer of vigor
and intelligence, despite a tendency to prolixity. What strikes one
most forcefully in the *Divine Revelations* is the unbounded optimism, the exuberant belief in progress in both this world and the
next, the radical and youthful confidence that history is turning
under spiritual influx and that the evils of the past are, for the most
part, behind us—an enthusiasm in tune with the mood of the
young nation at that juncture, and met already among the Shakers.
But Davis shared neither the Shakers' Christian piety (to the end of
his long life, he denied that Spiritualism or he himself were Christian), nor Swedenborg's Age of Reason restraint; his was a romantic
and free futurism and faith in worlds without end.

Davis's own future was fabulous enough. The year following
the publication of his book, the handsome young celebrity had
—following her sensational divorce scandal—married Catherine
DeWolfe, a lady twenty years older than he and of very considerable wealth. (The father of his bride, said to have once been the
second richest man in the country, had made his fortune as a slave
dealer and privateer, a matter which gave the daughter some spiritual uneasiness.) The union of the democratic idealist and the child
of fortune was not to last long, however, for she was called to a
higher sphere in only five years. The widower's inheritance was long
tied up in litigation and, when finally released, soon lost in unfortunate business ventures.

The career of Andrew Jackson Davis can be compared to that of
his contemporary, the incredible D. D. Home (1833–86). Born in
Scotland, Home was raised in America. Like Davis, he enjoyed his
major psychic opening at seventeen, a few months after the death

of his mother, when he heard her voice calling to him from the Other Shore. He caused a sensation in New England and New York in the fifties with his "physical mediumship" and spirit materializations. He went to Europe, where his charm and tales of the remarkable phenomena that attended him gained him entry into the highest circles. He was a favorite of the French Emperor and his glittering court; in England he was the subject of a sensational extortion trial involving a rich and dotty elderly lady who had given him a great amount of money; in Russia he managed to marry successively not one but two ladies of rank and riches, and the czar himself stood as godfather to one of his children. His amazing feats of levitation, of moving tables by non-physical means, of evoking spirit hands and music and the like, were much studied and never proven fraudulent.[22]

The Spiritualist Movement

Swedenborgianism, spread by Johnny Appleseed and others less colorful, rumors of strange goings-on within Shakerdom, and Andrew Jackson Davis's celebrated book—all were kindling for the fire of Spiritualism and helped to make it not just a book-philosophy or an esoteric experience reserved for the few but a new adventure for the masses. It needed only a spark, a paradigmatic event demonstrating that, for anyone, however humble, the spirit world was real; and that even now, in our day, that world was contacting us. The spark was provided by the "Rochester rappings." The Fox sisters, who heard the rappings, were hardly mighty savants like the Swede, nor even native initiates like Davis and Home, but plain farmgirls of no great education or wit; precisely because of that, when they began communicating with some entity in their house through taps not unlike Morse Code and publicized the phenomena, they joined the number of those through whom emergent religion has surfaced into popular culture.

Spiritualism was, in fact, more of a popular culture movement than a religious movement in a strictly ecclesiastical sense; like excursus religion generally, it avoided direct competition with structural institutions by being either looser or tighter than they, and usually looser. It was not until the last quarter of the century

that Spiritualist churches and national denominations were formed;
then as now, these were not overly successful and accounted for only
a fraction of the diffuse public interest in mediumship and other
Spiritualist phenomena. During the 1850s, when Spiritualist enthusiasm reached its high point, the movement was a disorganized
but effervescent world of "home circles" practicing amateur
mediumship and table-tilting, of famous lecturers and performers,
of numerous Spiritualist books and magazines. Sensational stories
in the newspapers of Spiritualist scandal and success whetted the
public appetite for more. Experimental communal groups, like
Brook Farm, Hopedale, Ceresco, and New Harmony, as well as new
Spiritualist utopias like Mountain Cove and Kiantone, followed the
Shakers in reporting Spiritualist phenomena—a social process also
noted in many of the experimental communes of the 1960s, as
groups grew more and more into themselves as total institutions
separate from ordinary society.

Typical of American Spiritualism in the 1850s was the "Spirit
Room" of the Koons family in their remote farm in southeast
Ohio. In 1852 the head of the household, Jonathan Koons, an
erstwhile freethinker, investigated Spiritualism and found himself
an effective medium. The Spirit Room, actually a detached log
cabin, was built according to spirit specifications, and was inhabited
by a band of one hundred sixty-five high spirits, who manifested
themselves in seances attracting neighbors from miles around and,
in time, visitors from distant states. Not only did this merry band
deliver messages glibly through two tin horns, but would take up
drums, fiddles, horns, and other instruments in the darkened room
to produce a spiritual shivaree audible for more than a mile. The
seance would culminate in the appearance of a luminous spirit hand,
detached at the wrist, which would rapidly write messages on sheets
of paper. The experience of transcendence in American Spiritualism
was by no means always solemn; once when a curious investigator
placed his face too close to the writing spirit-hand, the revenant
mischievously poked his nose with the dull end of the pencil.[23]

We can note several points about Spiritualism as emergent religion. First, its essential conceptual ideology was hardly new in the
pivotal year 1848 when the Fox girls heard the rappings, but can be
traced back in an almost infinite regress to Davis, Swedenborg,

renaissance and ancient Neoplatonism, and finally, no doubt, to
archaic shamanism. It is important to note that 1848 really was of
little significance to its *conceptual* evolution, but only to its rise and
decline in a specific social manifestation.

Second, we may note that what lifts this tradition out of conceptual philosophy is the appearance of phenomena, chiefly initiatory,
in the shamanistic pattern, as evidenced by the call and careers of
men like Swedenborg, Davis, and Home. These men recall the
magus of antiquity and suggest the revival of paradigmatically
shamanistic careers, complete with spiritual call, inner initiation,
marvelous flight, journeys to and commerce with other worlds.

Third, through a "structurally weak" person and situation is
achieved a moment of symbolic transcendence into the cosmos of
the emerging world view—as, for example, in the Fox sisters'
experience. The structural weakness and noncompetitive character
of the new experience legitimates it as a form of excursus for
everyone.

Fourth, we may see that Spiritualism does not form a single
monolithic ecclesiastical structure, but a diversity of institutions,
some very diffuse and some total—though still ephemeral. Related
to this is Spiritualism's connection with progressive idealism; both
as an experience close to entertainment, and as a liberal eschatology, Spiritualism had no strong need for institutionalization.
This suited well its character as the following of charismatic, shamanistic figures, and as the interpretation of intense and visionary
but irregular subjective experiences—not to mention the ample
temptations to fraud and egomania which attempts to routinize
Spiritualism always afford.

Transformations of Spiritualism

As one would expect of a movement of this sort, Spiritualism went
through several stages of development, or more accurately, produced individuals who, initially awakened to commerce with other
worlds through Spiritualism, went on to alternative means of realizing spiritual reality and the hope of a new spiritual age. Whitney
Cross has noted that few remained active Spiritualists for very long,
but that Spiritualism was frequently a step on the road to some

form of religious modernism. Spiritualism's scientific language, social awareness, criticism of the Bible and the historical churches, and its speculative mood "must have tended to obliterate any remnants of literal-mindedness and orthodoxy embedded in its converts."[24]

A good example would be Thomas Lake Harris (1823-1906). Harris was a man of elaborate inner life who started his career as a Universalist minister, and who was finally to achieve a measure of fame as the founder and ruler of the Fountain Grove utopian community in California. He was close to Andrew Jackson Davis in the 1840s, around the time of the production of the *Divine Revelations,* and was much under the medium's influence. But he broke with Davis, and thereafter became a Swedenborgian minister. At the same time, his spiritual life was becoming tumultous; he was preoccupied with his inner states and from time to time would fall into deep and uncontrollable trances.

In 1854 Harris had a mystical experience, obviously inspired partly by Swedenborgianism and Spiritualism, of a "counterpartal marriage" to a "Queen Lily of the Conjugial Angels." (The spelling "conjugial" is Swedenborgian.) He believed that a spiritual being of the opposite sex is "counterpart" to each human, and that marriage between the two is basic to the fulfillment of spiritual life. His mystical nuptials were, in fact, a second birth which gave him a new name and a new mission; he declared it was the first of seven steps to his attainment of immortality and deity. After the event, he was freed of his interior obsessions and pathological trances and lived in communion and "conjugial bliss" with his spirit-bride in his nightly dreams; in sleep he was in heaven. This dual life continued the rest of his days; even after he was married to a wife of flesh he remained celibate, having sexual relations only with the spiritual consort, whose prior rights the earthly partner was willing to concede. The other world was rich and alive for Harris; he was also able to see the fairies or "fays" who animated natural objects and even the human body. In this awareness he anticipated both Theosophy and an aspect of the "New-Pagan" movements of the twentieth century.

It was sexual mysticism that most stirred Harris, however. Like the Shakers and the kabbala, he taught that the divine has two coequal sides: the Eternal Masculine was divine love, the Eternal Feminine was divine truth, and their union, reflected in human and spiritual conjugial love, was divine ability. Sex possessed him even in his most spiritual moments. Affirming the spiritual significance of the religions of India and elsewhere, he said that the cross as a symbol of God was a lingam lifted to heaven.

His ideas became too heretical for the Swedenborgians, and he left that denomination to make his own way in several utopian communities, leading up to Fountain Grove. At Mountain Cove he was one of the directing mediums. In the end he came to certain ideas paralleling Theosophy: esoteric masters, a spirit world or "luminous kingdom," a sevenfold spiritual path, and a set of cycles or "rounds" of human spiritual evolution. He believed also in a subtle spiritual body which could be energized by practice involving breath and massage—these ideas, doubtless related to the sexual concern, show a characteristic entry into proximity sensory awareness, as does sexual mysticism itself.[25]

Harris was also a trance poet who delivered a vast amount of visionary and didactic verse, metered and rhymed, while in a sleeplike state. While not of the caliber of the work of his main spirit controls in this sphere, Petrarch and Dante, considered as extemporaneous verse it is impressive. Howard Kerr has compared the clairvoyant literary production of people like Harris and Davis to Walt Whitman's "self-dramatization as inspired bard unconstrained by barriers of space or time."[26]

Thus we find Harris, beginning in Spiritualism and Swedenborgianism, finding through it (as did the Shakers) a secondary world which offered sexual sublimation, a wellspring of creativity, a return to proximity senses, an effervescence which enhanced the life of withdrawal communities by placing them, as it were, in an alternative cosmos, and finally (as did the Theosophists and others) finding that alternative cosmos underlying our world, whose wise powers and evolutions explain this tangible sphere.

That was also to be the journey of another man, Henry Steel Olcott. In the early 1870s, the lonely farm of the Eddy brothers in Vermont was a spiritualist magnet comparable, in that respect, to the Koons farm twenty years earlier. Olcott, a lawyer and sometime writer for the *New York Daily Graphic,* visited the scene to write a series of articles, later published as a book, *People from the Other World*. It bespeaks the declining interest in Spiritualism that this fascinating book did not sell well, but, nonetheless, it is important in the story of excursus spirituality in America, for it is not only very revealing of the nineteenth-century Spiritualist experience, with its vivid illustrations of apparitions, but also marks a certain juncture.

Many of the Eddy manifestations were Native American spirits with names like Honto, Daybreak, and Santum; this underscores the importance of the American Indian theme in Spiritualism. "Indian guides" were and are common; descriptions of Native American shamanistic performances, reported by writers like Henry Schoolcraft and William Howitt, were widely read in the days of early Spiritualism, and there was interest in contemporary Native Americans of psychic power like the "Shawnee Prophet" (1768–1837), brother of Chief Tecumseh and a legendary seer. Olcott tells us also of a medium named Elizabeth Compton, of Havana, New York, whose "maternal grandmother, an Indian squaw, was brought up among the whites, but was not unfamiliar with the rude sorceries that prevailed among her people."[27]

What was of most significance about the Eddy phenomena, though, was its role in the final transformation of a part of what was awakened by Spiritualism from American Indians to India. For it was at the Eddy home that Henry Steel Olcott met the enigmatic Madame Blavatsky.

5

Colonel Olcott and Madame Blavatsky Journey to the East

A Fateful Meeting

The history of emergent spirituality is replete with obscure and seemingly happenstance events which have been the conduits through which one cycle of its expression has merged into another. Were these moments not perceived and understood, the emergent tradition would appear not as a tradition, but as isolated excursi. Consider, for example, Andrew Jackson Davis's meeting a group of Mesmerists; young Alan Watts's discovery of a certain bookstore in London which, through a Theosophist, led to Eastern contacts; Jack Kerouac's argument with Neal Cassady about reincarnation; and, perhaps most striking of all, the meeting of Henry Steel Olcott and Helena Blavatsky at a farmhouse near Chittenden, Vermont, where manifestations of the frontier Spiritualist genre were occurring. It is quite possible, however, that this was not a chance meeting, that Blavatsky had traveled to Vermont with the express purpose of encountering Olcott, a lawyer and writer, whose newspaper stories on Spiritualism had attracted attention in New York.

The meeting was on September 17, 1874, after dinner. Olcott had been struck by the fascinating appearance of this Russian woman, with her massive face and scarlet Garibaldian blouse, and when she went outside to roll herself a cigarette, he offered, in the French he had heard her speaking with a companion, to light it for her.

From that moment on Olcott found himself brought into a new world of deeper and deeper wonder. After her arrival at Chittenden, the American Indian guides and innocent little girl spirits who

had manifested themselves there were supplemented by exotic
figures from Russia and Caucasia, regions presumably unfamiliar to
any present except the mysterious madame. These visitants were the
forerunners of a spiritual excursus which would make Spiritualism
itself look tame and provincial.

When Olcott and Blavatsky renewed their acquaintance shortly
afterward in New York, the American was privileged to observe
further examples of his friend's power, from the materialization of
a white butterfly to the production of "real" apparitions at the
seance of a fraudulent medium—much to the latter's fright! As
time went on, Blavatsky gradually introduced Olcott to new concepts about spiritualism and the "phenomena" as well. He learned
that actual, discrete spirits were not usually involved, but instead
"elementals," which the strange lady could control by her "mayavic" power, that is, her ability to manipulate the realm of appearances and the finite entities ensnared in it. She was an adept of
"Eastern Spiritualism" or "Brahma Vidya," which is based on a
deeper science than the crude American Spiritualism and produces
its works through something similar to Mesmerism.

His attention directed to the East, Olcott learned still more: that
there exists an Occult Brotherhood of Eastern Adepts, who live and
operate on both this and higher, more invisible, planes, and who
give instruction to elect disciples on the earthly plane. The "East"
to which they pertain seems almost more a state of mind than a
geographical direction, for Masters are found at the hearts of all
ancient cultures, from the Greek and Egyptian to the Japanese and
the Central American Mayan. However, as we shall see, those
concerned with these cultures came to be most interested in India,
and beyond it, mysterious Tibet. Olcott, under Madame Blavatsky's guidance, started as a student of the African (Egyptian)
Section of the Occult Brotherhood, but was later transferred to the
Indian.

It is with that transfer and with its manifestation, so to speak, in
the journey of Olcott and Blavatsky to India in 1879 that we shall
focus our attention in this chapter. We shall examine the Theosophical movement in America by taking just one facet of that story
and exploring it in some depth. That facet will be the emergence of
the East as a powerful symbol of an alternative spiritual center, a

development not limited to Theosophy but early and paradig-matically expressed in it, and of immense consequence for the subsequent development of excursus religion.

To understand fully the Theosophical founders' journey to India, though, requires examining the meaning of their lives in more detail both before and after the meeting at Chittenden. We shall do that first in terms of the categories of liminality and communitas suggested by Victor Turner. For if liminality burgeoning into com-munitas was manifest as they landed on the Bombay dock, as we shall see, the seeds which there came to full flower must have been planted long before.

Liminality and the Theosophical Twins

In chapter 2, we noted that liminality is fundamentally a process state, a state of transition. Literally or figuratively, one has to travel out of what is familiar, indeed, from all landmarks whatsoever, in order to get somewhere new. But for some, as we have seen, transition can become a permanent state, and liminality a perma-nent vocation. This is the classic role of the monk, the wandering friar, holy man, or shaman—or the clown, court jester, or hobo. The sacred misfit is often a harbinger of cleavage in the social fabric and of a reversal of the values of ordinary structures. This role is often reified by such signs as continual wandering or pilgrimage, celibacy or other non-ordinary sexual and family arrangements, living with economic instability, even skirting the edge of madness. In recompense, the permanently liminal person seems to be able to peer further into invisible reality than those circumscribed by struc-ture—as does the initiate in his night of transition. (Theosophy sees life as a series of initiations, and the permanently liminal state of Blavatsky and Olcott seems to express this value to an intense degree.) Thus the ''misfit'' friar, shaman, or clown manifests sym-bolically the continuing possibility of liminality, even as do festival recapitulations of return to chaos and renewal for those who only enter liminality periodically and ritually.

Olcott and Blavatsky, the ''Theosophical Twins'' as Olcott liked to call them, richly exemplified this liminal wandering vocation in their voyage to India. All her life, Helena Petrovna Blavatsky

(1831–91) personified the vocation of permanently dwelling in or
near liminality. With her exotic accent, hints of an adventurous
past, imported cigarettes, rough-edged tongue, amazing psychic
phenomena, and aura of being an envoy of mysterious powers, she
was always a wanderer, a colorful misfit in whatever society she
found herself. She spoke, like a magus of old, of having received
occult initiations in the East and of wandering to arcane shrines of
wisdom. She originally came to America in 1873, she said, because
it was the birthplace of Spiritualism, and she was drawn to it as "a
Mohammedan approaching the birthplace of his prophet." She
confessed in 1874 that, "For the sake of Spiritualism I have left my
home, an easy life amongst a civilized society, and have become a
wanderer upon the face of this earth."[1] As we have seen, though,
behind her interest in Spiritualism lay an interest in deeper mysteries and in the East. Olcott shared this interest, and to him fell the
task of creating in Theosophy new forms of social structure to
mediate the wisdom of the other world he had touched.

Both Blavatsky and Olcott had backgrounds of status within the
established social structure, as different as those backgrounds were.
The Russian lady was born the daughter of an officer and grand-
daughter of a provincial governor of the Czar. Henry Steel Olcott
was born of successful American farmers and rose to reasonable
success and recognition in several fields. Neither of the future
Theosophists, however, found the status satisfactory.

Helena Blavatsky

Helena, who grew up on vast estates near the Volga, was a difficult
and unmanageable child. She would hide for hours, or tell long
and fantastic stories about the lives and past lives of the mounted
animals in her grandfather's museum. As an adolescent she once
deliberately scalded her foot in boiling water so she would not have
to go to a viceroy's ball. At sixteen she married N. V. Blavatsky, a
widower in his forties, who served as vice-governor of Erivan in
Armenia. Helena made her typically impulsive decision and on the
rebound from a disappointed infatuation, apparently in response to
taunts that no man would have such an odd young lady.

But the ill-matched couple did not stay together for long. The future chronicler of the cosmic pilgrim left Russia and began her restless wanderings. Differing accounts are given of these years, but it is evident that they included the development of exceptional psychic and mediumistic skills and a corresponding fascination with occult lore and the wonder-workers of the earth. Blavatsky's way of life undoubtedly reflected how she felt about herself: marginal to normative society, without important external bonds, but possessed of a deeply felt and complex subjectivity.

Somehow during this time the grip of ordinary life grew weaker and weaker, and the gates of access to deeper alternative realities wider. It was a process comparable to that through which Swedenborg was vouchsafed his visions of the Other Side, the Shakers discovered their spirit paradises, and Thomas Lake Harris found his way to the bower of his immortal bride. In the case of Madame Blavatsky, the steps of the process are less clear, the end result possibly even more self-transformative. Perhaps it began in 1851, after the break-up of her marriage, when her father took her to London, where she reported seeing a princely, turbaned man she said would ever after be her Master. He was with a delegation of Indian and Nepali princes in the British capital at the time.

Except for the period between 1858 and 1864, when she was back in Russia with her family and, for a time, with her husband, amazing her social circle with psychic phenomena, not much is known of her life between 1851 and 1871.

These years were certainly spent in restless travel. She was apparently with Garibaldi's forces at the battle of Mentana in 1867. But according to her account, she traveled further afield, crossing America in a covered wagon, and finally reached India and Tibet, where she received initiations from her Masters.

The memoirs of her cousin, Count S. Y. Witte (1849–1915), distinguished statesman and prime minister of Russia 1905–6, and other accounts, paint rather a different picture of those years. They tell of her wandering about Europe with an opera singer, impulsively dabbling in radicalism, and engaging in such varied enterprises as riding horses in a Turkish circus and managing the Servian royal choir. But Witte's testimony is weakened by the fact that it was written more than fifty years after events that would have occurred when he was only a child or teen-ager. On the other hand, it can be presumed to represent family tradition about the notorious relative.

Helena Blavatsky's own accounts of those years contain inconsistencies, not to mention improbabilities, even as her psychic phenomena undoubtedly contained elements of fraud. Her writing is replete with some—though perhaps not as many as some critics have supposed—examples of unattributed borrowing.[2]

It is not our primary task, however, to explore, much less to judge, these matters here. We are instead concerned with the overall significance, especially on the symbolic level, of Theosophy in American spiritual history, rather than with a detailed or critical biography of the Russian woman.

In light of her symbolic role, even her deceitfulness can be comprehended. Whether one condones it or not, it is of a nature which, in the context of her life and teaching, identifies her with archetypal figures from myth and religious typology: the trickster (as we have seen), the shaman, the magus. The love of trickery of this nineteenth-century parlor shaman led her more than once into foolishness and embarrassing situations, and came close to discrediting her cause completely.

Yet that it did not for many followers both Eastern and Western, and that her movement finally came to have a certain influence, can only be attributed to the likelihood that her particular style of trickery was so consistent with her role as magus as to be unperceived as trickery. Or, if it was so perceived, it was taken only to reinforce the archetype, as being a kind of trickery legitimate to the shaman or magus, if not essential to her social and spiritual role. One gets a feeling that Olcott, who never conceded trickery on his companion's part but who sometimes seems to leave that interpretation open to all but the most credulous readers of his memoirs, probably understood some of her "phenomena" in that light. That interpretation would, of course, apply only to those who were, so to speak, in the magus's world; for the many critics outside it, it is only trickery, or at best raw psychic power without significance, as are the miracles of all religions to nonbelievers.

Three ways in which this trickery can be related to Madame Blavatsky's vocation come to mind. First, she was like a shaman, with her preternatural guides, and shamans commonly employ

both sleight-of-hand and inflated narratives about their own supernatural initiations to facilitate belief and confidence in their clients.
Second, she was, as we have seen, like a trickster in that she enjoyed
fooling people and thereby deflating the pretensions of society, a
labor congenial to the genuine outsider and denizen of two worlds
—the trickster is at once righteous, comic, and amoral. Third, the
evidence suggests she may have had at least a mild case of dissocia-
tion or multiple personality, a condition in which each personality
may operate by quite different values and have different goals from
the others, and may not even be aware of everything the other does.
While pathological if extreme, some degree of multiple personality
may comport with many important religious phenomena: visions,
possessions, and inspiration. When one learns how to "trigger" the
shift, even while attributing it to supernatural overshadowing, it
facilitates mediumship and shamanism. Some capacity for multiple
personality, then, is vital to the shamanistic role.

Whatever their nature, it was during her "hidden" years that
HPB (as Theosophists like to call Helena Petrovna Blavatsky)
brought her shamanistic capacities to full flower. Independent
documentation for these wandering years is scant and ambiguous.
It is clear, though, that HPB surfaced in Cairo in 1871, where she
founded a short-lived Spiritualist group. After a brief visit to
Russia, she went to Paris and there was in touch with leading
Spiritualists. Then she came to America.

More significant to us is what must have happened to her inwardly during this time. Whatever she was doing, she was living a
life of marginality to the established social order—all accounts,
flattering and otherwise, agree on this—and was apparently participating more and more actively in another order. In this other order,
the universe itself becomes subjectivity; it is a cosmic mind animated by other subjectivities, later called the Masters and the
Hierarchy. She was half of this world and half of what Theosophists
later called the "inner plane" and the "inner government of the
world," a network or ascendancy or hidden Masters continuous
with intrapsychic forces and directly accessible to consciousness
more than to sense. The frontiers of this realm are probed by
Spiritualism, but, according to Theosophy, though one may be
brought toward it by that faith, its entities are only wretched lorelei
compared to the true splendors of the Masters' occult world.

One could say that the syncretism of Theosophical doctrine, thickly populated with hidden Masters and the lore of many ancient cultures, is an expression on the theoretical level of communitas. It expresses a desire to be free of conditioned structure and to have rapport—an I-thou relationship, one might say—with initiates of all times, places, and levels of reality. The nineteenth-century's romantic bent, inspired by the sensational decoding of the Rosetta Stone, the discovery of the jungle-buried temples of the Mayans and of Angkor, and the unearthing of Troy, was fascinated by lost cities, peoples, even continents. That fascination was fed by books like John L. Stephens's popular *Incidents of Travel in Yucatan,* which as we shall see, Olcott was reading one memorable evening. Of course, the esoteric reputations of Egypt and India go back at least to the days of Plato. Helena Blavatsky and her followers combined old and new by talking of the Brotherhood of Luxor, the Eastern Lodge, the lore of the Mayans, Tibet, Atlantis. A more innocent day than ours is recalled by the syncretistic brooch HPB liked to wear, now preserved in the seal of the Theosophical Society, containing both the swastika and the Star of David, surrounded by the encircling serpent.

Henry Steel Olcott

Colonel Henry Steel Olcott (1832-1907) came later to alienation from the ordinary than did Madame Blavatsky, but no less decisively. He was an energetic, gregarious man who had made a place for himself in the world of practical affairs. He wrote books on agriculture. As a Union officer in the Civil War he was involved in investigative work; his exposure of corrupt suppliers won him recognition. He also had a role in the controversial conspiracy investigation after the assassination of Lincoln. Olcott handled the initial interrogation of Mary Surratt; whether she was a knowing accomplice of John Booth, or her hanging a judicial murder spurred by the overheated atmosphere of Washington in 1865, is still argued. Olcott's material, though, was not formally used in her trial. After the war, Olcott established a reasonably successful law career in New York; he also wrote frequently for newspapers and magazines.

It may be that his separation from his devoutly church-going wife in the early seventies helped induce his break with a conventional life. Perhaps it was nostalgia for the Spiritualism which had during his youth held a fascination for him; around 1850 he spent some time on his uncle's farm in Ohio, and with him had seen some of the early manifestations. As a youth, he had also, like the young Andrew Jackson Davis, experimented with Mesmerism, and once put a girl into a trance for a dental operation. Or perhaps he turned to spirits and theosophy because deep-seated dissatisfaction gnawed at him—though outwardly Olcott seemed a skeptical and sophisticated man about town, more given to a witticism or a convivial drink than to philosophy or prayer.

In any case, as we have seen, his interest in the spirit world was revived in 1874 by reports of the materializations being produced at the home of the dour Eddy Brothers in Vermont. Going to the lonely, ghost-infested New England farm with the intent of writing about it for the *Daily Graphic*, Olcott found himself intrigued by the exotic Russian lady in the red shirt, and the equally exotic apparitions in her train. Before long, back in the city, he had moved into an apartment just above hers, and they were spending all their free time together, talking about Spiritualism and the steps beyond it, experiencing psychic phenomena, and arranging meetings in which these things were made available to a wider circle.

A Remarkable Year

The result of these talks and meetings was the formation of the Theosophical Society in the fall of 1875. Much else, however, happened in that year. Theosophy's precursor was a Miracle Club Olcott organized early in 1875 to investigate psychic phenomena; it was inspired by a group of the same name founded in London around Bulwer-Lytton for the study of magic twenty years before. Olcott's club, however, failed, largely because the medium they selected as the chief object of study turned out to be an utter scoundrel.

In the meantime, HPB continued writing for and corresponding with Spiritualist periodicals, married an unstable Russian and lived briefly with him in Philadelphia, and while in that city passed through a psycho-physical crisis which initiated a remarkable new stage in her spiritual life.

Her correspondence with Spiritualist periodicals involved complicated issues concerning allegedly fraudulent mediumship, and, above all, the attempt of Olcott and Blavatsky to use the magazine called *The Spiritual Scientist* as a vehicle for the teaching said to be coming through them from the "Brotherhood of Luxor," to which HPB belonged. The venture was unsuccessful and ended in bad feelings toward the editor, who later went bankrupt. The failure of this attempt to employ the established means of Spiritualist communication undoubtedly was a factor leading to the founding of the Theosophical Society.

Blavatsky married a Mr. Betanelly, from Russian Georgia, who had entered into correspondence with Olcott and Blavatsky after reading of the Caucasian manifestations at Chittenden. He claimed to be able to verify the identity of one of them. It is conceivable, though totally unproven, that Betanelly knew something, about Chittenden or something else, that HPB desperately wanted unrevealed, even at the cost of a distasteful marital union. HPB agreed to marry her countryman after Betanelly allegedly threatened suicide several times and consented to allow her to keep her name and full freedom. This union ended in divorce in 1878. It was actually never valid, for although HPB apparently chose to assume General Blavatsky was deceased, her aged spouse was, in fact, still alive in the homeland.

Early in 1875 Madame Blavatsky injured her leg twice, once from a fall and once when a bedstead she was trying to move dropped on it. After her move to Philadelphia in March, the leg became gangrene and her condition was very serious. Doctors advised amputation, but this she refused. During June the illness reached a mysterious crisis when, according to Betanelly, during the day she would lie in bed for long hours, immobile and in a deep trance, but at night would get up and proceed to her "spirit room," walking strongly on the diseased limb. She herself wrote on June 19 that she was "tired of all this dying business" and wished she could die once and for all.

Yet she did not die, but during this crisis, according to her own account, went through a remarkable change. Here it is in her own words, from a letter to her sister Mme Jelihovsky in Russia:

> And just about this time [after a sudden cure at the end of June which she attributed to the Master she called the "Sahib"; Olcott says "she got better in one night, by one of her quasi-miraculous cures"] I have

begun to feel a very strange duality. Several times a day I feel that beside me there is someone else, quite separable from me, present in my
body. I never lose the consciousness of my personality; what I feel is
as if I were keeping silent and the one—the lodger who is in me—were
speaking with my tongue.

For instance, I know that I have never been in the places which are
described by my "other me," but this other one—the second me—does
not lie when he tells about places and things unknown to me, because
he has actually seen them and known them well. I have given it up;
let my fate conduct me at its own sweet will; and besides, what am I
to do? It would be perfectly ridiculous if I were to deny the possession
of knowledge avowed by my No. 2, giving occasion to the people
around me to imagine that I kept them in the dark for modesty's sake.

In the night, when I am alone in my bed, the whole life of my No. 2
passes before my eyes, and I do not see myself at all, but quite a different person—different in race and different in feelings. But what's
the use of talking about it? It is enough to drive one mad. I try to throw
myself into the part, and to forget the strangeness of my situation. This
is no mediumship, and by no means an impure power; for that, it has
too strong an ascendancy over us all leading us into better ways. No
devil would act like that. "Spirits," maybe? But if it comes to that, my
ancient "spooks" dare not approach me any more. It's enough for me
to enter the room where a seance is being held, to stop all kinds of
phenomena at once, especially materializations. Ah no, this is altogether of a higher order![3]

HPB referred to this second personality as "the Voice" or "Sahib," and later as her "Master." Apparently this was in time
understood by her to be the same personality as, or sent by, the
the Hindu Master whom she had seen "in the Astral body" as
a child, when he was a sort of guardian angel protecting her
in moments of great danger, and whom she had met in London
in 1851 when he was with the Indo-Nepali delegation and spoke
to her.

The near-death and transformation experience invites comparison with that of Jemima Wilkinson, the Public Universal Friend,
although HPB is characteristically more articulate about it. Regarding its psychological meaning, the light it may shed on her accounts
of remarkable travels and initiation during her hidden years, and its
meaning for her subsequent vocation, the reader must draw his own
conclusions. The summer of 1875 may be the clue to everything,
and one seeking to rationalize in some way the enigma which was

HPB is tempted to seize upon it—but then again, other clues
suggest it may seem more important than it really was. The whole
scenario may have been partly a working of her "maya." It was
neither the first nor last time she underwent such a crisis, or
reported diverse personalities working through her. The life of HPB
is, in the words of the title of one biography of her, a "hall of magic
mirrors."

Nonetheless, there is a strong and deep initiatory motif to the
literature of the crisis. During it, Olcott received letters in New
York and Boston signed by the Master Serapis, one of his mystic
mentors, interpreting the illness as Sister Helena's great initiatory
ordeal, when she must fight the dark Dweller on the Threshold (a
term from Bulwer-Lytton's novel *Zanoni,* which has much influenced Theosophists and occultists), and "either conquer—or
die herself his victim." Olcott hardly mentions the Serapis letters in
Old Diary Leaves—he is very reticent about the whole affair—but
they were published by a later president of the Theosophical Society, C. Jinarajadasa. These epistles interpret not only the illness
but also the odd marriage to Betanelly as parts of the initiatory
abasement she must pass through. The letters urge Olcott to remain
wholly supportive of HPB in her suffering and critical transition; he
is told his own initiation depends upon his loyalty to her.[4]

By autumn Olcott and Blavatsky were back together again in
New York, the separation and Philadelphia interlude seemingly
forgotten. It was then that the Theosophical Society was organized,
with full slate of officers and constitution, by a group which had
first come together to hear Egyptology lectures by J. H. Felt, and
wished to further their pursuit of occult and arcane matters. Colonel Olcott was the first president; H. P. Blavatsky was corresponding secretary. HPB never held any position in the Theosophical
Society other than this, except when later she headed the Esoteric
Section. Although she was certainly a catalyst in its organization, it
would be incorrect to say the society was founded to focus solely on
her or on her particular teachings. She undoubtedly would not
have been capable of holding an office other than the secretarial
one, for public speaking and conducting meetings were tasks she
detested and usually refused, and she was quite lacking in either
tact or administrative ability.

The Early Years of Theosophy

The infant Theosophical Society in the three years before the
journey to India was marked by the erratic shifts in emphasis and
membership, yet was lively enough to produce some memorable
events. Olcott, in his memoirs *Old Diary Leaves*, reminisces of such
things as the alleged first cremation in America, which was held
under Theosophical auspices. The deceased was the Baron de Palma,
an aristocratic confidence man from Europe who had attached
himself to the Theosophists—much to their discomfiture, when the
vast wealth and Alpine castles he had promised to leave the society
turned out to consist of nothing but a few grubby suitcases followed
by a horde of creditors. Olcott also tells of hilarious games of
charades played in Madame Blavatsky's apartment, in which Theosophy was spoofed most of all.

But these years were not, however, simply years of chaos. In them
occurred a socio-psychological process of great interest, namely, the
increasing detachment of the principle Theosophists, Blavatsky and
Olcott, from the structures of society at large, as institutional and
subjective Theosophy became reified as an alternative reality. There
also occurred an event of far-reaching significance, the writing and
publication of Madame Blavatsky's first major work, the massive
Isis Unveiled. Both of these matters influenced the decision to go to
India, heartland of the alternative reality probed by the book.
These were years of an increasing experience of liminality through
the Theosophical mystique, which cried out to be expressed by
excursus and to become total, a drive consummated when Olcott
knelt on the Bombay docks. But it occurred in different ways for
different Theosophists.

For HPB, Theosophy was the culminating phase of a marginal
way of life she had lived virtually from birth, in an inward sense. In
fact, the responsibilities for leadership she assumed with her position in the society represented a greater accommodation with structure than had ever been forced upon her before, and often she
found that accommodation no easy burden to bear, given her
anarchic temperament and her relations to the Masters on the other
side of mundane structure.

For Olcott, Theosophy and his closeness to Madame Blavatsky
were vehicles of transition from a conventionally structured life

toward an existence of liminal meaning. When he finally completed the transition with the landing in India he said, doubtless
with much relief, that the past was now forgotten. (Later, though,
he gravitated toward elaborate structural responsibilities within
Theosophy.)

In 1875–78, his marriage was over, but Olcott kept up his
professional life with diminishing interest. He symbolized his intrapsychic break through his gleeful participation in such unconventional acts as the cremation and the "Pagan funeral" (as the press
called it), complete with Orphic and Vedantic hymns and a police
cordon to restrain outraged religionists of more orthodox persuasion, from which obsequies for de Palma were delivered.

Pulling Olcott toward his new life was his continual exposure
to Blavatsky's "phenomena," including letters, signs, and visions
from the superhuman Masters of the Brotherhoods of Luxor and
the East who were undertaking to teach and guide this willing
novice of the Mysteries, this middle-aged attorney who was, in
Shelley's phrase, a "nurseling of immortality."

Gertrude M. Williams, in her book on the life of Madame
Blavatsky, argues that there was in this period a deliberate and
successful attempt by HPB, through psychological pressure reinforced by tricks and magisterial epistles, to wean Olcott away from
his past and to get him entirely under her psychic domination.[5]
More to the point for the phenomenologist, as we have seen, would
be comparison with a complex phenomenon like shamanism.

For the more occasional Theosophist in the New York of the
1870s, Theosophy was a sometime experience of listening to the
mysterious lady, colorful, exotic, defiant of convention, talk of
arcane marvels and truths far beyond the ken of the ordinary.
Within her garishly decorated, book-filled apartment at 46 Irving
Place, the lady with the enchanting accent, who suggested remote
worlds of monarchical splendor and Eastern mysteries, ushered
many into another realm from that of the drab city streets below.
Olcott writes:

> Without a single exception those who published accounts of their visits
> to 'The Lamasery'—as we humorously called our humble suite of
> rooms—declared that their experience had been novel and out of the
> usual course. Most of them wrote about HPB in terms of exaggerated
> praise or wonder. In appearance there was not a shade of the ascetic

about her: she neither mediated in seclusion, practised austerities in
regimen, nor selected her company. Her door was open to all, even to
those whom she knew meant to write about her with pens over which
she could have no control. Often they lampooned her, but if the articles
were witty, she used to enjoy them with me to the fullest extent.[6]

What sort of people were involved in early Theosophy? Early
members included such luminaries as Thomas A. Edison and General Abner Doubleday, alleged to be the inventor of baseball. A
glance at some of the other individuals who appear most promi-
nently in the literature, while not a quantitative survey, does result in
some interesting observations, for these persons tend to be, in a technical sense, "marginal" or "status inconsistent." These types, commonly inhabitants past and present of Balch and Nelson's "cultic
milieu," are basically people who find that the structures of society
do not allow them to be what they experience themselves inwardly
to be, or who are forced into a life of several roles which seem
inconsistent. They may be people of high intelligence and creativity
but with limited formal education and a corresponding lack of
access to the regular ways of expression; or they may be people like
HPB from the most aristocratic ranks of society, unable to abide its
restrictions, or people like immigrants; minorities; the young; the
intelligent Victorian (or modern) woman, who, despite some apparent advantages, are never quite sure where they stand, what
invisible doors might be closed, and how what they are fits with
how they are perceived. In the terms of chapter 3, their social and
non-social identities are experienced as highly dissonant. (Maybe
even the poorly educated, but brilliant, successful, and spiritually
questing Edison was in this category.)

People who experience marginality or status inconsistency often
tend to believe their lives are subject to forces outside their control
which easily become personified in supernatural forms. They are
drawn to associate with groups perceived as reifying their marginality, which can be elevated into the transcendentally liminal, and
they may be susceptible to belief (on many levels of terminology
and sophistication) in magic and supernatural intervention. (For
equally understandable reasons, persons structurally secure and
status consistent are prone to establishment religion and the rejection of non-rational interpretations of things.)

HPB perceived something of this, at least in regard to Spiritualism, when she wrote before the beginning of formal Theosophy that, "not unlike Christianity in the beginning of its era, Spiritualism numbers in its ranks more of the humble and afflicted ones, than of the powerful and wealthy of this earth."[7] Within the ranks of the active early Theosophists were rising immigrants like William Q. Judge and his brother, and H. D. Monachesi. Olcott tells us of a housepainter extremely well-read in Greek philosophy who became a member. The Russian Countess de Pashkov, world traveler and writer, lived for a time with HPB and helped with the cooking. Charles Sotheran was a bibliophile of independent means. Alexander Wilder, archetype of the profound auto-didact, was a mostly self-educated practitioner of eclectic medicine, editor, and writer on esoteric topics.

The Writing of Isis Unveiled

The most significant labor of this period, and the work suggestive of the process leading to the journey to India, is *Isis Unveiled* (1877). Started in 1875 or 1876 (inconsistent dates are given), the writing was apparently a continuation of the same process inaugurated by HPB's strange illness of the summer of 1875, as well as a work of the budding society. Wilder, Sotheran, the Judge brothers, and Olcott were involved with the process extensively: they made suggestions, located sources, transcribed the manuscript for the publisher, and did indexing. The flow of material came from the Russian lady, reportedly under inspiration of various of the Masters who successively inspired the "shell" of her body. As Olcott describes it:

> Now it was a curious fact that each change in the HPB manuscript would be preceded, either by her leaving the room for a moment or two, or by her going off into the trance or abstracted state, when her lifeless eyes would be looking beyond me into space, as it were, and returning to the normal waking state almost immediately. And there would also be a distinct change of personality, or rather personal peculiarities, in gait, vocal expression, vivacity of manner, and, above all, in temper ... Not another as to visible change of physical body, but another as to tricks of motion, speech, and manners; with different mental brightness, different views of things, different command of

English orthography, idiom, and grammar, and different—very, *very*
different command over her temper; which, at its sunniest, was almost
angelic, at its worst, the opposite.[8]

Sometimes it was sufficient that her mentors simply present the
material to her by occult means:

> To watch her at work was a rare and never-to-be-forgotten experience.
> We sat at opposite sides of one big table usually, and I could see her
> every movement. Her pen would be flying over the page, when she
> would suddenly stop, look out into space with the vacant eye of the
> clairvoyant seer, shorten her vision as though to look at something held
> invisible in the air before her, and begin copying on her paper what she
> saw. The quotation finished, her eyes would resume their natural ex-
> pression, and she would go on writing until again stopped by a similar
> interruption. I remember well two instances when I, also, was able to
> see and even handle books from whose astral duplicates she had copied
> quotations into her manuscript, and which she was obliged to "ma-
> terialise" for me, to refer to when reading the proofs, as I refused to
> pass the pages for the "strike-off" unless my doubts as to the accuracy
> of her copy were satisfactory.[9]

Who were these adepts whose invisible fingers were the true
holders of the pen that wrote *Isis Unveiled?* While Theosophy has
no formal or obligatory belief regarding them, it cannot be denied
they were the most intriguing and distinctive idea, or experience,
shared by the intimates of Madame Blavatsky. The concept of the
adepts, later called Masters, however, is far from novel. In this case
it was partly related to Spiritualist belief in spirit guides, but even
more to the primordial *rishis* of Hinduism, the Buddhist bodhisattva, and the psychopomps of theurgic Neoplatonism. Roman
Catholic, Eastern Orthodox, and Muslim saints, especially in popular legend and piety, are entities of about the same order. The
concept is none other than an eclectic revival of the very widespread
belief in human beings who have through great preparation attained participation in a transcendent level of being, like that of the
divine, and so can wield miraculous-seeming wisdom and power.
According to Theosophical tradition, there are beings like this in
many parts of the world and in many faiths; they can communicate
and cooperate with each other, and influence the course of the
world in subtle but significant ways, forming an "invisible government" which does what it can to further humankind's slow evolu-

tion toward the good. India, Tibet, and the Gobi region are their greatest redoubts. Many Masters are in the physical body, others work entirely on other planes. But even those in the physical form can travel or appear out of it through mayavic power; Olcott reports that some Masters whom they saw appear in New York were later visited in India, where they manifested nothing other than ordinary flesh, but were recognizable.

This is the world opened up by *Isis Unveiled*, though that book actually says little about the Masters. (The rationalization of the hierarchy of Masters from hints in the writings of HPB and Olcott, and from further clairvoyant experience, was the work of writers like C. W. Leadbeater in the second generation of Theosophy.) But the purpose of the book was not, as the writer acknowledged, to remove the veil of Isis completely. It was only to lift it a little in order to suggest the wonders behind the scrim of time and matter. Indeed, the title was originally intended to be *The Veil of Isis,* and was changed at the last minute, when it was discovered that another book of that title existed.

Isis Unveiled is mainly a collage of accounts from the annals of Mesmerism, history, travel in out-of-the-way places, the lore of numbers, rites, Masonic symbolism, Pythagoreanism, Neoplatonism, and Hindu and Zoroastrian texts. It is aimed at suggesting an intricate splendor behind the world as we know it. Significant concepts of the book are: a supreme mind, pre-existent souls which have fallen from glory into life on earth, their initiatory purification and return whence they came, and their acquiring along the path supernormal powers. These principles are demonstrated by the anecdotes, which report about events that demonstrate the existence of mind and spiritual realities independent of body and of birth and death as we know it. The book extols the power of mind manifested in Mesmerism and magic and brings to light the activity of disembodied souls and "elementals." The reader of *Isis Unveiled* also joins excursions into speculative history that round off an alternative world view; compares the traditional lives of Krishna, the Buddha, and Jesus; and confronts the reader with sardonic remarks on "orthodox" Christianity and science alike.

In all of this India appears as a beckoning contrast. It is an unfailing source of stories of marvels illustrative of the main theses, many taken from the voluminous and wonder-filled books of L. Jacolliot, or of the Abbè Huc, though some are presented as first hand observations of HPB, or possibly of one of her possessing entities. India, moreover, had not paled under the grip of either church or gown as we know them in the West, but its wise ones rejoiced in a deep philosophy not far fallen from its source in primordial truth. Indeed, though the ruling doctrine of the book is said to be Platonic, *Isis* asserts that the wisdom of the West's profoundest mind is but a compendium of "the abstruse systems of old India" which are thousands of years older.[10]

It is clear, then, that the compiling of *Isis Unveiled* was an important step along the way to India, though not the only one.[11] Let us now trace the steps of that progress.

Going East

It is not entirely clear just when and why the two leading Theosophists determined to depart for India. But it is evident that it turned out to be a remarkably sagacious move. Despite the publication of *Isis Unveiled* in 1877, and the attention it attracted, the Theosophical Society seemed to have reached a dead end in New York. Olcott, in a later, double-funnel chronological diagram of the society's vicissitudes, shows it declining to a mere point at the time of the pilgrimage to India, and then, after the trip, the diagram grows broader and broader with the proliferation of new chapters there and elsewhere.

But in these three years of decline, India, always a major reservoir of the ancient wisdom Theosophy was concerned to revive, came more and more into their conversations. The supernormal Masters whom Madame Blavatsky was able to introduce to Olcott increasingly wore turbans. Then in 1878 the society united by correspondence with Swami Dayananda Sarasvati's Arya Samaj (founded in 1875 to affirm the Vedas as revealed scripture and to reform Hinduism on that basis), calling itself "The Theosophical Society of the Arya Samaj." Olcott, president of the Theosophical Society, felt at the time that the Arya Samaj's reconstructed Vedism was one with the spiritual universalism he identified with Theosophy, and HPB affirmed that Dayananda was none other than a Himalayan Master

inhabiting the great swami's body. But vast was Olcott's disillusionment, confirmed later in India, when further information
revealed the Arya Samaj, for all its virtues, intended only conservative, integralist reforms and the advancement of education in India,
and so was of little interest to Western universalists, unless from a
larger perspective than Olcott could then comprehend.

The relation with the Arya Samaj had its roots in 1870, when
Olcott had met Moolji Thackersey of Bombay on a ship to England.
In 1878 Olcott began corresponding with him again, and invited
the Indian to join the Theosophical Society. Thackersey, in turn,
told Olcott in enthusiastic terms of the allegedly parallel work of
the Arya Samaj, and introduced him by mail to Hurrychund Chintamon, president of the Bombay branch of the Arya Samaj. It
appears that this relationship, unhappy as it turned out to be,
sowed the seeds of the desire to go to India. Olcott and Blavatsky
now had a definite reason for going: to meet Saravati Dayananda,
the great spiritual leader of the Samaj, learn Eastern esotericism
from him, and strengthen the links between the two societies.
Having specific contacts in India also made the practical side of the
trip seem more manageable. Even after the first disillusionment in
New York upon getting further information about the Arya Samaj,
they still felt drawn to Aryavarta, and HPB still felt that Sarasvati
was a great Master who was summoning her. Correspondence was
continued, and a little later Chintamon was entrusted with making
arrangements in India for the arrival of the New York Theosophists
—a trust they were sorely to regret.

Another reason for the journey to India in 1878 was the founding
of a London branch of the society that year, which the two wanted
to visit en route. Moreover, that same year HPB became the first
immigrant Russian woman to acquire U.S. citizenship, making her
eligible for an American passport. The change of citizenship was
emotionally difficult for her. It was inconsistent with other positions of hers, HPB admitted, but she retained to the end a deep
love for Russia, the Czar, and the Orthodox Church—which never
shared in the scathing attacks she heaped on the priestcraft of Rome
and the fanaticism of Protestants, and whose last rites she is said to
have requested quietly at the end of her occult mission.[12] But the
British Raj's almost-paranoid suspicions of Russian designs on India

at the time made it far more politic for this unusual traveler to carry a U.S. than a Russian passport—even though it did not relieve her of a discreet police "tail" during some of her stay in the land of elephants and sages, and even though her adversaries often accused her, among other things, of being a spy.

Still another reason for going to India was that the famous levitationist and "physical medium" D. D. Home, whose pupil and assistant some report HPB to have once been (though she denied it bitterly), and who was well-connected in Russia, published a book called *Lights and Shadows of Spiritualism* in 1877. It included a chapter ridiculing the Theosophical Society and reviling Olcott as a fool. HPB was furious. On October 2, 1877, she wrote the Russian psychical researcher A. N. Aksakov, "That's why I'm going off forever to India, and from shame and grief I wish to go where no one knows even my name. Home has ruined me forever in Europe by his spite and hatred."[13]

The decision had also a powerful occult side. As we have seen, India had been a part of HPB's subjective world at least since she was twenty, when she had met her lord on the inner plane in London, probably he who later became known as the Rajput prince Morya. "By the light of the moon that was setting," she had seen "the Master of my dreams!!" she wrote later in her diary with schoolgirlish rapture of meeting him at Ramsgate (probably a disguise for London) on her twentieth birthday, and she had sought the princely great soul around the world ever since.[14]

It was said to be the Masters, including some from India, who actually ordered the Theosophists to leave America for India in 1878, just as HPB had said it was under orders that she had come to America five years before. Following are some intriguing lines from her diary late in 1878; Gertrude Williams suspected them of having been written after the move to India and backdated, but in any case they offer a Theosophical hermeneutic of the journey.[15]

In the diary for October 22, 1878 (they left December 17 of the same year), we read, "*Narayan* left watch—and in came *Sahib*. The latter with orders from Serapis to complete all the first days of December."[16] In this enigmatic passage, Narayan is an Indian Master, later identified with an actual living swami in the hills not far from Madras, whom HPB and Olcott met physically about April

30, 1882, and who supported the Theosophists in a time of trouble.
Sahib, whom we have already encountered, probably refers to
Morya. Serapis was prominent in the early days of Theosophy when
Olcott was still studying with the Egyptian section, and signed the
letters he received during HPB's psycho-physiological crisis. The
curious change of watch among these Masters suggests the subjective "overshadowing" by these supernormal entities which was
involved in the writing of *Isis Unveiled* and was apparently a major
component of HPB's inner experience.

Later, on November 14, we have these lines: "Naray decamped
and Morya walked in—broken finger and all. Came with definite
orders from Serapis. *Have to go;* the latest from 15th to 20th
Dec.... O God, O Indra of the golden face! Is this really the
beginning and the end!"[17]

Of a somewhat earlier period, Olcott tells us:

> Little by little, HPB let me know of the existence of Eastern adepts,
> and their powers, and gave me by a multitude of phenomena the proofs
> of her own control over the occult forces of nature.... For years, and
> until shortly before I left New York for India, I was connected in pu-
> pilage with the African section of the Occult Brotherhood; but, later,
> when a certain wonderful psycho-physiological change happened to
> HPB that I am not at liberty to speak about, and that nobody has up to
> the present suspected, although enjoying her intimacy and full confi-
> dence, as they fancy, I was transferred to the Indian section and a dif-
> ferent group of Masters.[18]

Even more revealing is the following account by Olcott, unfortunately not dated, but presumably in 1876 or 1877, since they were
at work on *Isis Unveiled;* for Olcott, this event was apparently the
decisive supernatural goad in the direction of India.

> The story has been told before, but it had its place in the present retro-
> spect, for it was the chief among the causes of my abandonment of the
> world and my coming out to my Indian home. Hence it was one of the
> chief factors in the upbuilding of the Theosophical Society. I do not
> mean to say that without it I should not have come to India, for my
> heart had been leaping within me to come, from the time when I
> learned what India had been to the world, what she might be
> made again. An insatiable longing had possessed me to come to
> the land of the Rishis and the Buddhas, the Sacred Land among lands;
> but I could not see my way clear to breaking the ties of circumstance
> which bound me to America, and I might have felt compelled to put

it off to that "convenient season" which so often never comes to the procrastinator and waiter upon the turn of events. This experience in question, however, settled my fate; in an instant doubts melted away, the clear foresight of a fixed will showed the way, and before the dawn of that sleepless night came, I began to devise the means and to bend all things to that end. The happening was thus:

Our evening's work on *Isis* was finished, I had bade good-night to HPB, retired to my own room, closed the door as usual, sat me down to read and smoke, and was soon absorbed in my book; which, if I remember aright, was Stephens's *Travels in Yucatan;* at all events, not a book on ghosts . . .

All at once, as I read with my shoulder a little turned from the door, there came a gleam of something white in the right-hand corner of my right eye; I turned my head, dropped my book in astonishment, and saw towering above me in his great stature an Oriental clad in white garments, and wearing a head-cloth or turban of amber-striped fabric . . .[19]

Olcott continues at great length to tell us of the splendor, the majesty, and the spiritual radiance of this man, which caused him to bend his knees and bow as before a god. But the mighty presence bade the colonel be seated, and, sitting down himself, proceeded to tell Olcott about the great work for humanity which lay before him and about the mysterious tie that had drawn the colonel and HPB together. Finally he left, and as he did so he placed his turban (which can still be seen at the Theosophical headquarters in Adyar) on the table as a tangible proof of his appearance. Olcott then immediately banged on HPB's door to tell her of this marvelous experience.

India was, first of all, the land of phenomenal Masters, who could reach out to touch the thoughts and even appear before the eyes of one half a world away, and whose presence made their native home a magnet. They practiced "Brahma Vidya" or "Eastern Spiritualism," and it was the power of these Masters who summoned the Westerners, for their "invisible government of the world" had conceived a plan for the advancement of the world in which they would be its roving ambassadors. The pilgrimage to India was part voyage of discovery, part response to a call from what Victor Turner calls "the center out there," the goal of all pilgrimage. The journey took on the traditional structure of a pilgrimage, and was consummated like all such in a situation of full liminality and communitas.

Passage to More Than India

Beyond all other reasons for the journey, then, was the unparalleled
spiritual magnetism of India and enigmatic Tibet. The journey
itself was long and difficult. They left the United States on December 17, 1878, and, after a stop-over in England, arrived in India in
mid-February of the following year. The meaning India had come
to have for them—and for many other occidental seekers—is finely
expressed by Olcott in his *Old Diary Leaves.* He writes that upon
finally landing in Bombay on February 16, 1879:

> the first thing I did on touching land was to stoop down and kiss the
> granite step; my instinctive act of pooja! For here we were at last on
> sacred soil; our past forgotten, our perilous and disagreeable sea-voyage
> gone out of mind, the agony of long deferred hopes replaced by the
> thrilling joy of presence in the land of the Rishis, the cradle country
> of religions, the dwelling place of the Masters, the home of our dusky
> brothers and sisters, with whom to live and die was all we could desire.[20]

In these lines is certainly expressed the sacred and archetypal
meaning of pilgrimage, and understanding the inner meaning of
pilgrimage is a valuable key to understanding the meaning of
Theosophy, with its restlessness toward the conventional and its
quest for occult lore and initiations, for the source and inner
meaning of religions, and for human brotherhood.

In the passage to India Olcott, through peril and strain, found
movement away from the ordinary through a ritually demarcated
threshold, to a place at once inductive of a new sort of awareness
("the thrilling joy of presence in the land of the Rishis"), a return
to a point of origins ("the cradle country of religions"), a region of
access to transcendence ("the dwelling place of the Masters"), and
the locale of a new, transvalued community ("the home of our
dusky brothers and sisters") establishing ultimate *communitas*
rather than conditioned relationships ("with whom to live and die
was all we could desire").

Much the same symbolic experience, as Victor Turner has shown,
can be found in established ritual pilgrimage: the medieval journey
to Jerusalem, the Muslim *hajj,* Hindu progresses to Hardwar or
Pandharpur.[21] But the Theosophical Twins were travelling no well-
worn sacred track, nor was it one particular shrine or peak that drew

them, except the presence of Swami Dayananda. Olcott, at least, may hardly have known India well enough to single out such places. Rather it was India itself, one might say the idea of India, and its invisible realities, which was the object of pilgrimage.

Gustave Moreau's overwhelming late-romantic painting "The Triumph of Alexander," catches something of this sort of vision of the East: the Macedonian hero rides before a topless mountain laden with Egyptian columns, Hindu temples, a Jaina tirthankara, a Buddha from the Ajanta caves, all bathed in the opalescent light of the enchanted Orient. The same undifferentiated but romantically mystical East earlier appeared in the writings of Henry David Thoreau, whose importance for the emergent and excursus tradition in America should not be underestimated, and who mused of it:

> While the commentators are disputing about the meaning of this word and that, I hear only the resounding of the ancient sea, and put into it all the meaning I am possessed of, the deepest murmurs I can recall, for I do not in the least care where I get my ideas, or what suggests them.[22]

In counterbalance to this mood, however, it should be pointed out that Thoreau, probably more than Emerson, was quite aware of the diverse cultures and major spiritual texts of the East, and could cite them with some precision. A combination of textual specificity and the romantic vision of the East is found in this famous passage from *Walden,* which gloriously evokes the universalism, the anti-historicism, the mystical intuitionism, and the romance of the "Yankee Hindoo," despite several factual improbabilities.

> In the morning I bathe my intellect in the stupendous and cosmogonal philosophy of the Bhagvat-Geeta, since whose composition years of the gods have elapsed, and in comparison with which our modern world and its literature seem puny and trivial; and I doubt if that philosophy is not to be referred to a previous state of existence, so remote is its sublimity from our conceptions. I lay down the book and go to my well for water, and lo! there I meet the servant of the Bramin, priest of Brahma and Vishnu and Indra, who still sits in his temple on the Ganges reading the Vedas, or dwells at the root of a tree with his crust and water jug. I meet his servant come to draw water for his master, and our buckets at it were grate together in the same well. The pure Walden water is mingled with the sacred water of the Ganges.[23]

Even more suggestive is Walt Whitman's "Passage to India,"
written in 1871 to commemorate the completion of the transcon-
tinental railroad, the Trans-Atlantic cable, and above all the Suez
Canal through which the Theosophical Twins were to pass a few
years later on their way to that fabled heartland of the soul. It
contains lines such as these:

> Passage O soul to India!
> Eclaircise the myths Asiatic, the primitive fables.
> Not you alone proud truths of the world,
> Nor you alone ye facts of modern science,
> But myths and fables of old, Asia's, Africa's fables,
> The far-darting beams of the spirit, the unloos'd dreams,
> The deep diving bibles and legends,
> The daring plots of the poets, the elder religions;
> O you temples fairer than lilies pour'd over by the rising sun!
> O you fables spurning the known, eluding the hold of the known,
>   mounting to heaven!
> You lofty and dazzling towers, pinnacled, red as roses, burnish'd
>   with gold!
> Towers of fables immortal fashion'd from mortal dreams!. . .
> Passage to more than India!
> Are thy wings plumed indeed for such far flights?
> O soul, voyagest thou indeed on voyages like those?
> Disportest thou on waters such as those?
> Soundest below the Sanscrit and the Vedas?
> Then have thy bent unleash'd.
> Passage to you, your shores, ye aged fierce enigmas!
> . . . Passage to more than India!
> O secret of the earth and sky!

The Western discovery of spiritual India has been for some a
passage into an archetypal Far Place which transforms them and
incorporates them into a new community. For them, as for Blavatsky and Olcott, passage to India has been a journey to another
spiritual state as well as to another land. It has been Hermann
Hesse's paradigmatic "Journey to the East"—which has been made
by many who have never physically left Europe or America. But for
all of them (whatever it may be in itself), India has been the land of
communitas relations with others and with spiritual reality, the
land of return to sunrise origins, the sacred place which is at once
the pivot of the spiritual world and the place of access to transcen-

dence. It has been the true goal of pilgrimage, what Turner calls "the center out there."

In India Olcott and Blavatsky lived with a communitas-like detachment from all ties except those of the quest, and entered more and more deeply into subjective freedom from the structures imposed by their previous lives. Olcott tells us of the wonderful first days in the Asian land:

> Every evening we held an impromptu durbar, when the knottiest problems of philosophy, metaphysics, and science were discussed. We lived and breathed in an atmosphere of mind, amid the highest spiritual ideals . . .
>
> Visitors kept on crowding our bungalow, and stopping until late every evening to discuss religious questions. Old and young, it was all the same; and thus did we come, so early in our connection with the Hindus, to know the difference between Western and Eastern ideals of life, and the greater dignity of the latter. Questions of wealth, color, business, or politics scarcely ever crossed our threshold; the Soul was the burning topic of debate. . . .
>
> Fanatics, if you please; crazy enthusiasts; dreamers of unpractical dreams; devotees of a hobby! dupes of our imaginations. Yet our dreams were of human perfectibility, our yearnings after divine wisdom, our sole hope to help mankind to higher thinking and nobler living. And, under those umbrageous palms, we were visited in person by Mahātmas; and their inspiring presence made us strong to proceed in the path we were treading . . . [23]

One must keep in mind that this was British India in the heyday of imperialism and the Christian, Anglo-Saxon chauvinism which too often went with it, not least among India's fair-skinned rulers, to comprehend fully the radical reversal of established structures implied by Olcott's attitude. They traveled continually—perhaps in itself a symbol of breaking structure. When one thinks of conditions of travel in nineteenth century India, it is tiring even to read Olcott's narrative.

They intrigued the cream of Anglo-Indian society at Simla. Olcott also lectured to native audiences on the virtues of their own heritage and did Mesmeric "magnetic" healings to all who drew near at innumerable stops. Blavatsky mysteriously kept in touch with the Masters, from whom letters arrived frequently during these early Indian years. Far from familiar kin and culture, in defiance of convention in all sorts of ways—from their lack of Christian piety,

to their unimperial attitude toward natives, to their strange un-
married companionship—they had nonetheless found for themselves in India an inner space for communitas between male and
female, between European and Asiatic, between religions, between
this world and a transcendent one represented by the Masters.

Their life in India was an acting-out of the different perspective
on the human scene cast by the Theosophical teaching that Masters
of the Ancient Wisdom stood behind all religions, a teaching
reinforced by the phenomena associated with Madame Blavatsky
from the obscure farm at Chittenden to the bungalow in Bombay.
During the nineteenth century, despite the Transcendentalists and
their kin, most people thought of culture, above all spiritual culture, as flowing only from West to East in the form of missionaries,
traders, and imperial proconsuls. As quaint as the mission of the
Theosophical Twins may sound to some, it was a destiny-fraught
sign of a rising undertow to that flow, a reverse process which would
not stop until independence had come again to the East and the
West was awash with yoga and chanting. In the Indian subcon-
tinent that mission had an important part in the recovery of pride
in indigenous culture at the roots of the independence movement.
Olcott is something of a national hero in Sri Lanka (Ceylon) for his
work for the revitalization of Buddhism and was recently honored
there on a postage stamp. In the West, Theosophy, though never
large numerically or politically important, has had through books
and lectures a certain role in popularizing such concepts as karma
and reincarnation, and in promoting a view of spiritual traditions
neither reductionistic nor incompatible with tolerance.

India as "Center Out There"

Let us reconsider some of the reasons why Olcott and Blavatsky
went to India. As pilgrimage to a place of wider liminality, it was
because early Theosophy did not find a secure place structurally in
New York—that is, the organization did not appear then to have a
promising future—but at the same time it had opened up for the
core-group a subjective world too big to be contained in the Irving
Place apartment. There was a need for movement in space to equal
the increasing expansion of mind. Having become a liminal person

inwardly, Olcott in particular needed a place where he could integrate himself by acting out the liminal role in a totally new life; it would have been less meaningful for him to kiss the pavement in New York!

In India, Blavatsky and Olcott could act out liminality and the "exaltation of the weak" motif so closely related to it which we discussed in connection with Spiritualism. They were outsiders in that rigidly structured society, religious "bums" who attracted attention at all levels. True, Olcott and HPB were not structurally weak by circumstance but by choice, like many "dropouts" of our day. But they had made their decision, and, indeed, had little future in the West. In India, though, it was another game; whether they had anticipated it or not, Theosophy became a sensation there, and the Theosophical Twins found themselves the guests and the subject of gossip of common people, maharajahs, pandits, and the British elite. By an odd coincidence, the Viceroy of India at the time of their arrival was the romantic imperialist Robert Bulwer-Lytton, son of Edward George Bulwer-Lytton, whose occult novels like *Zanoni* had so much affected HPB and other Theosophists. His presence in India made talk of such matters fashionable in the drawing-rooms of Simla and "Ooty."

For the Theosophists themselves, India was "the center out there" which incarnated their vision. As represented in such accounts as those of Jacolliot, it was a land of marvels like those of antiquity in the days of the "Ancient Mystery Schools" had been. Excursus religion as means of access to liminality in American society needs continually to refresh its ties to the reservoirs of liminal infinity to which it relates. For this reason pilgrimage is frequently of more importance to emergent than to established religion. Theosophists go to India, and American adherents of Nichiren Shoshu or Zen to Japan, proportionately much more than American Methodists go to Jerusalem or even Aldersgate. On a deeper level, one feels the subjective freedom from ordinary structure of the excursus religionist needs to be symbolized and sustained by frequent comings and goings; for this reason leaders, like Blavatsky and Olcott, are virtually peripatetic.

Finally, communitas, as the goal to which liminality inexorably pressed Olcott and HPB, required a social setting which nine-

teenth-century India admirably provided. They could only find it
in a society in which they were wholly marginal, yet in which they
would have effective access to many different levels. English-speak-
ing and cultivated, but non-British and non-Hindu (in traditional
terms), India was open to them as it would not have been to one
who had a place high or low in its complex and rigid structure; they
could fall into the interstices of social structure while amusing or
enlightening people of all sorts, and could exercise the ability of the
"status inconsistent" to rejoice in those miracles and alternative
world views which the establishmentarian fears.

In both practical and psychic terms, then, India represented an
ideal "center out there," peripheral to European-American society,
yet accessible in terms of language and steamship bookings; full of
Masters of Wisdom yet, under the British Raj, just familiar enough
that one could meaningfully be marginal to it.

Nor can one overlook the subjective history of Olcott and HPB in
1875-78, however one explains it. Out of it came the determina-
tion to go to India. Something suggested by the transfer of Olcott
from the African to the Indian sections of the Occult Brotherhood,
by his midnight turbaned visitor, by HPB's mysterious crisis and
the insistent orders from Serapis, underscored the logic of the outer
events.

It was in India that the marvelous happened continuously to
the Theosophists, even to a Master awakening Olcott in the middle
of the night in a tent near Lahore to hand him a silk-wrapped letter,
and the celebrated and controversial "astral post office" of the
"shrine room" at Adyar where such communication appeared
regularly. To be sure, much of the literature of early Theosophy
now has a quintessential Victorian flavor, charming but distancing.
Yet the magic that India was to them, as old as Apollonius of Tyana
and as new as the most recent American guru-enthusiasm, is with
us still. It is paradigmatically exemplified in the pilgrimages of
Olcott and Blavatsky and their followers. They were sometimes
credulous, undoubtedly, but they anticipated in important ways
the more pluralistic, culturally interdependent, and subjectivity-
oriented spiritual world of the twentieth century in which India
remains an unequaled symbol of the spiritual side of all those
things. One could almost say India, or perhaps the East, is to

excursus religion since the Theosophical transformation of Spiritualism what Palestine is to the American religious establishment.

Notes on the Destiny of Theosophy

Theosophy, then, provided a wedge for liminality to the nineteenth and twentieth centuries—and to what lies beyond liminality. Our purpose here has been just to focus on one "moment" in
the actualization of liminality, the journey to India of 1878-79. But
what was started then was to continue. The complex history of
Theosophy, fascinating as it is, cannot be fully traced here. However, the movements devolving from Theosophy might be cited as
illustrating ways in which a Theosophy-based experience of liminality can change and grow.

Alice Bailey (1880-1949), founder of the Arcane School and the
Full Moon Meditation Groups, and Guy Ballard (1878-1939) of the
"I Am" movement, are representative of those who have started
activites based on new and special communications from Theosophical Masters. Alice Bailey wrote a series of books under inspiration
of one called "The Tibetan" which, within the context of Theosophical doctrine, put special emphasis on the imminent coming of
the Christ and the importance of meditation by groups, which
customarily meet every full moon to prepare lines of spiritual force
preparing for this event. Ballard's "I Am" has stressed contact with
"Ascended Masters" and the use of sound and color in the spiritual
life; it is also highly eschatological. In both cases the liminality
experience inauguraged by talk of Theosophical Masters has led,
more than in regular Theosophy, to an almost apocalyptic sense
that the ordinary, non-liminal world is about to pass away.

On the other hand, Jiddu Krishnamurti (b. 1895), himself a son
of India, "the center out there," was raised by the post-Blavatsky
generation of Theosophists as one who was to become the voice of
the World Teacher for this age "if he proved worthy"—virtually
the one whom the Bailey school anticipates. But in 1929, when he
was expected to begin his full mission, he renounced it in any
formal sense together with any idea of philosophical or spiritual
conceptual knowledge or organization. Since then Krishnamurti
has traveled the world, lecturing on behalf of a way of thought free
from all cages built by thought-forms, memories, and desires. Over

the years, his books and lectures have become immensely popular.
Here is a formless incarnation of the liminality first broached in the
Theosophical journey to India. Liminality is the freedom and reversal of breaking structure; structure can be broken by the marvelous,
but it can also be broken when the here-and-now is freed from both
the marvelous and the ordinary.[25]

The theosophical journey of the 1870s set in motion the historical
forces which led to both these ends. It established models for the
excursus religion pilgrimage to the East and established the symbolic role of India or Tibet as source of liberating wisdom. Since
then, India has increasingly been either a place where one goes on
the seeker's pilgrimage, or the place from which have come teachers
like Swami Vivekananda and others of the Ramakrishna Mission
and the Vedanta Societies, or Swami Yogananda of the Self-Realization Fellowship, or Swami Bhaktivedanta of the International
Society for Krishna Consciousness, or Guru Maharaj Ji of the Divine
Light Mission. The journey of the Russian lady and the American
gentleman a century ago can help us to understand the inner
meaning of this ongoing exchange.

6   *Zen Journeys to the West*

Krishnamurti and Zen

Is Krishnamurti the true end of Theosophy? Despite conventional Theosophy's elaborate metaphysical doctrines about the evolution of worlds and humanities according to triads and septads and so forth, does the mentalism that underlies it finally agree with Krishnamurti that all our concepts and ideas are empty and a hindrance to the fullness of joy? There is some reason to think so; Krishnamurti's books are popular among Theosophists, and even a Theosophical classic such as Mabel Collins's *Light on the Path,* first published in 1885, ten years before Krishnamurti was born, ends with such enigmatic, concept-transcending verses as

> Hold fast to that which has neither substance nor existence.
> Listen only to the voice which is soundless.
> Look only on that which is invisible alike to the inner and the
> outer sense.

In the light of a spiritual path as sublimely austere as is suggested by these lines, the ornate side of Theosophical thought would have to be seen as a true yet disposable vision, important only at certain stages of the long ascent to a whiteness without shadow.

These are ideas, or rather anti-ideas, which also suggest the way of Zen Buddhism, especially as it has been presented in the West. For at the heart of Zen are texts like the Heart Sutra and the Diamond Sutra; the former has lines like

> There is no suffering, no accumulation, no annihilation, no path;
> there is no knowledge, no attainment, no realization, because there

is no attainment. In the mind of the bodhisattva who dwells depending
on the wisdom that has gone beyond, there are no obstacles, and going
beyond thought-coverings, he reaches final Nirvana.

Links between Theosophy and Krishnamurti, and the recent
enthusiasms for Zen in America, are perceptible on the historical as
well as the theoretical plane; Alan Watts, who certainly did more
than anyone else except his mentor D. T. Suzuki to popularize Zen
in America in the mid-twentieth century, was introduced to Suzuki
as a young man in London in the 1930s by Christmas Humphreys,
an old-guard Theosophist who established the Buddhist Lodge in
England, and by Krishnamurti. For that matter, the wife of D. T.
Suzuki, the American Beatrice Lane Suzuki, a notable Buddhist
scholar in her own right, was an active Theosophist and organizer of
the work in Japan.[1] Mircea Eliade tells us that Edward Conze, whose
admirable scholarly books on Buddhism have also done much to
spread Buddhist thought in the West, likewise professed Theosophy and was a great admirer of *The Secret Doctrine*. Conze believed, among other things, that Madam Blavatsky was a reincarnation of Tsonkapa, the great Tibetan Buddhist reformer of the four-
teenth century.[2] Historical and personal ties between the theosophy
of the earlier decades of the century and the Buddhist enthusiasms
of the fifties and sixties are, then, far from lacking. An egregious
symbol of the linkage is the famous mid-fifties "underground"
movie *Pull My Daisy*, which Jack Kerouac, to be discussed in a
moment, narrated and which was based on an earlier play of his; it
consists largely of a conversation between a bishop of the theo-
sophically oriented Liberal Catholic Church and several leading
"beats."

Theosophy has had a significant general influence on this century. It is sufficient to mention its impact on the images and
spiritual development of William Butler Yeats, and the fact that
Mohandas K. Gandhi first discovered the *Bhagavad-Gita,* which
was to become virtually his Bible, in a Theosophical edition. Indeed, closer to home, the prevalence of ideas like karma, reincarnation, astrology, and a "new age" in popular culture owes a debt to
the lectures and literature-distribution of Theosophists in American
towns and cities as far back as the 1890s. One can find theosophical
books in public libraries almost everywhere; they have been read,

and have influenced the inner worlds of countless people, including some who are outwardly pillars of more conventional churches. It is worth noting that the immensely popular teachings about reincarnation and Atlantis of the Kentucky seer Edgar Cayce seem to be taken from Theosophical lore. Such recent and very widely read books as those of Ruth Montgomery, Richard Bach's *Jonathan Livingstone Seagull,* and Raymond Moody's *Life after Life,* with its data on postmortum experience, also agree in a Swedenborgian-Spiritualist-Theosophical view of the soul and its career after physical death.

Yet, while the teachings may be timeless, the Theosophical vessel as we know it has an unmistakably nineteenth-century aura about it—part of its glamour to some, suggestive of stuffiness and tedium to others. There is the heavily verbal orientation of the lectures and ponderous books, and the mystical systems seemingly as baroque as the fittings of a Victorian parlor. In America, theosophy inherited to some extent the place of the Spiritualism of the 1840s and 50s. So has Theosophy in the mid-twentieth century given center stage to other expressions of emergent religion. These have often been imports brought more or less intact from the East, complete with foreign-language terminology and teachers in foreign-looking robes. It would seem than many American seekers have wanted the flavor of an alternative culture as well as the words of an alternative faith, and have preferred the appearance of integralism in the exotic faith to syncretism—the latter having, unjustly, a pejorative connotation.

This is, no doubt, symptomatic of increasing alienation from much of American culture on the part of those who are seekers. They do not desire, as did an earlier generation of aficionados of the East, reassuring symbols of continuity with the past: a service with a basically Protestant structure at 11 on Sunday morning, group organization with American-style boards and committees, and an emphasis on reading scripturelike books and listening to sermonistic lectures as the major means of communication. However Eastern the message, these Western features of worship and sociological packaging, typical of groups like the Vedanta societies and Self-Realization Fellowship, make it seem continuous with liberal Protestantism—even as the message itself is likely to be couched in terms that make it seem an extension of Emerson.

But in the generations after World War II, a new pattern in the expression of emergent and excursus religion appeared. It had a definite religious content, Eastern more often than not, but it sought symbols of discontinuity with the American churchly past, at the same time incorporating not only the ideology but also aspects of the culture and lifestyle of the land of its origin. Americans practicing yoga or Zen, chanting "Hare Krishna" or "Nam myoho renge kyo," had their meetings at any time other than on Sunday morning. Their gatherings to sit silently in lotus posture, or chant in an exotic tongue in an atmosphere of incense and strange gods, would not have been reassuring to even the most liberal of old-fashioned Boston Unitarians. And they would often favor the dress, the food and tea and art, of India or Japan. But, as we shall see, now the wheel has almost come full circle, and in a movement like est, ideas typical of the alternative altars are being programmed in management-seminar format.

Zen Buddhism has no doubt been the most widely influential, at least culturally, of these imports. Paradoxically, Zen has conspicuously played the role of exotic import, and yet has been the most readily assimilated of the Eastern imports in America.

Zen Buddhism

A glance at the history and meaning of Zen in Asia is essential if we are to understand why Zen in particular emerged in America as a symbolic focus for emergent and excursus religion.

The word *Zen* is the Japanese transliteration of the Chinese *Ch'an,* which, in turn, is a transliteration of the Sanskrit *dhyana,* meaning meditation. Zen, then, is that tradition of practice which emphasizes meditation as the chief means to realizing Buddhist enlightenment. In a Zen temple in Japan or in an American Zen center, one will see rows of Zen practitioners seated in the posture called *zazen*—legs crossed in the lotus position, back erect, eyes half-open, focused on the floor or a wall some four feet in front, hands in the lap with thumbs joined. As they sit, a proctor with a stick may walk slowly up and down before the silent figures, bringing it down smartly on the shoulder of one who becomes drowsy or who bows forward to indicate he needs its therapy to recall him to mindfulness. A slowly burning stick of incense before

the altar measures the calm minutes as they slip by; when the zazen
session is over, a sharp striking of clappers and gongs will break into
the tranquility. When the meditators arise to labor, eat, or solicit
alms, they are to do it in a manner demonstrating the true nature of
the self approached in *zazen*.

This is concentration of a particular sort. It is not thinking
gorgeous thoughts, or contacting spirit worlds, but is "sitting
quietly, doing nothing," allowing an "empty but marvelous"
consciousness to surface. The things one may do with the mind
during *zazen*—counting breaths, following thoughts until they
vanish, holding in consciousness one of those enigmatic Zen *koans*
or riddles—are all ways of stopping the activity of the "monkey
mind." They are ways of bringing to a halt the ordinary racing of
the stream of consciousness and the ordinary tendency to interpret
experience conceptually and rationally, and to enable one to think
spontaneously and to see things "just as they are."

Zen has two sides. There is the still meditation and the harsh
discipline, and then there is the spirit of liberation from all constraints. Alan Watts called them square Zen and beat Zen.[3]

These two sides appear throughout the long history of Zen.
According to tradition, Zen began long ago when the Buddha
handed a flower to a disciple and smiled—and the disciple caught
in the flower and smile a universe of wisdom outside all words and
books. The secret of that smile was passed on until it was brought
by Bodhidharma to China in 520 A.D. Actually, Ch'an is a distinctively Chinese form of Mahayana Buddhism which combines the
latter's deep psychology and metaphysics with a Taoist sense of
naturalness and nature and a characteristic Chinese pragmatism. It
flourished in the great T'ang dynasty (618–907), and eventually
came to be the normative Buddhism of most Chinese monasteries.
Ch'an was brought by Eisai and Dogen to Japan in the thirteenth
century, where—although never more than one of several Buddhist
denominations—Zen became popular with the samurai class then
ruling the island empire and had a powerful cultural influence.

Throughout its history, Zen has known its share of stern disci-
plinarians, in whose temples one ate and slept little, where rising
and sitting and walking were done with military precision, and
where interviews with pupils were not lacking in shouts and blows.

Zen has also produced a small but madcap assortment of hermits, wanderers, and poets. In T'ang China, there was Han Shan, the eccentric Cold Mountain recluse whose poems were translated by Gary Snyder—of this more later. In medieval Japan, Ikkyu, awakened to a desire for enlightenment by hearing the call of a crow in the deep of night, tempered the monastic life with wanderings through the countryside. Though of imperial blood, he mixed with all sorts of people gladly, ate meat, drank sake, and begat children. Yet the Zen teaching of this "son of the errant cloud," as he called himself, was hard and pure. His poetry was forceful, and his denunciations of priestly wealth and hypocrisy made him popular. He heard sutras in the sound of wind and water, and heaven's triumph over death in every moment of life which has conquered fear.[4]

The two sides of Zen are not wholly incompatible. Their interaction is evident in the famous Zen ox-herding pictures, a traditional series of allegorical paintings which have been interpreted by several different masters. They begin by showing a young man seeking out and taming an obstreperous ox, which represents the mind. He reaches the point where he can indifferently ride on the ox's back. Then the ox disappears, next the man, leaving only nature; finally all disappears to leave only the white circle of the Void. But in the last picture we see the seeker once again, now a jovial old man, utterly free of all inhibition or self-consciousness or dignity, dancing and playing with children in the road as he advances "with bliss-bearing hands" toward a city. Taming the ox was discipline— but its goal was to evoke the naturalness and unconstricted spontaneity of the Void itself by taking away everything, all fears and habits and concepts, which were not the pure "suchness" of original nature.

The same principle applies to Zen art. The contribution of the Zen spirit to the arts of East Asia is, as is well known, immensely rich and varied. There is a distinctive Zen style in painting, poetry, landscaping, the tea ceremony, even the martial arts. What characterizes all these diverse forms of expression is a simplicity and naturalism which appears effortless, but which finds just the right gesture to catch the essence of the moment it reflects through a direct, concentrated intuition resulting from deep inwardness and long discipline. Zen naturalness is not simply living by surface moods and feelings, which, according to Buddhism, are not "natural" at all but a tangled web woven of karma, suffering, and desire, compounded by ignorance. It is, rather, a ruthless pruning away of all these that allows the deep, true, and joyous spontaneity of one's buddhahood to well up. And because it had undistorted perception, this nature intuitively knows, and can flawlessly express through one's chosen medium, the true nature of all other things.

It is the sense of transcendent freedom from structures, whether of mind or society, and of seamless harmony with our ultimate environment, the infinite universe itself, which is suggested by this ideal that has most appealed to Westerners drawn to Zen. It is to these persons we must now turn.

Zen Mountaineering

We climaxed discussion of Theosophy with a single archetypal incident, Olcott's "instinctive act of pooja" in stooping down to kiss the ground upon landing at Bombay on February 16, 1879. Let us begin the discussion of American Zen with another symbolic date, October 22, 1955.

On that evening, the novelist Jack Kerouac and the poet Gary Snyder camped together in the High Sierras east of San Francisco. A third companion, John Montgomery, was following and camped below them.

It was a memorable evening. The high-country air was cool and fresh and more intoxicating than wine; the brilliant stars were as big and close as the stars of a fairy-tale world. Snyder, much the better outdoorsman, cooked a hearty supper. Then came talk, hours of the wonderful, ebullient camping talk of gifted young men, talk about everything under heaven: adventures, travels, women, poetry, philosophy. And Buddhism. For Kerouac and Snyder considered themselves Buddhists, after a fashion. Snyder was engaged in orientalist studies and was more advanced and serious than his friend in the faith of the Middle Way; Kerouac, having but recently turned to the Triple Refuge, regarded Snyder as his mentor.

But it was Jack Kerouac, chronicler of the 1950s "beat generation," who made the evening in the mountains famous. Although it is briefly described in Snyder's journal, it emerges as one of the unforgettable scenes in Kerouac's autobiographical novel *The Dharma Bums*.[5] That book is Kerouac's most famous work after his best-selling *On the Road;* it covers a year of his life in 1955–56 when he was close to Snyder, Allen Ginsberg, Kenneth Rexroth, and other lights of the "San Francisco Poetry Renaissance" of the late fifties. The basic theme of *The Dharma Bums* is Zen, or, more precisely, "Zen lunacy," and Gary Snyder, thinly disguised as Japhy Ryder, is the hero, the ideal youthful Zen enthusiast and adept.

Kerouac met Snyder through Ginsberg, whom Kerouac had known as far back as 1944, and who considered Snyder the most worthwhile person in the San Francisco scene. Their meeting was just before the legendary poetry reading in the Six Gallery in early October 1955, when the San Francisco Poetry Renaissance was allegedly born. Kenneth Rexroth was master of ceremonies, Allen Ginsberg first uttered his celebrated "Howl," Snyder delivered some lines on Coyote, the trickster-hero of the North American Indians, other young poets also read. About one hundred fifty people were present, and there was enough wine, raucous fun, and literary talk to last through dawn.

Kerouac devotes four freewheeling pages in *The Dharma Bums* to that epic night, but it was only the beginning of his relationship with Ryder/Snyder. The Japhy of the novel was living in Berkeley in a tiny cottage. He had been studying Japanese and Chinese at the university and on his own for three years, prepatory to going to a Zen monastery in Japan for further Zen practice the following year. That fall he was translating the Chinese Zen hermit-poet Han Shan, "Cold Mountain."

But Japhy was no mere scholar; he spent summers lumberjacking and fire-watching in the Northwest, and was as much at home in the mountains as amid Chinese and Japanese texts. Nor was he a rigorous ascetic; one could usually find women and cheap wine around his cabin, and it was the scene of some wild parties. But Japhy could be "tender as a mother" and quiet as a saint, and went his own way whenever you began to think you understood him. Over the whole narrative of *The Dharma Bums,* which focuses on his adamantine and mysterious holiness, lies knowledge that these boyish days are for him only an interlude and a preliminary; at the end of the year he will be going to his monastery in Japan. Something very deep and special set Japhy apart; all who met him, especially the immature but sensitive Kerouac, sensed that.

For one thing, he was always making simple gifts to people. On the mountain that mythic evening, Japhy gave Ray Smith (Kerouac) a worn Buddhist rosary—an act of *dana,* donation, one of the six Buddhist *paramitas* or perfections.

For another, he had that peculiar grace, "lightness," and air of physical and psychic balance which comes from great equilibrium and reserve strength on many levels, from knowing what the universe is and where one fits in it. The morning after they camped on the mountain, the pair pushed their way toward the peak. Kerouac lost his nerve, but Japhy ran like a mountain goat over the crags and through the fog to the peak. Then Smith (Kerouac) says, "Suddenly I heard a beautiful broken yodel of a strange musical and mystical intensity in the wind, and looked up, and it was Japhy standing on top of Matterhorn peak letting out his triumphant mountain-conquering Buddha Mountain Smashing song of Joy. It was beautiful."[6] (There is a Zen saying, "When you get to the top of a mountain, keep climbing.")

The Dharma Bums has its weaknesses as literature. The structure is limp and lacks consistency. Female characters are stereotypical mothers and waitresses, or "chicks" who appear out of nowhere for a party, then conveniently disappear when the menfolk get down to the serious business of drinking wine and discussing philosophy. As for Zen Buddhism, there is no evidence in the novel that Japhy or anyone else ever regularly practiced *zazen,* or were aware that it was an important part of the faith they loved to celebrate—though Smith/Kerouac did have a "nice old rocking chair" on the dilapidated porch of his house, where he liked to sit in the morning and read the Diamond Sutra, even as Thoreau had, we gather, read the "Bhagvat Geeta" some Walden morning. But whatever the gaps in the book's knowledge of Buddhism (and Kerouac would have been responsible for these, not Snyder), it was the anti-structural, spontaneous side of Zen that its heroes wished to celebrate—"Zen lunacy," they called it.

Moreover, the romantic, youthful exuberance of *The Dharma*

Bums manages to rise above its limitations and makes the book not
only an important social document relevant to excursus religion in
America, but also strangely moving. Above all, the figure of Japhy,
elusive yet unforgettable, coarse yet pious, both American and
oriental at once, both a Walt Whitman and a Han Shan, stays in
one's mind. He remains unique, yet also archetypical, even as he
was at the end of the book, when the physical Japhy was seven
thousand miles away answering the sonorous meditation bell of an
ancient temple, but the narrator, descending a mountain Japhy had
loved, perceived some twisted gnarly trees:

> And suddenly it seemed I saw that unimaginable little Chinese bum
> standing there, in the fog, with that expressionless humor on his
> seamed face. It wasn't the real-life Japhy of rucksacks and Buddhism
> studies and big mad parties at Corte Madera, it was the realer-than-life
> Japhy of my dreams, and he stood there saying nothing. "Go away,
> thieves of the mind!" he cried down the hollows of the unbelievable
> Casades.[7]

Jack Kerouac

Jean-Louis Kerouac (1922–69), called Jack, was born and raised in
Lowell, Massachusetts. His family was French-Canadian, of Breton
origin, and there is more than a little Celtic romanticism in his love
of words, wandering, and magical glamor.

After a very indifferent Merchant Marine and Navy career during
the war, and equally indifferent starts at college and odd jobs,
Kerouac hitchhiked to the West Coast in 1947. That epic journey,
together with later excursions to New Orleans and Mexico, was the
basis of *On the Road,* the novel which ten years later was to make its
author famous and financially secure, and which, for all its un-
couthness, was a literary gust of fresh air that managed to catch the
inchoate rebellion of a new postwar generation.

What is of most concern to us is how that rebellion got linked up
with Zen Buddhism—so that for the "Dharma Bums," the rhetoric
of the Eastern faith and the lifestyle of the "Zen lunatics" became
both an expression and a legitimation of their dissatisfaction and
their "hip" way of life.

Jack Kerouac was raised in a highly traditional French Catholic family. His mother, upon whom he was dependent and with whom he lived off and on all his life, was very devout. (Kerouac liked to say that his prose style came from his boyhood experience of making a full confession to a priest every week, cleansing himself of all he had done by giving a full account of it.)

But away from home, other things attracted him. In 1954, when he was feeling lost and low, he discovered Buddhism. He had actually come into contact with it the year before, when Allen Ginsberg, while studying Chinese painting, had read some of D. T. Suzuki's essays on Zen and talked to Jack about them. But Kerouac was unimpressed at the time. Then, in January of 1955, Kerouac moved in with Neal Cassady (Dean Moriarty in *On the Road*) and his family and began serious Buddhist study.

It started when Cassady expressed his enthusiasm for the American mystic Edgar Cayce, especially for his teachings regarding reincarnation, and Jack responded by arguing against him. Kerouac had shortly before reread Thoreau, whom he had long admired, and, recalling the Walden sage's citations of Hindu philosophy, had turned to Eastern texts. He rummaged through libraries to find books like a translation of Ashvagosha's life of the Buddha, and told Cassady that Cayce's literalistic idea of continuous reincarnations of an immortal soul was unsophisticated from a Buddhist point of view, since in the eyes of the great faith of East Asia there is really no ego, and so nothing to reincarnate and nothing to be immortal.

For himself, though, Kerouac prized most the first of the Buddha's Four Noble Truths: All Life is Suffering. To him this verity, uttered by one as quiet and deep as the World-Enlightened One, gave some perspective on his own confused and tormented life—with his restlessness, his apparent failure (he was not yet successful as a writer), his second ex-wife's taking him to court to win child support, his pointless appetites for drink and drugs.

By late in 1954 he had taken up Mahayana literature, especially the *Diamond Sutra*, with its lines like these:

> All composite things
> Are like a dream, a phantasm, a
>   bubble, and a shadow,
> Are like a dew-drop and a flash of lightning;
> They are thus to be regarded.

He had decided he was going to become a bodhisattva and painfully practiced meditation briefly every day. He wrote several hundred pages, called *Some of the Dharma* (never published, though he tried) of notes and reflections on his new faith. Kerouac went back East for Christmas 1954, and stayed through the following summer; his shiftlessness and his Buddhism aggravated his prosaic relatives and led to some stormy living room scenes. But in mid-summer he unexpectedly got word that *On the Road,* many times rejected by publishers, had been accepted by Viking Press. Jubilant and with an advance in his pocket, he went to Mexico City, did some writing, and then returned to California, where he hopped a freight out of Los Angeles to the Bay Area, a journey immortalized in the opening scene of *The Dharma Bums*. Next came the great Six Gallery reading and the meeting with Snyder, who deepened and stabilized the novelist's Buddhism.[8]

Several observations can be appended to this precis of how Jack Kerouac came to Buddhism. First, we note the indirect influence through Ginsberg of D. T. Suzuki (1870–1966), that Japanese scholar who produced an almost endless series of books and essays in English on Zen. Although there were other influences, the Western vogue for Zen would have been almost inconceivable without Suzuki. He and those influenced by him have given Zen more English-language literature than all the rest of Buddhism put together. No doubt this gave Zen an edge in the spiritual market-place, though it is probably true that no other form of Buddhism could have had the Western cultural impact of Zen, with its conceptual flexibility and its easy-to-appreciate art. Suzuki made the transmission process all the easier by stressing an interpretation of Zen which drew on Western existentialism at the expense of the discipline, cultic, and sociological sides of Zen in Japan, mixing in just enough of the latter to give it an excitingly exotic flavor but not enough to intimidate the adventurous spirit. Suzuki was himself no holy, unworldly monk; he was a layman and a highly sophisticated student of Western thought who knew how to present Zen to make it a live option in the Euro-American context. Nor was he unaware of the Western tradition of alternative spirituality within which Zen was to fit; it is curious to note that there is a 1914 Japanese translation of Swedenborg's *New Jerusalem* by D. T. Suzuki, who did several such works on commission for the Swedenborgian church.

Second, we may note the role of Thoreau in first directing
Kerouac's attention to Eastern thought. The seminal importance of
the New England Transcendentalists and their spiritual kin, like
Whitman, in shaping the American experience of excursus religion
can hardly be overemphasized, as we have seen. Kerouac read Henry
Thoreau several times in an attempt to get into the side of the
American dream Walden represented; he had always wanted to go
somewhere and live the Walden life. Instead he discovered Thoreau's East.

Third, the discovery of Buddhism came in the midst of discussions about excursus tradition figures and ideas—namely, Edgar
Cayce and reincarnation. Buddhism emerged as an option when the
language, sociology, and conceptual frame of reference was already
defined by talk of alternatives to normative religion, and of the
pre-existence and destiny of the soul. We have already observed
that Cayce's doctrines were probably borrowed from Theosophy.

Fourth and most important, Kerouac became serious about Buddhism following a self-alienation from American values, above all
from the apotheosis of surburbia of those Eisenhower years, as
exemplified by his wandering and seemingly unproductive life. The
example of another American dropout, Thoreau, was not enough as
his personal troubles mounted, though the earlier writer's Hindu
citations pointed in the right direction. But Kerouac's inner compass was far more wobbly indeed than the old-fashioned New
England conscience of his model, his view of himself and the world
correspondingly less sunny. He needed more than pantheism; he
needed also the Buddha's clear-sighted diagnosis of the painful
disease called separate existence. It was, then, after a prior state of
essential alienation from America and inner despair that Kerouac
was able to take refuge in the alternative from the East, and to read
signposts to it in America's past. It is this process which both veils
and reveals the fundamental continuity of emergent religion.

It must be noted that Kerouac's Buddhism did not wear particularly well. He was a falling star which quickly burned out, and the
pitiful last decade of his life was marked by a desperation and
incapacity which the bottle and life with mother seemed to solace
better than the Dharma. But the significance of *The Dharma
Bums,* both as symbol and influence, is not erased by this end. We

must now turn to him who, in the novel, Kerouac acknowledges is ahead of him in the Buddha-stream, and observe how his career is also a paradigm of Zen in the West.

Gary Snyder

Gary Snyder was born in San Francisco in 1930, but grew up amid considerable poverty on a dairy farm in Washington state. He loved the Pacific Northwest, with its towering mountains and dark forests, and early acquired a deep and romantic appreciation for woodcraft and Native American lore unsullied by conventional religion. He was not personally influenced by Theosophy in his turning to Eastern or archaic American spiritual symbols. In 1942 he moved with his family to Portland, Oregon, and there he graduated in 1951 from Reed College with majors in anthropology and literature. His most intense interest at the time was the mythology and anthropology of the Amerindians who lived amid the woods and mountains he loved.

In 1952 he moved to San Francisco and worked at various jobs there. In 1953 he moved again to Berkeley, where he lived in the little cottage described by Kerouac in *The Dharma Bums* and studied Chinese and Japanese in the Department of Oriental Languages at the University of California in Berkeley, without neglecting breaks to return to the forests and mountains. During summers he made some money in logging and manning a fire lookout in national forests—readers of *The Dharma Bums* will recall that, at the end of the epic year therein transcribed, when Snyder left for Japan, he got Kerouac/Smith the lookout job in Washington's Mt. Baker National Forest that he had filled with mystical perfection a season or two before.[9]

Snyder became increasingly involved with the East as well as with ancient America. He says he was first drawn to the Far East by an appreciation of Chinese poetry and the philosophy of Taoism, and became interested in Zen when he realized that the spirit of philosophical Taoism survived in it. He first learned of Zen from the works of D. T. Suzuki. He was also attracted to India by the powerful archetypes of Hindu mythology; through the study of Indian thought he perceived the richness of Indian Buddhist philosophy and followed it from the original Mahayana systems to Zen.

He wrote poetry on Amerindian myths, seeing American lore in the crisp clarity of Zen perception. Not content with mere romantic appreciation of the Eastern school, he proceeded to ground himself in Zen through appropriate language skills and disciplined training. He translated, as we have seen, the poems of that kindred soul of a dozen centuries before, Han-Shan (Kanzan in Japanese, literally "Cold Mountain.")

He began the published version of the Cold Mountain Poems with a preface by the hermit-poet's contemporary, Lu Ch'iu-yin, governor of T'ai prefecture, who said, "No one knows just what sort of man Han-Shan was." He was a mountain madman, who looked like a tramp, "yet in every word he breathed was a meaning in line with the subtle principles of things if only you thought of it deeply."[10] Kerouac, at least, read Gary Snyder to be the same kind of man.

It was in the fall of 1955, then, that Gary Snyder met Kerouac through Ginsberg, just before the legendary poetry reading at the Six Galley. In May of 1956 he left for Japan on a scholarship provided by the First Zen Institute of America, in New York, to study Zen and Japanese in Kyoto. His patron and teacher in Japan was Ruth Fuller Sasaki, doyenne of American Zen. He stayed in the Japanese Zen temple a year and a half, then, in 1958, worked his way back to America on a ship. He returned to Japan in 1959, studying under Oda Sesso Roshi, head abbot of the famous Dai-toku temple in Kyoto, and for a while afterward alternated between living in Japan, working at sea, and publishing his poetry and giving poetry readings in America. In 1961–62 he traveled in India, visiting Hindu and Buddhist holy places. He now lives in the foothills of the Sierra Nevadas with his wife, Masa, and two sons. In the seventies he was involved in environmentalist thought and politics, and served as a member of the California Arts Council, appointed by the governor.

The length of time he has spent in Japanese temples certainly confirms the seriousness about Zen of this paragon of Zen-American mysticism. Yet it is important to note that he is just as authentically a successor of the American radical tradition often related earlier to Transcendentalism, Spiritualism, and Theosophy. There is the same anarchistic protest, the same deep feeling for the heritage of the American Indians and their spirituality, mixed with the same—or a similar—thirst for an appropriate exoticism which would confirm and complete one's sense of being both more profoundly and spiritually American than most others, and yet not at home in conventional American society. As with them, the quest for excursus into the archaic led to an excursus to the distant and exotic: the past and the far away became almost one. In 1961 Snyder wrote: "As a poet I hold the most archaic values on earth. They go back to the late Paleolithic: the fertility of the soil, the magic of animals, the power-vision in solitude, the terrifying initiation and rebirth, the love and ecstasy of the dance, the common work of the tribe."[11]

Yet all of this was not wholly inconsistent with the great Eastern religions; later Snyder pointed out that Buddhism and Hinduism carry much of Stone Age religion with them in such practices as shaving the head.[12] The most important product of his experiences is the rich kaleidoscope of his major prose book, *Earth House Hold*, which can move from vignettes of a very "tight" sesshin, or intensive meditation session, at the Shokokuji in Kyoto, to experiments with living a primitive life on an island with his Japanese wife, to accounts of the racy conversation of a tanker crew.

In 1975 Gary Snyder received the Pulitzer Prize in poetry for his book *Turtle Island*. Its poems are ostensibly drawn largely from native American mythology, though more subtly they reflect a biological systems-theory of ecology, and the theme of the interdependence of all beings supremely expressed, as Snyder has himself emphasized, in the Buddhist Avatamsaka or Garland Sutra.[13] In a prose afterword, the poet speaks of his Zen training as a major formative influence.

Alan Watts

During his San Francisco and Berkeley days, Gary Snyder was familiar with the American Academy of Asian Studies in San Francisco, though he never formally studied at it. This institution was organized in 1951 by Frederick Spiegelberg, and was oriented toward a serious but accessible communication of Asian culture to the general public. The Academy played an indefinable but not insignificant role in shaping the "San Francisco Renaissance" of the fifties, with its Zen interests, and the even more explosive Asiaticism of the sixties "counterculture," whose mecca was San Francisco's Haight-Ashbury district. As much as anything, this was because one of the Academy's leading teachers in the fifties was a middle-aged Englishman named Alan Watts (1915–73), a good friend of Snyder's.

Generously and gracefully, Alan Watts in his autobiography disclaims credit for Gary Snyder and says that Kerouac's characterization of him as Japhy Ryder "hardly begins to do him justice." Watts adds that Snyder studied Chinese at the University of California and Zen in Kyoto, "but when I am dead I would like to be able to say that he is carrying on everything I hold most dearly, though with a different style. To put it in another way, my only regret is that I cannot formally claim him as my spiritual successor. He did it all on his own, but nevertheless he *is* just exactly what I have been trying to *say*." The supreme tribute is perhaps this: "I can only say that a universe which has manifested Gary Snyder could never be called a failure."[14]

Nonetheless, we cannot think of Gary Snyder's generation, and of Zen in America, without putting Alan Watts in the foreground. If Snyder *is* what he *says*, what Watts said has been immensely important to millions, as it was to Snyder himself.

Watts was a very different sort of man from Kerouac and Snyder. The genius of the latter two, in their different ways, was to make Zen appear a natural consummation and interpretive paradigm for that authentically American lifestyle and literary tradition represented by Thoreau, Whitman, and Tom Wolfe. Their Zen fitted like a glove to the way of that very American type, or at least ideal: the young man who thinks deeply but cares little for "success" or social grace, and, like a pilgrim-monk of old, wanders about in shabby clothes, logging, seafaring, hitchhiking, writing verse, and exulting in nature and the infinite. Gentle yet fiercely independent and vaguely radical, he is Johnny Appleseed, the young Frederick Evans, Henry Olcott after he carried the style to India, Gary Snyder, and many others. This lifestyle is deeply intertwined with excursus religion and is of sufficient and authentic cultural importance in

America that its latter-day interpenetration with imported Zen is highly significant and serves to help legitimate Zen both as American and as spiritually viable.

Alan Watts's role in the Zen movement was different from theirs, but had some inner continuities with their experience. Despite his very important position as a catalyst and interpreter, Watts was always in some deep, mainly inner sense an outsider to everything. He was more than a little alienated by British church and society as a young man, yet rootless as a transplanted Englishman in America, where his British public-school accent and manner sometimes put people off as being incongruous for a guru, and where (like many others in a similar situation) he sometimes overplayed the part. He was, after D. T. Suzuki, the West's foremost exponent of Zen, yet he never formally indentified himself with any Zen movement and did not call himself a Buddhist or anything else, nor did he practice meditation more than sporadically.

Despite the fact that Watts had only qualified enthusiasm for Kerouac's "beat Zen," there were certain odd parallels and paradoxes between his life and the French-Canadian's. Both were relatively short-lived; both originated as definite outsiders to the West Coast mysticism scene, and later became eminent stimulators and interpreters of it; both were prolific writers, with marvelous gifts of image and metaphor, who, in two paragraphs, could entice a reader into their worlds of fantasy or mystical reality through sheer word-wizardry, but who finally lacked a countervailing breadth (both men essentially say and do the same thing in all their books) or a capacity for tight literary discipline and intellectual rigor. Both men, moreover, for all their mysticism, lived personal lives which could scarcely be characterized as ascetic, and they made no secret of this in their autobiographical works (Watts's *In My Own Way;* virtually the whole corpus of Kerouac).

Paradox, though, is close to the center of meaning in the life of Alan Watts. That life was always something of a pendulum swinging between what we have here called established and emergent religion; nor did the pendulum stop when he ostensibly cut all ties with establishment, for he soon became so prominent a writer and spokesman for the other side as to become virtually an establishment in himself.

Watts was born in an English village, and grew up with a love for the beautiful countryside of that land—a love like that of another figure we have met in these pages, Frederick Evans of the Shakers. There is little further parallel with the earlier emigrant, though.

Watts, though he did not attend university, acquired a solid education at one of the best public schools, King's College in Canterbury. In school, and during a few years afterward, when he was, owing to his family's inability to afford formal higher education for him, "his own univerity," the bright young man discovered Buddhism and other exotic spiritual disciplines. In London, during the dark years of the late thirties, he sought out bookstores and circles of people interested in these disciplines. When only twenty, he published his first book, *The Spirit of Zen.*

Christmas Humphreys, a London solicitor, Theosophist, and Buddhist, took the young man under his wing and gave him an unusual education in the spiritual mysteries of the East. He introduced him to the writings of D. T. Suzuki as early as 1930, although Watts did not meet his great mentor in Zen until 1936.

Daisetz Teitaro Suzuki, whose influence on Kerouac and Snyder we have already noted, first came to the West as early as 1897, when his teacher, Soyen Roshi, arranged for him to become an editor of the Open Court Publishing Company in LaSalle, Illinois. There he remained as a guest of the distinguished publisher, Paul Carus, until 1909, writing books, articles, and translations on Buddhism and related topics. After he returned to Japan, he became a professor of English and married an American lady, Beatrice Lane, a Buddhist scholar and writer of some importance herself, and, as we have seen, an active Theosophist. On his way back to America in 1936, he attended a World Congress of Faiths in London, when Watts met him. In 1950–58 he was again in America, teaching and lecturing at universities, and the intense intellectual interest in Zen of those days can be largely traced to this activity and to the lingering influence of his earlier writing. Many Westerners came to Zen through such books of his as *An Introduction to Zen Buddhism, Essays in Zen Buddhism, The Training of the Zen Buddhist Monk, Manual of Zen Buddhism, Zen and Japanese Culture.*

Alan Watts was to have an interlude of a few years, however, before he fulfilled the commission Suzuki might be supposed to have given him. In 1938 he married, in an Anglican parish church in London, the daughter of a very wealthy Chicago businessman. Despite the establishment locale of the wedding, both partners were more or less Buddhist; the bride's mother was Ruth Fuller Everett, a leader in the First Zen Institute in New York. Indeed, after becoming widowed a few years later, this lady was to become well-known in her own right as a Zen writer and priest.

On the eve of World War II, Alan and Eleanor Watts came to New York. He immediately began the only kind of life with which he was ever happy or, for that matter, successful: an informal mixture of writing, teaching, and lecturing. He also maintained a close relationship with the Zen Institute.

However, drawn by the aesthetic appeal of Anglo-Catholicism and by a desire for a professional vocation in which he could fulfill within the context of his culture his main interest, religion, he determined to enter the priesthood of the Episcopal Church. On Ascension Day, 1945, Alan Watts was ordained in Chicago and became Episcopal chaplain at Northwestern University.

Five years later he was to leave the priesthood. But during those five years he constructed a ministry and a Christian theological style worth remembering. Indeed, his five brief years in the Episcopal Church and on the Northwestern campus were so highly charged that those in both institutions whose memories go back that far have little trouble remembering that brilliant, intense, loquacious, and flamboyant presence among them, who never lacked for money (his wife's), wit, or attention. Canterbury House under him was a virtually nonstop bull-session; his services drew worshipers from near and far to a rich liturgical splendor embellished with a sense of playfulness and to the incomparable mystical sermons of he who then as later could induce with words a sense of spiritual experience and of being on the "inside" of some cosmic secret.

Theologically he was still wrestling with the reconciliation of Buddhism and Christianity. In a book like *Behold the Spirit* (1947), deriving from this Christian period, he expounded a Christianity based on a pantheistic view of deity reinforced by both Eastern and Western mystical philosophies, but profoundly incarnational and sacramental in its mundane expression, and imbued with a deep appreciation of the spiritual significance of aesthetics and play. His next book, *The Supreme Identity* (1950), moved further in assimilating Eastern and Western paths to knowing the One in the Eternal Now—the one thing worth knowing, though uncontainable in words; *The Supreme Identity* is probably Watts's most substantial work as far as scholarship and sustained, serious philosophical discourse are concerned.

By the time it was published, Watts's career as a Christian priest was about over. He was in trouble for teaching libertarian views on sex and marriage; his own marriage was on the rocks; and his inner doubts concerning Christianity and his clerical calling could not be resolved. It became evident that the ministry was not for him and, despite his success as a university chaplain, he could not go on. He later wrote of the difference between the shaman and priest, the latter being an institutional officer and the former a loner who originates rather than follows traditions; he was all shaman. In the summer of 1950 his marriage and his ministry ended.

He was on his own at thirty-five, for the first time in his life without money, profession, or social role. It was a difficult passage, even a sort of initiation. He landed on his feet the next year, though. He remarried, and was appointed to the faculty of the American Academy of Asian Studies in San Francisco.

For the rest of his life, apart from the few years of full-time teaching at the American Academy, Watts was again doing what he liked best, and very successfully: scrambling to make a life and a living from writing, holding seminars, lecturing, finagling grants, being a celebrity. A three-year fellowship from the Bollengen Foundation enabled him to do research for the book most relevant to our purpose, *The Way of Zen*, published in 1957. But his numerous other books, including such well-known titles as *Beyond Theology*, *Erotic Spirituality*, *The Wisdom of Insecurity*, *This is It*, and *The Two Hands of God*, culminating in his autobiography, *In My Own Way*, testify to his literary virtuosity. (His father wrote the introduction to the last, which, as Watts remarks, must be a unique literary phenomenon.) Apart from the divide between his Christian and post-Christian phases, however, one detects a curious lack of movement or development on a deep level, although there are superficial tie-ins with passing vogues: Zen in the fifties, psychedelia in the sixties. But all the way through there are the same attacks on the Judeo-Christian God the Father, the same Krishna-murtian intentional intentionlessness, the same Zen/Vedanta pantheistic glow. It is all said eloquently, and said over and over.

Nonetheless, *The Way of Zen* remains the most accessible general introduction to Zen in English, at least in the D. T. Suzuki manner of interpretation, and as such has been immensely influential. The tone of Watts's approach is captured by the opening sentence: "Zen Buddhism is a way and a view of life which does not belong to any of the formal categories of modern Western thought."[15] The hard monastic discipline side of Zen is glossed over, but we are immediately intrigued by what doubtless intrigues most Westerners when they first turn to the contemplation of Zen: the idea of a whole new "view of life" and one so unique it cannot even be handled by the mental machinery we have used thus far. Watts properly does not overdo the "mysterious East" business, but he does emphasize that Zen and even *zazen* are more an attitude or kind of awareness than a particular practice; this he got from Suzuki, whom he says elsewhere was really more Taoist than Japanese Zen. Watts liked the free inwardness he associated with true Taoism and Zen, and disdained the "skinhead military zip" of many Japanese monks. Gary Snyder had some good things to say about Suzuki and Watts:

> The reason people criticize Suzuki is that there almost aren't enough words to say how big he was. What other Japanese person has had so much influence on the world at large? We don't think of it that way because we take him to be so much our own, but he is Japan's greatest cultural contribution to the world so far. In Europe and America he has influenced everything—psychology, music, aesthetics, architecture, landscape design—and through his disciples like Christmas Humphreys, Edward Conze, Hubert Benoit, Bernard Phillips, John Cage, and Alan Watts, he has permeated all levels of society. He has been the catalyst of some real social changes, in attitudes towards the self, towards effort, towards involvement, in attitudes on the nature of creativity, on the value of verbalization and articulation as against the intuitive approach. All these things which are not 'pure Zen' or Zen practice are nonetheless very important humanly. You can say about Alan Watts's books that they have done a lot of people a lot of good in terms of turning down their anxiety, and in stimulating them towards a more creative attitude towards themselves. Whether or not his books are 'real Zen' is beside the point. You meet people all the time

who say, 'I owe so much to Alan Watts's writings. They helped me lead
my life.' And that is how great Suzuki is. He is more than just a part
of bringing Zen to the West. He entered deeply into new social attitudes in the world.[16]

Formal Zen

Thus far most of what we have discussed of Zen is in the nature of
diffuse cultural influence or persons mainly responsible for that
influence. Probably that is the most significant feature of Zen: its
ability to suggest, in Watts's phrase, "a view of life which does not
belong to any of the formal categories of modern Western
thought." Zen's putatively supplemental or noncompetitive relation to Western thought and even to Western religion, is essential
to its role in the ecology of American culture and to the understanding of emergent and excursus religion. But it is also important
to see the place of the formal Zen centers, such as the First Zen
Institute of America in New York, significant at one point, as we
have seen, in the career of Alan Watts. Excursus religion tends to
avoid direct competition with established religion, but maintains
interpersonal relationships among its followers either more diffuse
or more intense than those found in mainline churches; we now
move to consider those Zen relationships, centering around that of
roshi or master and disciple, but also sometimes involving community, that can be very intense.

This is, of course, the story of those Zen priests (not laymen like
Suzuki) who have come to America to live and teach Zen in a
formal manner. The tale begins with the redoubtable Soyen Shaku
(1859–1919), a Japanese monk who wrote of himself in 1888:

This fellow was a son of Nobusuke Goemon Ichenose of Takahama,
the province of Wakasa. His nature was stupid and tough. When he
was young, none of his relatives liked him. When he was twelve years
old, he was ordained as a monk by Ekkei, Abbot of Myo-shin Monastery. Afterwards, he studied literature under Shungai of Kennin Monastery for three years, and gained nothing. Then he went to Mii-dera and
studied Tendai philosophy under Tai-ho for a summer, and gained
nothing. After this, he went to Bizen and studied Zen under the old
teacher Gisan for one year, and attained nothing. He then went to the
East, to Kamakura, and studied under the Zen master Ko-sen in the

Engaku Monastery for six years, and added nothing to the aforesaid nothingness. He was in charge of a little temple, Butsu-nichi, one of the temples of the Engaku Cathedral, for one year and from there he went to Tokyo to attend Kej-o College for one year and a half, making himself the worst student there; and forgot the nothingness that he had gained. Then he created for himself new delusions, and came to Ceylon in the spring of 1887; and now, under the Ceylon monk he is studying the Pali language and Hinayana Buddhism. Such a wandering mendicant! He ought to repay the twenty years of debts to those who fed him in the name of Buddhism.[17]

This fellow (and those who know something of Zen philosophy will catch the double meaning of the nothingness he attained and forgot) did something to repay those debts when, in 1893, he came to the United States to attend the World Parliament of Religions, a conference that was seminal to the Easternization of emergent religion in America in several respects. Like Swami Vivekananda, the founder of the Ramakrishna Mission and the Vedanta Societies in the West, Soyen found that the 1893 event kindled something in the West; it was a moment at the height of imperialism when its reverse side, the penetration of the conqueror by the conquered, began to show itself for those who had eyes to see.

Soyen returned to Japan and taught Zen in Kamakura after the parliament. Among his students were D. T. Suzuki and Nyogen Senzaki (1876-1958). Soyen came to America a second time in 1905, when he was the guest of Mr. and Mrs. Alexander Russell of San Francisco; Mrs. Russell was the first American to study the Zen "riddles" or *koans* formally. Senzaki came to America the same year. He was the first Zen monk to reside permanently in this country. His life after his arrival at age twenty-nine was typical of that of the Japanese immigrant of those days. He worked as a houseboy, cook, waiter, and finally teacher of the Japanese language, and did not begin lecturing on Buddhism until he had been in America for twenty years. But he then devoted more than thirty more years to mission work, and during this time (except for the war years, when he was interned) he taught in *zendos* in San Francisco and Los Angeles, and through his students was responsible for Zen centers from New York to Hawaii.

Senzaki acquainted himself with the American intellectual heritage, and was surprised to find what he considered an excellent

preparation for Zen in the American freethinkers, from Thomas
Paine to Robert Ingersoll, and in Ralph Waldo Emerson. Above all,
though, he believed that the pragmatism of William James was but
the Zen of another culture, ''another name for one manifestation
of the sparkling rays of Zen in the actual, practical world.'' Surely,
he thought, people with the rationality, informality, pragmatism,
simplicity, and love of nature of Americans will not forever be able
to resist the appeal of Zen.[18]

Another influential personality was Sokatsu Shaku Roshi (1869–
1954), also a student of Soyen, who came to America with six
disciples in 1906. They bought a farm in Hayward, California, and
when it failed, established a Zen center in San Francisco. In 1910
they returned to Japan, leaving only one member of the party
behind, Shigemitsu Sasaki, who was later to become the *roshi* of
the First Zen Institute of America in New York, a teacher of Alan
Watts, and the husband of Ruth Fuller Sasaki.

In February, 1911, Sasaki crossed the Shasta mountains on foot;
he finally reached the Rogue River Valley and stayed with a friend
there, meditating daily on a big rock by the stream. He led a
wandering life for several years and ended up in New York. There
he lived in Greenwich Village and got to know some of the ''bo-
hemian'' poets of the day. He returned to Japan in 1919 to complete his study of Zen, but came back to New York in 1928 to
promulgate Zen there, and in 1930 Sasaki (his monastic name was
Sokei-an) founded the First Zen Institute, then the Buddhist Society. The most prominent of his American followers included Mary
Farkas and Ruth Fuller Everett, whom he later married, and who
was to become Watts's mother-in-law.

In passing, we must note the almost uncanny parallel between
Sasaki's life as a lonely Zen priest in the America of the World War
I era, and that of the ''dharma bums'' of American Zen some forty
years later. Here is the same Zen mountaineering in the rich,
meditative woods of the Northwest, and the same interaction with
the alienated urban poets of the day. Already Zen had established a
relationship with the perennial American themes of understanding
spiritually the fabulous natural splendor of the land, so majestic as
almost to mock the Puritan concept of cosmic fallenness, and to the
inner malaise of the person of fine poetic and intellectual sensitivity
in this land of supposed materialistic crassness.

In 1941 the Institute tried to begin a new work in a new building owned by Ruth Everett on East 65th Street. The new Institute was opened on December 7th, 1941—and shortly after was swarming with FBI men. Sasaki was interned in 1942. His health failed; in 1943 he was released but was able to do little. In 1944, partly to stabilize the Institute's legal position in the difficult wartime situation and partly (according to Gary Snyder) out of love, Sasaki and the widowed Ruth Everett were married. In 1945 Sasaki Roshi died.

In the postwar decades, when the American mood turned suddenly from a chauvinistic antipathy toward all things Japanese to an equally uncritical enthusiasm for them, as occupation GIs came back with wondrous tales of the land of kimonos and courtesy, the Zen Institute flourished. Our attention, however, must turn to one whose orientalism was older and deeper, and whose impact on American Zen is incalculable, Sasaki's widow, Ruth Fuller Sasaki.

Ruth Fuller Sasaki (1893–1967) first learned about Zen in 1930, when she visited D. T. Suzuki on the way back from a trip to China. Her earlier college studies in Sanskrit and Pali had, however, given her a background valuable for understanding Buddhism. Two years later she returned to Japan to study at a Zen monastery for three and a half months. In 1938 she settled in New York and became, with her ample financial means, the principal supporter of the Institute.

The most remarkable phase of her life, however, came after the war. Beginning a new life as a serious scholar and Zen adept at over fifty years of age, she came to Japan, where she lived for the remainder of her life, studying under the abbot of the great Daitokuji in Kyoto. In time she rebuilt and became priest herself of a dilapidated temple within the Daitokuji complex, the first Westerner to hold such a position. In this capacity and as leader of the First Zen Institute of America in Kyoto she befriended the many foreigners, including Gary Snyder, who came to Japan in the fifties and sixties hoping to study Zen. It was here also that she wrote several important scholarly monographs and translations, and her important book *Zen Dust* (with Miura Roshi). Indeed, one of her most valuable contributions was her insistence upon solid Zen scholarship, which contrasts with the attitude of the more artless Western Zennist. She had a mastery of Japanese and classical Chinese, and an ability in Sanskrit, Pali, and European languages, equal to that of any academic savant. Her Zen was far removed from the "beat" style of Kerouac (though, oddly, it shared the same capacity for deracination and the linking figure of Gary Snyder); the Zen of her erstwhile son-in-law Alan Watts perhaps lay midway between the two.

More Zen

Several disciplic lineages from major teachers, both those we have discussed and a few others, have entered American Zen. Most are interrelated, going back to the previously discussed Soyen Shaku, to his teacher Imakita Kosen, and ultimately to the great Ekaku Hakuin in the eighteenth century, who developed the present system of *koan* study and who, indeed, virtually created modern Rinzai Zen.[19]

There is another tradition, however, the Harada lineage, and it is Soto, the other major school of Zen besides Rinzai. (Rinzai has emphasized *koan* study, while Soto has emphasized Zen sitting.) The great modern figure of the Harada lineage was Hakuun Yasutani (1885-1973), who, like Harada, actually combined both Soto and Rinzai techniques. His most influential American disciple was Philip Kapleau, who first came to Japan in 1946 as a reporter in the war crimes trials. (Many are the Americans in Zen and other Eastern spiritual movements who first met the Orient amid the storm and glory of war and occupation.) In 1951 he attended D. T. Suzuki's lectures at Columbia University. In 1953 he went to Japan, searching for a teacher, coming in time to Harada and his student Yasutani. When he returned to America in 1966, he established an important Zen center in Rochester, New York.

Kapleau's book *The Three Pillars of Zen* (1965), based on Yasutani's teaching, has undoubtedly been one of the most influential Western books on Zen, after those of Suzuki and Watts. It is, in fact, a good corrective to the latter two, for it emphasizes the importance of Zen sitting and the traditional relation of *roshi* and student. Its detailed accounts of Zen experience by both Western and Japanese practitioners make it an important document for the psychology of religion.

The largest American Zen center is the San Francisco Zen Center.

Interestingly, it is not itself related to either the Kosen or Harada lineages, but began in a different manner. Its effectual founder and first *roshi* was Shunryu Suzuki (1904–71), the son of a Soto priest, and himself priest of an important temple in Japan at only thirty-one years of age. In 1959 he unexpectedly came to America to serve as priest of a Japanese-American Soto temple in San Francisco. So great was the interest in Zen in the community, and so effective his spiritual charisma, that an informal body of occidental disciples gathered around Suzuki; this group was incorporated in 1962 as the Zen Center. It flourished in the sixties, developing several branches in the Bay area. Headquartered now in a fifty-room building in downtown San Francisco, where many residential Zen students live, it also operates Green Gulch Farm near Sausalito and the famous and spectacularly located Zen Mountain Center, dedicated to intensive training, at Tassajara Hot Springs in the mountains behind Carmel. When Suzuki Roshi died in 1971, he was succeeded by an American *roshi,* Richard Baker.[20]

The Zen Center is typical of the groups we are discussing in that its membership is both intense and often short-term; it is largely residential, and many members (even if not residential) practice *zazen* up to twice a day, a level of participation far closer to that of the Christian, or Buddhist, monk than of the ordinary churchgoer. Yet in 1970 a leading officer estimated the dropout rate to be about 80 percent a year. He adds that many students who survive the first year seem to drop out in the third, which appears to be a difficult one that involves a major adjustment; Zen students of four years or more, though, may be considered senior and stable.[21] However, the center has since become much more stable, which is characteristic of the equilibrium reached in the seventies of many new spiritual movements that had their starts in the sixties.

The other ten or twelve American Zen centers established after the Korean War and after the Zen enthusiasms of the fifties have explored diverse ways of practicing Zen on these shores. The Rinzai-related Cimarron Zen Center in Los Angeles sponsors the austere Mt. Baldy Center deep in the California mountains, which is probably more like a strict Japanese Zen monastery in discipline and practice than any other establishment in this country. The Sotoist Mt. Shasta Zen Center, under the direction of Jiyu Kennett, an Englishwoman who is a Zen *roshi,* has experimented with such Westernizing techniques as chanting the sutras in English plainsong.

On the other end of the scale, the general cultural influence of Zen continues apace. In 1974 Robert M. Pirsig's remarkable *Zen and the Art of Motorcycle Maintenance* made the best-seller lists and, while there is not much Zen in it once one gets past the title, it is a rich philosophical novel. The popularity of the title and the semi-autobiographical content shows that the Kerouac tradition of making the word Zen serve as shorthand for the values of the American spiritual picaresque, in which cross-country travel by alienated intellectuals goes with self-discovery and Whitmanesque unfolding of the spiritual meaning of America, is far from dead. It may even be becoming a genre. Whatever purists may say, Zen is a useful label, for, by the exoticism of its reference, it serves to distinguish the picaresque—which is an excursus of the spirit—from that other American genre, the Dos Passos or Erskine Caldwell wandering in which one is always at home, celebrating or vexing the too familiar. In any case, there is Zen precedent for the wanderer —Basho in Japan and Soyen Shaku in America—as well as for the still meditator, and also for Zennists like Gary Snyder and Ruth Fuller Sasaki, who represent both Zen roles.

Then there is Zen as spiritual excursus for those already within a circle of faith. We can only allude to books like Dom Aelred Graham, *Zen Catholicism* (1963), Thomas Merton, *Mystics and Zen Masters* (1967), and William Johnston, *The Still Point* (1970), as evidence of a burgeoning, and thus far mostly Roman Catholic, dialogue between Christianity and Zen. These are writers familiar with the Christian mystical tradition of Dionysius, Eckhart, the *Cloud of Unknowing,* and John of the Cross; the parallels and differences, especially of theological interpretation, have for them and for many of their readers proved a deep well of creative insight. If the day is past when Christian thinkers can work just in terms of their own tradition and its interaction with Western thought, as Cantwell Smith has suggested, and if the next great burst of theological work will come from dialogue with the world religions, then the foundations are already being laid in the case of Zen.[22] But it is significant to note that most of this writing is basically in response to D. T. Suzuki's presentation of Zen to the West; the initiative for dialogue, in other words, came from Zen.

Still another example of Zen in America may be the Erhard Seminars Training, or "est," a mind-improvement process which by the late seventies had graduated well over 100,000 Americans. Werner Erhard, the founder and leader, acknowledges that some Zen training was important in his development of the est idea, as was reading Alan Watts, although it was certainly not the only influence—he was also involved in Scientology, Silva Mind Control, humanistic psychology, and many other current "self-actualization" techniques. Est might, in fact, be considered a sort of ultimate, demythologized simplification and rationalization of the whole popular self-tranformation process into a few easy steps and concepts (or rather non-concepts). It could be seen as the ultimate Americanization of Zen, for, as far as I can see, the gist of it is Zen, but the language is wholly American—as is the junior executive atmosphere of the seminars—and there are no exotic trappings.

Like one of Kerouac's dharma bums, except for his background as a successful businessman, Erhard got his basic insight, he says, while driving south on highway 101 in California. He directly experienced his self, and no longer identified it with his body or personality or past or future or feelings or thought or circumstances or self-image—and he realized that verbalization is irrelevant.[23]

All this, very Zen indeed, is what the seminars communicate, and through such Zen-like techniques as quiet sitting and working inwardly on *koan*-like questions which (to use est terms) probe the "barriers" that maintain our "belief systems" and keep us from being "at the cause" of our "experience"—for only "experience," so easily obscured by "considerations" (value systems, judgments) and "chatter" and the space/time illusions we mistake for "reality," is the true source of awareness. "Getting" this is to "get clear" and be "at the cause" of one's experience rather than "at its effect."

This very diverse panorama, from lonely prewar Japanese missionary to "beat" poet, from "skinhead" Zen communalist and meditator to est seminarian, reflects the capacity of emergent spirituality, because it is emergent and its unities are largely invisible, to crop out in diverse ways. Swedenborgianism and Spiritualism expressed the excursus idea through the symbol of spirit worlds, and Theosophy in liminal pilgrimage. So did American Zen in pointing to what is inexpressible in wandering what is left of the North American wilderness, and in quiet sitting.

Epilogue

Changes in Critical Perspective

Books are still written which treat movements such as we have discussed as "cults of unreason" and as reactionary mysticisms which refuse to accept "science" and the new world it is creating. Certain of these books present useful empirical data, but the operative concepts of "reason" and "science" contained in them generally would have been simplistic in the heyday of logical positivism, and are vastly out of touch with the frontiers of philosophy of science, cosmology, physics, and psychological thought in the last quarter of the twentieth century. A classic Kuhnian paradigm shift is going on in these fields, basic to constructing the era's scientific master paradigms and world views. It is not so much a doctrinal battle as the simple replacement of one generation by another which does not think quite the same way: an older generation is still half in the world of Thomas Huxley, but a younger generation, more profoundly affected by the Einsteinian revolution in science on every level of attitude—including a new perception of the place of subjective consciousness in the cosmos wrought by its profound challenge to the "myth of the objective mind"—is sounding more like his contemporary Madame Blavatsky (at her best), or at least like Zen. (Outside of Jaina thought, I wonder if there is a better premodern anticipation of the philosophical dimensions of relativity theory than the essay on "Being-Time" by the thirteenth-century Japanese Zen master Dogen.) One should also mention a new openness by a new generation about parapsychological evidence regarding the nature of consciousness that approaches the same world, at least, as Swedenborgianism and Spiritualism.

Inevitably, this new mentality will lead to a more sympathetic understanding of the heritage of excursus religious movements and perhaps of the emergent tradition. It will not necessarily produce an adulation of them as having preternatural prescience (nor should it, for as does everything human they have their quotient of silliness), but perhaps it can be recognized that the sociological paradigms which lead people to perceive them only as "bizarre" and their members only as "cranks" are also capable of challenge and change. It can be perceived that these religions have not always been wrong or reactionary and that they have a place in the many-sided American spiritual symposium.

A perception of "non-normative" religions in America, even those imported (as it seems) from the East, as essentially American in America, and so to be understood (and criticized) in terms of the themes and sociology and styles of American religious life, involves another paradigm shift which is also under way. Zen, Swedenborgianism, Theosophy, or Vedanta, for example, are in American life far from what they are or were in Japan, eighteenth-century England, or nineteenth-century India. Too much knowledge of their distant origins, knowledge which may be greater than that of most twentieth-century American adherents themselves, can easily be a hindrance to comprehension of these adherents—who may use Eastern symbols, for reasons we have explored, but whose essential spiritual life is better approached through the American emergent and excursus heritage from Emerson, Thoreau, Whitman, the Shakers and Spiritualists, to the cults of the depression era, or to the "beatniks" and the "hippies."

Yet there are also books written which castigate American movements with Eastern links for failure to present the Eastern teaching in an "authentic" form and for adding to its classical texts "spurious" modern sources like the writings of Blavatsky. This sort of purist critique is, of course, legitimate within the context of commitment to the classic form of any tradition, but as applied to the phenomenology of religion it is unacceptable. Its ideal hardly fits the way religion really works, for religion is always in process, always undergoing modification through intercultural contact and trans-

plantation, and always producing new books which become normative and classical in time. Often, like the Mahayana sutras placed in
the mouth of the Buddha and the Tibetan *gter-ma* texts alleged to
have been penned by an ancient sage and hidden many centuries,
these classics are back-dated and ascribed to minds greater than
that of the one whose hands gave them to the world.

More important, as we have indicated, this attitude does little to
add to understanding of these movements in this country. If one is
going to talk about purity and authenticity of tradition (usually a
futile and dangerous project), one ought to talk about it in terms of
the American lineage in which a later phenomenon is placed. For
the "beat Zen" school, for example, the real ideal was clearly the
American ideal of Thoreau and Whitman, and of this Zen was
simply a new exotic symbol; it would make more sense (and be
more fair) to look at its values, life-style, and spirituality in that
light rather than to compare it with the Zen practiced long ago by
East Asian masters in a very different culture.

A contemporary genre of books exists whose chief purpose is to
indicate the alleged occult, theosophical, and oriental derivation of
the ideology of Nazism, and then to point with alarm to the
proliferation of those same teachings in America. It seems incum-
bent upon responsible writers of the history of such groups to point
out the logical and historical fallacies in this position, which, if
widely accepted, could have serious consequences for freedom of
religion.

First, it should be noted that, inasmuch as "the occult" only
joins Hegel, Wagner, Nietzsche, and the anti-Semitic strain in normative Christianity in receiving the blame for Hitlerism, one ought
finally to end up faulting not so much one small and easily identifiable culprit so much as a large part of the intellectual foundation
of the modern world.

Second, although the Theosophical doctrines of Madame Blavatsky and her followers are often cited in this connection, we should
note that whenever in modern history Theosophists have had a
discernible role and influence, as in the cultural renaissances and
independence movements of Ireland and India, it has been on the
side of freedom and democracy—and that leaders of the Theosophical Society, like many other occultists, disappeared into con-

centration camps in Germany as soon as the Nazis, their alleged
disciples, came to power.

Third, let us reiterate that whatever meaning these ideologies
may have in Asia or in Europe, in America they have appeared
simply as revitalizations of a tradition going back as far as Transcendentalism, and usually aligned with the idealistic, even radical,
wing of American democracy. To be sure, American occultism and
non-normative religion can assume a rightist guise, and did to some
extent in the 1930s. But this does not appear to be typical, or true
to their historical roots. Despite superficial similarities, nothing is
more different between Europe and America than the role of
religion—both mainstream and non-normative—in the two societies. We must insist that American religious groups can only be
judged in terms of American history, not in terms of any apparent
European parallels, which inevitably will be misleading.

Time, as American culture matures and recognizes how unique it
is (nowhere more so than in religion), will eventually provide its
corrective on these points. Most American Eastern groups are now
rapidly maturing—not in the direction of purism, but of indigeniz-
ing their own way; this is bound to happen more and more, even as
it has with the Judaism and Christianity transplanted to these
shores. The perception and appreciation of this process, and,
thereby, the evaluation of excursus groups as integral parts of the
American spiritual heritage, will be aided by the aforementioned
changes in world-view paradigms. It will also be encouraged by the
contemporary mood in religious studies, which by and large is far
removed from the stereotyping and polemics of another day.

Changes in American Religion

One important reason for new attitudes in religious studies is new
contours of American religion, and new perceptions by Americans
of what their religion is. Most commentators in the late twentieth-
century point to an increasing functional breakdown of what there
was in America of the classic Troeltschean cleavage between church
and sect, with an ever more radical exposure of more and more
people to the extensive pluralism of American religion and a growing indifference to the large institutional structures of religion. In

its place, one finds—in the flourishing of evangelicalism, pentecostalism, the "born again" experience, prayer groups, excursus
religion, and para-religious self-realization activities like est—a
movement toward subjectivity and small groups. This means, in
our terms, that the structure of establishment religion, and the
social identity that has gone with it, is crumbling. Indeed, the
spiritual style and meaning that is associated with excursus religion
is almost becoming normative, provided one includes its Judeo-
Christian forms—a paradoxical situation whose ultimate cultural
meaning is hard to assess. No model of a society whose religion is
mainly subjective and small group (at best the local church or small
intensive denomination), with no major religious institutions
linked to the major institutions of government, business, and
education, comes to mind which would be meaningfully comparable to the United States.

That is certainly because this situation (which is not yet here,
to be sure, but seems to be approaching), would be a product of
modern social secularization, including those aspects of it which are
genuinely unique to the contemporary era. Secularization unequiv-
ocably does not mean decline in interest in religious issues or in
desire for religious expression. That has obviously not been the
upshot in the twentieth century. Rather, what it has meant is that
religion has been increasingly divorced from the major structures of
society—first (as early as the late Middle Ages) from economics,
then from the state, then from education, and finally from religious
institutions that parallel major structures of society in their organization and symbolic social roles. That divorce liberates religion to
exist principally, possibly even to prosper unprecedentedly, within
subjectivity and in small groups.

American religion clearly is far better prepared to prosper in this
situation, and to suffer fewer pains of transition to a new mode of
life, than the religion of most societies. It has lived with secularism,
in the sense suggested above, much longer than most other lands;
and in its amazing pluralism, numerous religionists—not least
those in our excursus religion—have experimented with and experienced religion focused on private subjectivity and the small group
rather than on the ecclesiastical institution. Indeed, we may expect
to see our "non-normative" groups appear more and more normal,

and even prestigious, at least from a sociological standpoint. It is hard to see how the new situation could bring them bane, and it could easily bring blessing.

But another way of looking at the picture (for there is little new under the sun in the history of religion) is that what is happening is simply a return to folk religion. It is a religion of Robert Redfield's "little tradition" of village and nonliterary folk transmission, excited as folk cultures are by the occasional thaumaturge or messiah, but without much vital interaction with the cultural "great tradition" of the society. Certainly there is much about American religion in the last quarter of the century which suggests this interpretation. It has no small vitality (folk religion, peasant culture religion, is often quite alive in terms of feeling and participation), but it has increasingly less real intellectual interaction with science, education, and the major institutions. As has been often remarked, there seem now to be no theological giants like Barth, Tillich, or the Niebuhrs capable of building bridges of serious dialogue between religion and culture. Instead, one senses that the issues being raised in the great tradition—the new cosmology, the medical revolution, present-day currents in literature and even social affairs —are very little engaged in by religion and vice versa. Religion, with the peasant's obstinate and almost deliberate naivete, is content to dwell with its own nonhistorical, and nonliterary—in the cultural sense—joys and apocalypses.

Probably that kind of religion is inevitable as a concomitant of the final divorce of religion from the major institutions, for folk or popular religion is that of a people largely separate from the major institutions of the society. As folk or popular religion usually does when first liberated from the grip of institutions, it will probably inflate and flourish to fill all the voids (as the evangelical tradition seems now to be doing), but that will still not commend it to the great tradition except for pro forma alliances.

But in the religious folk culture of a technological society, among the spiritual peasantry of a postindustrial nation, excursus religion could have a strange and important role. Every subjectivity, every small group, every charmed circle, needs the stimulus of something outside and different engaging it from time to time, lest it die of inertia. As American religion becomes more divorced from the great tradition, it receives less stimulus and engagement from that direction. Major intellectuals do not bother to address it, as Emerson and James once did, nor do they stir the ponds of its piety; neither is there any H. L. Mencken who troubles to bait it—though surely there are aspects of neo-evangelicalism worthy of his bite. But the two worlds, weary of each other and perhaps even of themselves as combatants, merely drift apart, until they become nearly invisible to each other.

Yet American religion is aware of the excursus, alternative tradition—it is something it can understand even in its present intellectual anemia as a competitor and challenger on its own turf. Through television and newspaper publicity, Spiritualism, Zen, other Eastern religions, and the like, are perceived as part of the religious scene—and perceived as rivals by those committed to the Judeo-Christian tradition. But in that very rivalry they can do what our highly nonmilitant secularism is far too bland to undertake—they can stimulate and challenge all American religion to think, to define its views of human nature, of the infinite and the spiritual path, in ways that take into account the experiences of others with other views and on other paths.

This they have done before, and can do again.

Notes

1   *Temple and Cave in America*

1.   Peter L. Berger, *The Sacred Canopy* (Garden City, N.Y.: Double-day Anchor Books, 1969), p. 28.

2.   C. G. Jung, *Memories, Dreams, Reflections* (N.Y.: Pantheon Books, 1963), p. 39.

3.   J. Lofland and R. Stark, "Becoming a World-Saver: A Theory of Conversion to a Deviant Perspective," *American Sociological Review* 30 (1965): 862-74.

3.   J. Lofland and R. Stark, "Becoming a World-Saver: A Theory of Conversion to a Deviant Perspective," pp. 862-74. See also John Lofland, " 'Becoming a World-Saver' Revisited," *American Behavioral Scientist* 20, no. 6 (July-August 1977): 805-17; and James T. Richardson and Mary Stewart, "Conversion Process Models and the Jesus Movement," *American Behavioral Scientist* 20, no. 6 (July-August 1977): 819-38, especially p. 822, where the Lofland and Stark model is summarized.

4.   Robert Balch and David Taylor, "Seekers and Savers: The Role of the Cultic Milieu in Joining a UFO Cult," *American Behavioral Scientist* 20, no. 6 (July-August 1977): 839-60.

5.   Frederick R. Lynch, "Toward a Theory of Conversion and Commitment to the Occult," *American Behavioral Scientist* 20, no. 6 (July-August 1977): 887-908.

6.   Stephen C. Pepper, *World Hypotheses* (Berkeley and Los Angeles: University of California Press, 1942).

7.   For this discussion I am deeply indebted to a stimulating essay by Victor Turner, "Social Dramas and Ritual Metaphors," in *Dramas, Fields, and Metaphors* (Ithaca, N.Y.: Cornell University Press, 1974), pp. 23-59.

8.   Paul Radin, *Primitive Man as Philosopher* (New York: Dover Publications, 1957).

9.   Turner, *Dramas, Fields, and Metaphors*, pp. 24-25. Robert A.

Nisbet, *Social Change and History: Aspects of the Western Theory of Development* (London: Oxford University Press, 1969), pp. 3-4.

10.   J. Milton Yinger, *Religion, Society, and the Individual* (New York: Macmillan, 1957), pp. 142-55.

11.   Geoffrey K. Nelson, *Spiritualism and Society* (New York: Schocken Books, 1969), p. 220. In a more recent book, *The Scientific Study of Religion* (New York: Macmillan, 1970), pp. 279-80, J. Milton Yinger discusses and generally accepts Nelson's contention that some cults can be long-lasting and the sources of new religions.

12.   James T. Richardson, "An Oppositional and General Conceptualization of Cult." Unpublished paper read at the annual meeting of the Association for the Sociology of Religion (New York, 1976), p. 7.

13.   Roy Wallis, "Ideology, Authority and the Development of Cultic Movements," *Social Research* 41, no. 2 (Summer 1974): 299-327.

2   *Excursus Religion*

1.   Cited and translated in W. R. Irwin, "There and Back Again: The Romances of Williams, Lewis, and Tolkien," *Sewanee Review* 64, no. 4 (Oct.-Dec. 1961): 566.

2.   Irwin, "There and Back Again," p. 567.

3.   Mary Douglas, *Natural Symbols* (New York: Vintage Books, 1973).

4.   Sheldon R. Isenberg and Dennis E. Owen, "Bodies, Natural and Contrived: The Work of Mary Douglas," *Religious Studies Review* 3, no. 1 (January 1977): 7-8. The following table is reprinted by permission of the authors.

5.   Isenberg and Owen, "Bodies, Natural and Contrived," p. 14.

6.   Victor W. Turner, *The Ritual Process* (Chicago: Aldine, 1969).

7.   Frederick J. Streng, *Understanding Religious Man* (Belmont, Calif.: Dickenson, 1969), pp. 4-5.

8.   Douglas, *Natural Symbols*, p. 190.

9.   Isenberg and Owen, "Bodies, Natural and Contrived," p. 14.

10.   Joachim Wach, *Sociology of Religion* (Chicago: University of Chicago Press, 1944), pp. 17-34.

11.   Erving Goffman, *Asylums: Essays on the Social Situation of Mental Patients and Other Inmates* (Garden City, N.Y.: Doubleday Anchor Books, 1961).

12.   Troeltsch, *Social Teachings of the Christian Church*, 2:734. See also William R. Garrett, "Maligned Mysticism: The Maledicted Career of Troeltsch's Third Type," *Sociological Analysis* 36, no. 3 (1975): 205-27. Garrett argues cogently that Troeltsch's mysticism type—shifted by Max Weber into a coordinate on the asceticism-mysticism axis *within* church and sect—deserves instead to be looked at anew as a third religious *type* and as such to be factored into the sociology of religion afresh.

177   Notes to Pages 38-57

13.   Robert S. Ellwood, Jr., "Notes on a Neo-Pagan Religious Group
in America," *History of Religions* 11, no. 1 (August 1971): 125-39; and
Robert S. Ellwood, Jr., *Religious and Spritual Groups in Modern America*
(Englewood Cliffs, N.J.: Prentice-Hall, 1973), pp. 194-200.
14.   Peter L. Berger and Thomas Luckmann, *The Social Construction
of Reality* (Garden City, N.Y.: Doubleday Anchor Books, 1967).

3   *Inner Worlds*   *The Psychology of*
                               Excursus Religion

1.   Godfré Ray King [Guy Ballard], *Unveiled Mysteries* (Chicago:
Saint Germain Press, 1939), p. 2.
2.   Paul Twitchell, *The Tiger's Fang* (New York: Lancer Books,
1969), p. 13.
3.   Carl G. Jung, *Flying Saucers: A Modern Myth of Things Seen in
the Sky* (New York: Signet Books, 1969), pp. 119-26.
4.   Orfeo M. Angelucci, *The Secret of the Saucers* (Amherst, Wisc.:
Amherst Press, 1955), pp. 1-5.
5.   Alfred Schutz, *Collected Papers*, vol. 1, edited and with an
introduction by Maurice Natanson (The Hague: Martinus Nijhoff, 1973),
pp. 207-59. See also William James, *The Principles of Psychology*, vol. 2,
chap. 21 (New York: H. Holt and Co., 1890).
6.   Ralph W. Hood, Jr., "Eliciting Mystical States of Consciousness
with Semistructured Nature Experiences," *Journal for the Scientific Study
of Religion* 16, no. 2 (1977): 199-263.
7.   See in particular R. D. Laing, *The Politics of Experience* (New
York: Ballantine Books, 1967).
8.   R. D. Laing, "Metanoia: Some Experiences at Kingsley Hall,
London," in Hendrick M. Ruitenbeek, ed., *Going Crazy: The Radical
Therapy of R. D. Laing and Others* (New York: Bantam Books, 1972), pp.
16-19. See also an essay by the woman who regressed herself in the same
books: Mary Barnes, "Flection-Reflection," pp. 103-18.
9.   Laing, *The Politics of Experience*, p. 157.
10.   Robert S. Ellwood, Jr., *Religious and Spritual Groups in Modern
America* (Englewood Cliffs, N.J.: Prentice-Hall, 1973), pp. 49-52, passim.
11.   Vsevolod Gergyeevich Solovyoff, *A Modern Priestess of Isis*,
translated by Walter Leaf (London: Longmans, Green, 1895; reprint ed.
New York: Arno Press, 1976), pp. 176-81.
12.   Heinrich Zimmer, *Myths and Symbols in Indian Art and Civilization* (New York: Bollengen Foundation, 1946), p. 179, note. I am
indebted for this quote and for the basic insight here discussed regarding
the trickster and the counter-spirituality personality to a letter by Melanie
Bandy in *The American Theosophist* 65, no. 11 (November 1977): 315.

13.   Ernest G. Schachtel, "On Memory and Childhood Amnesia," in his *Metamorphosis: On the Development of Affect, Perception, Attention, and Memory* (New York: Basic Books, 1959), pp. 279-322. See especially pp. 298-301.

14.   Kenneth Grant, *The Magical Revival* (New York: Samuel Weiser, 1973), p. 3.

4   *Shakers and Spiritualists*

1.   From Eirik's Saga, in Magnus Magnusson and Hermann Palsson, *The Vinland Sagas* (New York: New York University Press, 1966), pp. 81-84.

2.   Magnusson and Palsson, *The Vinland Sagas*, pp. 64-67, 71.

3.   I. M. Lewis, *Ecstatic Religion* (Harmondsworth, England: Penguin Books, 1971), p. 31.

4.   Lines found in her sketch-book, undated. Cited in Mary K. Neff, comp., *Personal Memoirs of H. P. Blavatsky* (Wheaton, Ill.: Theosophical Publishing House, 1937), p. 37.

5.   Carl Carmer, *Listen for a Lonesome Drum* (New York: William Sloane Associates, 1936), pp. 203-14.

6.   *Testimonies of the Life, Character, Revelations and Doctrines of Mother Ann Lee* (Albany: Weed Parsons, 1888. Reprint ed., New York: AMS Press, 1975), p. 5.

7.   *Testimonies of the Life ... of Mother Ann Lee*, in Marguerite Fellows Melcher, *The Shaker Adventure* (Princeton: Princeton University Press, 1941), passim.

8.   Cited in Frederick William Evans, *Autobiography of a Shaker* (New York: American News Company, 1888; reprint ed. New York: AMS Press, 1973), pp. 268-69.

9.   Hester M. Poole, "Shakers and Shakerism," in Evans, *Autobiography of a Shaker*, p. 268.

10.   J. M. Peebles, "Cycles," in Evans, *Autobiography of a Shaker*, p. 115.

11.   Melcher, *The Shaker Adventure*, p. 185.

12.   Melcher, *The Shaker Adventure*, p. 217. See also Edward Deming Andrews and Faith Andrews, *Fruits of the Shaker Tree of Life* (Stockbridge, Mass.: The Berkshire Traveller Press, 1975), especially pp. 220-21.

13.   Evans, *Autobiography of a Shaker*, p. 43.

14.   Evans, *Autobiography of a Shaker*, pp. 18-20.

15.   Carl Carmer, *Listen for a Lonesome Drum*, pp. 145-46. Whitney R. Cross, *The Burned Over District: The Social and Intellectual History of Enthusiastic Religion in Western New York* (New York: Harper and Row), 1965.

16.   George Trobridge, *Swedenborg: Life and Teaching* (New York: Swedenborg Foundation, 1935), p. 118.

17.   "Emanuel Swedenborg," translated by Richard Howard and César Rennert. Excerpted from the book *Jorge Luis Borges: Selected Poems 1923-1967*, edited by Norman Thomas di Giovanni. English translation copyright © 1968, 1970, 1971, 1972 by Emece Editores, S. A., and Norman Thomas di Giovanni. Reprinted by permission of Delacorte Press/Seymour Lawrence and Penguin Books, Ltd.

18.   See Robert Price, *Johnny Appleseed: Man and Myth*. (Gloucester, Mass.: Peter Smith, 1967).

19.   An accessible work on Mesmer, with good bibliography, is Vincent Buranelli, *The Wizard from Vienna* (New York: Coward, McCann and Geoghegan, 1975). On Mesmerism in America as it led up to Spiritualism see Slater Brown, *The Heyday of Spiritualism* (New York: Hawthorn Books, 1970).

20.   Catherine L. Albanese, *Corresponding Motion: Transcendental Religion and the New America*. Philadelphia: Temple University Press, 1977.

21.   The primary source is Andrew Jackson Davis, *The Magic Staff: An Autobiography* (New York: J. S. Brown and Co., 1857). See also Brown, *The Heyday of Spiritualism*, chap. 7.

22.   A fascinating though non-critical biography is Jean Burton, *Heyday of a Wizard* (New York: A. A. Knopf, 1944).

23.   Brown, *The Heyday of Spiritualism*, chap. 12.

24.   Whitney Cross, *The Burned Over District*, p. 348. One feels that the meteoric rise and fall of Spiritualism as a major cultural phenomenon in the 1850s, together with its ongoing influence through subdued but continuing institutions and in the lives of people who had seen their "literal-mindedness and orthodoxy" obliterated in its embrace, strikingly parallels the course and probable destiny of the "counterculture" religion of the 1960s. Both were linked with social radicalism, Amerindian lore, and wild eschatological visions; both seemed to vanish as sensational news only a few years after they had come, and were dampened by more sober forms of liberal and evangelical religion and a more pragmatic vision of society, which appeared in the seventies of both centuries. Yet over twelve decades later one can trace directly back to the first Spiritualist outburst a variety of lively activities from Theosophy to serious psychical research, and perceive an indirect influence on the rise of modern psychology and liberalism of several sorts. One should not foreclose the possibility of an equally subtle but far-reaching influence of Haight-Ashbury, for all its apparent ephemerality, on the twenty-first century.

On the relation of Spiritualism to rationalistic modernism, so evident in the thought of Frederick Evans the Shaker and many others, one may reflect on these words of Mircea Eliade:

I noticed long ago that spiritualism is the "spiritual" compensation that positivism allows itself. When one can no longer *believe* (in the Judeo-Christian sense of the term), one needs *concrete proofs* of the survival of the soul; it is on the basis of these "experimental" proofs that an after life is constructed—with its structures and its hierarchies—just as theologies are constructed (in a monotheistic climate) on the basis of a few prophetic revelations and mystical experiences.

Mircea Eliade, *No Souvenirs: Journal 1957-1969*. Translated from the French by Fred H. Johnson, Jr. (New York: Harper and Row, 1977), p. 145.

25. See Herbert W. Schneider and George Lawton, *A Pilgrim and a Prophet: Being the Incredible History of Thomas Lake Harris and Laurence Oliphant* (New York: Columbia University Press, 1942).

26. Howard Kerr, *Mediums, and Spirit-Rappers, and Roaring Radicals: Spiritualism in American Literature 1850-1900* (Urbana: University of Illinois Press, 1972).

27. Henry S. Olcott, *People from the Other World* (Hartford: American Publishing Co., 1875; reprint ed. Rutland, Vt.: Charles E. Tuttle Company, 1972), p. 481.

5   *Olcott and Blavatsky*
                                         Journey to the East

1. Letter by Madame Blavatsky in the *Spiritual Scientist* (Boston), vol. 1, December 3, 1874, pp. 148-49. Excerpted in *H. P. Blavatsky: Collected Writings, 1874-78*, vol. 1 (Adyar, Madras, India: Theosophical Publishing House, 1966), p. 47.

2. The principal source for the plagiarism charge is the time-consuming work which William Emmett Coleman did around the turn of the century to substantiate some 2000 plagiarisms in *Isis Unveiled*. His findings were published with full references in a series of magazine articles, and summarized in "The Sources of Madame Blavatsky's Writings" (appendix C to V. S. Solovyoff, *A Modern Priestess of Isis,* previously cited). Bruce Campbell, of the Institute of Religious Studies, University of California, Santa Barbara, has recently checked a substantial sample of these alleged borrowings. He concluded that the 2000 plagiarisms do exist, but are nearly all on the level of sentences and phrases in the midst of unplagiarized discourse, and so in a work of some 1400 pages probably do not represent more than five percent or so of the total. He did not find even this much plagiarism in *The Secret Doctrine*.

A curious light is shed on the whole business by the fact that the British Museum catalog lists an 1881 publication by William Henry Burr, a religious controversalist, devoted to accusing W. E. Coleman himself of plagiarism from his "Sunday Not the Sabbath."

3.   Given in Mary K. Neff, comp., *Personal Memoirs of H. P. Blavatsky* (Wheaton, Ill.: Theosophical Publishing House, 1937), pp. 341-42. Originally from Mrs. E. Johnson, "Letters of H. P. Blavatsky," *The Path*, December, 1894.

4.   Neff, *Personal Memoirs*, pp. 236-40.

5.   Gertrude M. Williams, *Priestess of the Occult* (New York: Alfred A. Knopf, 1946), passim.

6.   Henry Steel Olcott, *Old Diary Leaves: America 1874-1878, first series* (Adyar, Madras, India: Theosophical Publishing House, 1895) pp. 331-32. This volume henceforth cited as *ODL 1*.

7.   From the same letter cited in note 1, above.

8.   *ODL 1*, pp. 211-12.

9.   *ODL 1*, pp. 208-9.

10.   H. P. Blavatsky, *Isis Unveiled* (Wheaton, Ill.: Theosophical Publishing House, 1972 edition), 1:xi.

11.   It would be amiss not to mention here Helena Blavatsky's major work, *The Secret Doctrine* (1888), even though its composition comes after the period we are examining. The writing of this book seems to have been, as in the case of *Isis Unveiled*, a combination of psychic revelation and collective editorial effort by a circle of associates of the authoress to arrange her material. But *The Secret Doctrine* is much superior in sophistication and systematization; this is due partly to the high caliber of the later assistants, and partly, of course, to HPB's own maturation over the intervening decade. For fascinating firsthand accounts of the writing of *The Secret Doctrine*, see Countess Constance Wachtmeister et al., *Reminiscences of H. P. Blavatsky and The Secret Doctrine* (Wheaton, Ill.: Theosophical Publishing House, 1976). A standard edition of the work, annotated, indexed, and containing the posthumous third volume on symbolism, whose authorship by HPB is disputed, is H. P. Blavatsky, *The Secret Doctrine*, 6 vols. (Adyar, Madras, India: Theosophical Publishing House; sixth Adyar) edition, 1971).

12.   See Neff, *Personal Memoirs*, pp. 282, 289. In connection with HPB's relation to Russian Orthodoxy, it has sometimes been suggested there was something very Russian about her "mysticism," that she was more of an occultist *startsi* than anything else. While her psychic and mystic performances may have owed much to the *startsi* and other Eastern spiritual traditions, this does not seem to me to be the case in regard to the intellectual expression of her mysticism. Her maiden name was de Hahn, and on her father's side she was descended from German immigrants to Russia, though her mother, a gifted novelist, was of the old princely Dolgouroky house. However, HPB's world was that of those nineteenth-century Russian aristocrats more German in race and French in culture than Russian; despite her Russophile side, this is what comes through in her doctrine. In *Isis*, *The Secret Doctrine*, and her other writings, there is very little of the sensuous Slavic mysticism of guilt and joy, of love of the divine

in the humble, the suffering, and the soil, which lends passion to almost every page of Dostoevsky, Solovyov, and Blok, and gives spiritual character even to a figure like Rasputin, despite the fact she shared many of these passions in her own tempestuous life. Rather, hers seems doctrinally a much more Germanic style of mysticism. It has clearer affinities to the more intellectual, system-building occultism of the German Renaissance, to Paracelsus, Rosicrucianism, and Boehme, than to Russia. Despite its parallelism to the Platonic theology of the Eastern Church, her Platonism seems to be more that of the kabbala and the Rhineland than of Byzantium. On top of this, there is something of the flavor of the more recent French Spiritualism of Saint-Martin and Kardec.

13.   John Symonds, *Madame Blavatsky, Medium and Magician* (London: Odhams Press, 1959), p. 103. Gertrude Williams (*Priestess of the Occult*, p. 130) believed that, together with her congenital wanderlust, the humiliation of Home's book was the strongest reason for HPB's decision to go to India.

14.   Neff, *Personal Memoirs*, p. 55.

15.   Williams, *Priestess of the Occult*, pp. 89-90.

16.   "The Diaries of H. P. Blavatsky," 1878, in H. P. Blavatsky, *Collected Writings*, 1:414-15.

17.   Ibid., p. 420.

18.   *ODL 1*, pp. 17-18.

19.   *ODL 1*, pp. 376-77, 379.

20.   Henry Steel Olcott, *Old Diary Leaves, 1878-83, second series* (Adyar, Madras, India: Theosophical Publishing House, 1900), pp. 13-14. This volume henceforth cited as *ODL 2*.

21.   Victor Turner, "The Center Out There: Pilgrim's Goal," *History of Religions* 12, no. 3 (February 1973): 191-230.

22.   Henry David Thoreau, *Journal* (New York: Dover Publications, 1962), 8:134.

23.   Henry David Thoreau, *Walden* (New York: New American Library, 1942). pp. 198-99.

24.   *ODL 2:* 21, 24-25.

25.   See the excellent biography, Mary Lutyens, *Krishnamurti: The Years of Awakening* (New York: Farrar, Straus, and Giroux, 1975).

6   *Zen Journeys to the West*

1.   *The International Theosophical Yearbook 1937* (Adyar, Madras, India: Theosophical Publishing House), p. 151, tells of Mrs. Suzuki's establishing the Mahayana Lodge of Theosophists in Kyoto in 1924, and of her "enthusiastic work" in spreading Theosophy in Japan. Both Suzukis greeted Theosophical visitors to the island empire, including the international president, C. Jinarajadasa, in 1937.

183 Notes to Pages 137-64

2.   Mircea Eliade, *No Souvinirs* (New York: Harper and Row, 1977), p. 208. For an interesting assessment by Conze of D. T. Suzuki and Western Zen see Edward Conze, *Thirty Years of Buddhist Studies* (Columbia, S.C.: University of South Carolina Press, 1968), pp. 27-32.

3.   Alan W. Watts, *Beat Zen, Square Zen, and Zen* (San Francisco: City Lights Books, 1959). This essay contains an interesting critique of Jack Kerouac's *The Dharma Bums.*

4.   Heinrich Dumoulin, S. J., *A History of Zen Buddhism* (Boston: Beacon Press, 1969), pp. 184-86.

5.   Jack Kerouac, *The Dharma Bums* (New York: Viking Press, 1958), pp. 72-77.

6.   Kerouac, *The Dharma Bums,* p. 84.

7.   Kerouac, *The Dharma Bums,* p. 243.

8.   Ann Charters, *Kerouac* (New York: Warner Paperback Library Edition, 1974), pp. 217-31. This book is the standard biography of Jack Kerouac.

9.   David Kherdian, *A Biographical Sketch and Descriptive Checklist of Gary Snyder* (Berkeley: Oyez Press, 1965).

10.   Gary Snyder, *Riprap and Cold Mountain Poems* (San Francisco: City Lights Books, 1958), pp. 39-40.

11.   Quoted in David Kherdian, *Six Poets of the San Francisco Renaissance* (Fresno, Calif.: The Gilgia Press, 1965), p. 52.

12.   Gary Snyder, *Earth House Hold* (New York: New Directions, 1969), p. 132.

13.   Personal Communication, May 23, 1977.

14.   Alan Watts, *In My Own Way: An Autobiography, 1915-65* (New York: Vintage Books, 1973), p. 309.

15.   Alan W. Watts, *The Way of Zen* (New York: Pantheon Books, 1957), p. 3.

16.   Gary Snyder, interview statement in *Wind Bell,* publication of the San Francisco Zen Center, 8 nos. 1-2 (Fall 1969): 29. Reprinted by permission.

17.   Reprinted by permission from *Wind Bell,* 8 nos. 1-2 (Fall 1969): 1.

18.   Undated manuscript cited in Louis Nordstrom, ed., *Namu Dai Bosa: A Transmission of Zen Buddhism to America.* (New York: Theatre Arts Books, 1976), pp. 58-59.

19.   *Wind Bell* 8, nos. 1-2 (Fall 1969): 2-3. I am deeply indebted to this invaluable issue of the publication of the San Francisco Zen Center for much of the material on the history of formal Zen in America presented in this chapter.

20.   Biography based on *Wind Bell* 11 (1972): 7-10.

21.   *Wind Bell* 9, nos. 3-4 (Fall-Winder 1970-71): 39-40.

22.   Wilfred Cantwell Smith, *Religious Diversity,* ed. Willard G. Oxtoby (New York: Harper and Row, 1976). See especially the essay,

"Religiously Divided History Approaches Self-Consciousness," pp. 96–116.
23.   Adelaide Bry, *Est: 60 Hours that Transform your Life* (New York: Harper and Row, 1976), p. 115.

Index

Adept. *See* Magus

African religions, 13

Afterlife, as essence of spirituality, 3

Albanese, Catherine L., 93–94

Alienation: of Kerouac, 148; of Olcott, 11–12, 116–17; of religion from other cultural institutions, 172–73; symbols of, 21

Alternative religions. *See* Ecstatic religion; Emergent religion; Excursus religion; *and names of specific religious groups, leaders, movements, and thinkers*

American Academy of Asian Studies, 151, 156

American religion: alienation of, from other cultural institutions, 172–73; feminine spiritual leadership in (*see* Blavatsky, Madame Helena; Feminine spiritual leadership; Lee, Mother Ann; and Wilkinson, Jemima); flourishing of small groups in, 171–72; folk heritage revival in, 172; grid and group in, 22–25; popularization of non-normative traditions in, 168–69; secularization in, 171; spiritual traditions in, categorized, 25–28; Theosophy's suitability to, 138

Angelucci, Orfeo, 43–45

Animal magnetism, 91–92

Appleseed, Johnny, 40, 90–91, 152

Arcane School, 134

Aristotle, 53

Arya Samaj, 122–23

Authenticity: professions of, by excursus groups, 38–39, 47; and religious assimilation, 168–69

Bach, Richard, 138

Bailey, Alice, 134

Baker, Richard, 163

Balch, Robert, 10, 45, 118

Ballard, Guy, 42–45, 48, 134

Basho, 164

Beat generation, 60. *See also* Kerouac, Jack; Snyder, Gary; Zen Buddhism, two types of; *and names of San Francisco Beat individuals*

Behold the Spirit (Watts), 155

Berger, Peter, 3, 38

Beyond Theology (Watts), 156

Bhagavad-Gita, 128, 137

Bhaktivedanta, Swami, 135

Blavatsky, Madame Helena: childhood of, 107; early wanderings of, 31, 107, 110; inner voices of ("Masters"), 114–15, 119–32 passim; letter from, to Solovyoff, 54–56; liminality of, 106–7; marriages of, 107, 112, 113; meaning of Theosophy to, 116; meeting of, with Olcott, 104, 112; on Mesmer, 92; motives of, for journey to India, 122–26, 131–34; plagiarism by, 109 n.2; powers of, 53, 105; psycho-physical crisis of (initiation), 113–15; as trickster, 109–10; on women's fulfillment, 69. *See also* Olcott, Henry Steel; Theosophy

Bo and Peep, 10

Bodhidharma, 140